TWENTIETH CENTURY VIEWS

The aim of this series is to present the best in
contemporary critical opinion on major authors,
providing a twentieth century perspective on
their changing status in an era of profound
revaluation.

Maynard Mack, *Series Editor*
Yale University

KATHLEEN COBURN, the editor of this volume
in the Twentieth Century Views series, has
also edited the *Notebooks of Samuel Taylor
Coleridge* and the *Collected Works*. In addition to a selection of Coleridge's prose writings, entitled *Spirit*, and a volume of his
hitherto unpublished *Philosophical Lectures
1818–1819*, Professor Coburn is the author
of several articles on Coleridge, Wordsworth, and Hazlitt. She is Professor of English at Victoria College in the University of
Toronto.

COLERIDGE

A COLLECTION OF CRITICAL ESSAYS

Edited by

Kathleen Coburn

Prentice-Hall, Inc.
A SPECTRUM BOOK
Englewood Cliffs, N. J.

NOTE: Contributors' preferences account for the different listings of the titles of Coleridge's poems: thus, The Ancient Mariner, "The Ancient Mariner," and *The Ancient Mariner*.

Current printing (last number):
10 9 8 7 6 5 4 3 2 1

Contents

Introduction

by Kathleen Coburn

It is a common delusion that Coleridge is well-known
—F. J. A. Hort

Sometime in the 1920s a rising young poet wrote a potted biography of Coleridge for the National Portrait Gallery postcard from the Peter Vandyke portrait. It reads:

SAMUEL TAYLOR COLERIDGE

1772-1834

When five years old had read the *Arabian Nights*. Christ's Hospital and Cambridge. Metaphysician and poet. His life was ill-regulated; weak, slothful, a voracious reader, he contracted an unhappy marriage and much later the habit of taking laudanum. Described his own character in his great *Ode to Dejection* (1802). The greatest English literary critic, he was also the greatest intellectual force of his time. Probably influenced Newman, Maurice, and the Young Tories; and died as the guest of Mr. Gillman of Highgate.

T. S. Eliot.

In 1964, a few months before he died, Eliot gave an interview to the *Yorkshire Post*, during which, being reminded of his "idea that Coleridge had failed as a religious person" he replied:

I don't remember saying anything of the sort. Coleridge certainly was a religious man, and has a very important place in the history of religious thinking in the nineteenth century. I believe some of his writings stimulated Cardinal Newman and Frederick Denison Maurice. But I am always in the process of revising my views of Coleridge in the light of further knowledge. When I wrote a postcard for the National Portrait Gallery portrait of Coleridge, I still accepted the idea of Coleridge which was propagated by Carlyle in his "Life of Alexander Stirling," [sic] the idea of Coleridge as a lazy man. But Coleridge was a man of infinite industry, far more industrious than I am myself. I certainly wouldn't accept the idea that Coleridge failed religiously.

You have previously suggested that.
Did I?

Eliot's early views, and his later incredulity about them, represent fairly enough the changing responses to Coleridge of minds sensitive to the dynamics of literary history during the past forty-odd years. A rewriting of the National Gallery postcard in about the same number of words might now run something like this:

> A Devonshire vicarage, Christ's Hospital, and Cambridge. Author of *The Ancient Mariner* and other unforgettable poems. Great literary critic, psychologist, philosopher, theologian, lecturer, journalist, constructive critic of church and state, his works comprise some twenty volumes and seventy notebooks. Davy, Wordsworth, Mill, Newman, Maurice, I. A. Richards, Herbert Read, have all submitted to his varied creative influence in demanding realistic inquiry and imagination everywhere, in mundane and religious, as well as in aesthetic experience.

The impersonal generalities of the postcard, are well enough supported by the bare facts, and in I. A. Richards's essay in this volume are presented more fully.

In reviewing the progress of Coleridge's reputation through the years, it is pleasant to recall that the last Coleridge volumes to appear in the nineteenth century were his grandson's edition of the letters and his selection from the notebooks, *Anima Poetae,* both published as late as 1895. Undoubtedly these convey something of the engaging liveliness of Coleridge's sinewy comments on life and literature that the generation sixty years before had known through *Table Talk.* These were followed early in the twentieth century by the same editor's authoritative edition, in two volumes, of the *Poetical Works* (1912). Of the four great romantics, Coleridge was best served by his first editors—all members of his family. The great wealth of material lying behind these splendid publications was destined, however, to remain for many years untouched.

Then came two seminal books: in 1928 J. L. Lowes's *The Road to Xanadu,* and in 1934 I. A. Richards's *Coleridge on Imagination.* Lowes's book, subtitled *A Study in the Ways of the Imagination,* though frequently misunderstood as an attempt to *explain* the making of a poem, interested a large public, who demanded a second edition in 1930; his lecture audiences in Oxford in 1930-31 on the romantic poets overflowed to window sills and hallways, as Lowes, evidently fascinated by the poetic process as seen in images and revisions, described, not how the *Ancient Mariner* came about, nor the Mariner's destination, but the enormous range of interlocked reading out of which the poem set sail. One indirect effect was to impress readers with a new awareness, based on specific annotation, that Coleridge's famous erudition was not to be divorced from the seemingly simple and effortless poems. Lowes's book drove the thin edge of the wedge into the careless but solemn utterances to the effect that Coleridge's learning and philosophy had destroyed the poet. (Humphry House later applied his confident hammer to the same wedge.)

The second influential work, Richards's *Coleridge on Imagination,* provided among other things an analysis, by the much-respected author of *Practical Criticism* and *Principles of Criticism,* of Coleridge's principles and practice. Saintsbury had eulogized Coleridge's theory of criticism ("So then, there abide these three, Aristotle, Longinus, and Coleridge")[1] and Elton his practice, when he said that no one had ever excelled Coleridge in capturing poetic creation in the very act; but Richards analyzed Coleridge's poetics in the context of more recent critical and psychological theories, and discussed the nature and scope of the ways in which they anticipated later critics. Another office the book performed was to show that much of Coleridge's language of criticism was more precise and based on more specific experiences than Carlyle, and Sterling, and the Floskyites had appreciated.

What Lowes and Richards, in almost antithetical ways, were battling against was not only the general highly personal reaction of the First World War generation, led by Eliot, against the romantics, but also— and this represented a force in Eliot's background—the strong moral opposition of Irving Babbitt, whose essay "Coleridge and Imagination" in *The Nineteenth Century and After* (1929), among his numerous attacks on romanticism, demonstrated his antagonism to the imagination and all its operations, whether in literature or in the expanding society. In England, other hyper-rationalizations appeared in Lytton Strachey's review of Shawcross's edition of *Biographia Literaria* in 1907. Admitting that "a new annotated edition . . . has long been wanted," Strachey goes on:

> The only fault to be found with Mr. Shawcross's commentary is that it is apt to take Coleridge a little too seriously. . . . The truth is that Coleridge, in spite of—one is almost tempted to say in consequence of—his love of philosophy, was not a philosopher. He speculated too much and thought too little. . . . His famous theory of the imagination and the fancy, which forms the philosophical nucleus of the *Biographia Literaria,* hardly

---

[1] "Coleridge is the critical author to be turned over by day and by night. . . . . Coleridge—not Addison, not the Germans, not any other—is the real introducer into the criticism of poetry of the realising and disrealising Imagination." *A History of Criticism* (1917), III, 230-31.

deserves the elaborate consideration which Mr. Shawcross has devoted to
it in his introduction.

"Imagination," *Spectator* (7 March 1908)

Disagreement with Coleridge's philosophical or literary theories can be
shared by those most enthusiastic about him, but it was much too late in
the day to refuse to take them seriously. The "famous theory of the
imagination and the fancy," famous with very good reason, has had
more serious attention since then. T. J. Wise published the first *Bibli-
ography of Coleridge* in 1913; added a supplement, *Coleridgeiana*, in
1919; and published, in 1927, *Two Lake Poets, A Catalogue*, chiefly of
Wordsworth and Coleridge manuscripts. Spadework was going on. In
1929 Alice Snyder's *Coleridge in Logic and Learning* was published in
New Haven and London, a book far more influential than has been
fully recognized. However indirect the debt, more recent works owe
something to this pioneering selection of material from neglected manuscripts in the British Museum. In 1934, the centenary year of Coleridge's
death, Miss Snyder's edition of the *Treatise on Method* (Coleridge's introduction to the *Encyclopaedia Metropolitana*) was published.

J. H. Muirhead's *Coleridge as Philosopher* (1930) was one of those books
of which the failure is almost more instructive than success. The reason
was that Coleridge could not be reshaped by the mold of late nineteenth-
century British idealism into which Muirhead, with zest and affection,
tried to pour him. To some articles of Muirhead's philosophical faith
Coleridge simply could not be made to subscribe. Muirhead tried to dis-
allow the contradictions and inconsistencies; he recognized yet did not
seem fully to pursue the changing phases of Coleridge's thought between
the writing of the *Biographia Literaria* and the rewriting of *The Friend*
in 1818, and further still during the writing of *Aids to Reflection* and
later. Coleridge needs a tough-minded, objective, nonallied, nonprofes-
sional philosopher to tolerate and trace his intellectual image, for it is
not that of a systematic philosopher. Muirhead's positive contribution,
based on his knowledge of Coleridge's philosophical manuscripts, was less
his particular view than his contention that before comprehension and
criticism of Coleridge could proceed adequately, it was necessary to edit
the unpublished manuscripts.

A long and important article in 1929 by T. M. Raysor, "Coleridge and
Asra," [2] underlined this need from the biographical point of view: Cole-
ridge's domestic unhappiness and his love for that other Sara, Mrs.
Wordsworth's sister, were no secrets, as the poems alone told. But Raysor's

[2] In *Studies in Philology* XXVI (July 1929), 305-24.

contribution was to spell out, from the notebooks, the story of a relation-ship the significance of which had not been fully clear, either in itself or in relation to the breach with Wordsworth. The scholarly objectivity of Raysor's account, and the quality of the suffering revealed by the notebook entries, helped Humphry House to realize that Coleridge's manuscripts might reveal much that would be of significant literary in-terest in new dimensions of self-communication.

In 1930-31 Lowes and Muirhead were both lecturing in Oxford, an Oxford almost barren of interest in romantic poetry, at least in the in-fluential places. The indifference[3] was significant for the taste of the time more than for any deeply hostile or severely scholarly view of Coleridge's works, but it was in this atmosphere that a scholar of repute, with his eye on the centenary to come in 1934 and over-persuaded by colleagues, strayed into the uncongenial pasture of Coleridge biography. E. K. Chambers's biography of Coleridge was acclaimed as a miracle of condensation, as indeed it was; but the author's (self-admitted) antago-nism to his subject was noticed even by the reviews of that time, though to the general public its unjustness was obscured by Chambers's high scholarly reputation. However, its narrow moral and personal condem-nations, its lack of literary concern and perspective, the incomplete and unfair quotations, the contemptuous method of condensing references, were such manifest distortions as to discredit it with most Coleridgians. If Coleridge's life could be summed up in Chambers's final sentence, as "a handful of golden poems, an emptiness in the heart of a few friends, and a will-o'-the-wisp light for bemused thinkers," one wondered, why the "biographical study"? It was an immense loss that a compendium of biographical data by so skilfull a compiler should leave Coleridge's bi-ography still to be written.[4]

The centenary editing and criticism of Coleridge produced in the '30s T. M. Raysor's three rich and complicated volumes of literary criticism, E. L. Griggs's two volumes of *Unpublished Letters* (a foretaste of better things to follow), and two volumes of miscellaneous essays,[5] two or three of which threw shafts of light on unknown or little-known aspects of Coleridge's work. But Coleridge was still, a hundred years after his death,

---

[3] It seems appropriate to record here that at a critical stage one Oxford don, out of her rich interest in English literature of various periods, Dr. Ethel Seaton of St. Hugh's College, gave essential encouragement and vital help to my own Coleridge studies.

[4] The best study of Coleridge's early intellectual life has come from France, by Paul Deschamps: *La Formation de la Pensée de Coleridge (1771-1804)* (Paris, 1964).

[5] *Coleridge: Studies by Several Hands on the Hundredth Anniversary of his Death,* ed. Edmund Blunden and E. L. Griggs (London, 1934) and *Wordsworth and Coleridge: Studies in Honor of George McLean Harper,* ed. E. L. Griggs (Princeton, 1939).

discussed almost exclusively as poet and critic. The constructive work of
J. J. Isaacs in 1935 should also be remembered. His lecture to the English Association on "Coleridge's Critical Terminology" in conjunction
with the new *Oxford English Dictionary* (1933), stirred fresh attention
to Coleridge's use and creation of language.

The centenary passed by rather quietly, and until after the Second
World War one heard even less of Coleridge. One volume, however, came
out of occupied France: in 1945 *Coleridge: Vingt-Cinq Poèmes. Introduction et Traduction de Germain D'Hangest, Inspecteur général de
l'Instruction publique* was published in Paris. To read these tender trans-
lations, and the thorough, compact, and penetrating introduction of 150
pages, biographical and critical, was a moving experience, partly because
of the time ("Art stabilizes us on the verge of chaos," Picasso was saying
then) and partly because of the realization that the power of Coleridge's
poems in France was stronger and, naturally, truer than his anti-Galli-
canism.

Just before the war the publication of a slim volume of selections from
his political and social criticism, *The Political Thought of Samuel Taylor
Coleridge* by R. J. White, was a sign of fresh interest in the nonliterary
aspects of Coleridge's writings; but the fact that only *selections* were
ventured was perhaps symptomatic, just as the fuller publication later, by
the same editor, of *Political Tracts of Wordsworth, Coleridge and Shelley*
in 1953 was the sign of a fairer wind.

In 1942, in *Coleridge and the Broad Church Movement,* C. R. Sanders
discussed Coleridge as a liberal influence on English thought. Whether
deliberately or not, the book followed by an exact century a work the
dedication of which had also explained, glowingly, Coleridge's liberal
Anglican influence on an earlier generation: the second edition in 1842
of F. D. Maurice's *The Kingdom of Christ,* which was dedicated to Der-
went Coleridge in a thirty-two-page eulogy of his father. In spite of its
personal ambience, Maurice's statement of Coleridge's role as inquirer
and teacher was perhaps the most accurate of his time, and had it been
expressed in a broader setting might have modified considerably Mill's
emphasis on the Tory and High Church side of Coleridge's position. In
any case, Sanders took up where Maurice left off, and his essay on Coleridge as primarily an intellectual liberator was one that needed to be
written; it was, moreover, one of the freshest of the near-centenary crop.[6]

After the war, an indication of greatly increasing interest came with
negotiations, begun in 1947, for the purchase by the Pilgrim Trust for

---

[6] See also his "Coleridge as a Champion of Liberty," *Studies in Philology,* XXXII
(October 1935), 618-31.

the British Museum of the great collection of manuscripts and annotated books then owned by the late Geoffrey Lord Coleridge of Ottery St. Mary. In 1951 the transfer of these to the British Museum made possible an entirely new range of scholarly activity. The very fact that such negotiations were considered to be in the public interest reflected a change in the prevailing attitude to Coleridge. In 1934 the Nonesuch Press compendium of Coleridge's prose and verse had seemed to suffice; thirty years later nothing less than a collected edition, as nearly complete as may be, seems adequate.

Monographs and articles written about the poems in recent decades have naturally concentrated on the three most famous, and all in one way or another are attempts to gainsay the "black magic" theory of Lowes and others. Truth abhors a vacuum, and there has been an increasing impetus to account for the responses elicited by *The Ancient Mariner*, *Christabel*, and *Kubla Khan*, to understand (neither to minimize nor inflate) the precise quality and nature of one's experience of this poetry. Within the limits of this volume it has been a formidable task to try to select from scores of possibilities the most influential and interesting articles; yet one may say that those selected here are at least representative in that they attempt, by relating the themes and images of the poems, to show a pattern of thought and his psychological and aesthetic achievement. An enriching aspect of Coleridge studies has been the attention given the "Conversation Poems," as Humphry House, their distinguished first commentator, called them; the later poems are also steadily becoming recognized as having hitherto unacknowledged merit as poems and as having a good deal to say about Coleridge as well.[7] All the poems, well- or little-known, are being placed in the larger arcs of Coleridge's apperceptions. In fact, one obvious tendency of recent work on Coleridge is to show that the prose works and the poems can no longer be considered in the all-but-complete disjunction with which the nineteenth century regarded them.

One contribution to the present selection comes from Japan. Regrettably it is a mere synopsis—kindly provided by the author—of an article in the English quarterly published in Kyoto, *Apollon-sha*. It is included here not only for its intrinsic merit but also as a hopeful indication of things to come from the young generation of Japanese scholars. It displays a certain universal human response to Coleridge by subsuming

---

[7] See I. A. Richards's *Coleridge's Minor Poems* (a lecture delivered at Montana State U., April 8, 1960); George Whalley's "'Late Autumn's Amaranth': Coleridge's Late Poems," *Transactions of the Royal Society of Canada*, Vol. II, Series iv (June 1964), 159-79.

cultural differences, a response the more remarkable for "the sense of difficulty overcome" in transcending the East-West barrier. Articles by the younger men in Japan increasingly reflect their own personal dialogue with Coleridge's mind and its products, articles on central questions such as Kimiosha Yura's "Coleridge and *Remorse*," Yasunari Takahashi's "Coleridge and the Stream of Consciousness," and Asanari Yamanouchi's "The Cycle of Joy and Dejection in the Poetry of Coleridge." [8] It will be seen from the very titles that these responses are rooted in world-wide intellectual developments since Freud and Proust and Sartre. Is this merely an accident of a fashionable psychological attention? It may be so. Or are there not deeper causes behind the present approaches to Coleridge, American, English, French, German, Italian, Japanese, and Spanish? The response of his cosmopolitan audience is exemplified in this selection of essays in the conviction that these lie in part in Coleridge himself. We are no longer primarily interested in whether Coleridge had his ideas from the German transcendentalists or whether they were original with him; they are more and more seen to belong to a climate of opinion, and in any case, personal priorities and national claims now have taken their place far behind more meaningful concerns.[9]

It is true to say that some of the excitement aroused by Coleridge in the young today is connected with his post-Kantian, pre-Freudian views, and by what is taken by some to be pre-Sartrian existentialism. This is admirably clear in the study by M. Paul Deschamps referred to above. It was Coleridge's habit to ask acute questions about logical, psychological, and metaphysical uncertainties—the powers of the human mind, and the relation of mind, on the one hand to emotion, instinct, the body, on the other to the mysteries of the universe. His were the critical post-Kantian questions posed by a sensibility and a poetic imagination that left Kant inadequate for him and threw him back on Greek philosophers, seventeenth century English divines, the observation of children, chemistry, the natural world, and a self-examination at least as rigorous as Swift's and coming almost as close to unbalancing him. Is one factor in Coleridge's accessibility to foreigners the fact that in his poems he taps

---

[8] The production of Japanese Coleridgeana since the first translation of *The Rime of the Ancient Mariner* in 1924 has gained extraordinary momentum. Excellent work on Coleridge being done in several other countries is also represented here. Private bibliographies kindly supplied by French and German scholars, along with monographs and periodical articles, show interesting developments from the influence of, *inter alios,* Aynard, D'Hangest, Brandl, and Webber.

[9] Two excellent recent studies, J. A. Appleyard's *Coleridge's Philosophy of Literature* and R. H. Fogle's *The Idea of Coleridge's Criticism* take their departures from ground cleared of the old saws about origins and deviations and discuss Coleridge's views for their inherent interest.

more directly the inner reaches of human experience, those "obscure feelings" he frequently struggles with, dimmer but more universal, less specified in time and place and culture than, say, period manners or a regional landscape? Basically a haunted man, Coleridge is seen in modern terms to have been a brave one, pursuing with fervor and through despair his inquiries into the common human dilemmas he knew under the skin as well as intellectually; personal experience led him to perceive, in any area, the unrecognized, or unappreciated, psychological factor.

Coleridge's is generally considered one of the great minds, but from schooldays onward something of a nine-days' wonder, to be admired or condemned according to its supposed direction or to be appreciated in fragments. To those who do not like wonders or fragments, Coleridge can be irritating; and it must be admitted that he can be charged with exploiting the modes of both wonder (Lamb's "inspired charity boy") and the sick genius ("power without strength") in neglecting to complete his poem or his plan. His unabashed need to be liked, the evasions and exaggerated apologies of the drug addict, the self-indulging petty excuses, these combined with grandiose designs never fulfilled, are naturally repellent in varying degrees, most of all to those for whom these frailties seemed in his case to be linked with unacceptable idealistic moralistic positions. No analysis of Coleridge as a person, nor of any of his roles as poet, literary critic, theologian, social critic, critic of philosophy, or educationist, can dissolve such objections. To Coleridge's admirers the palliative is that he is himself the discloser of his most unendearing weaknesses, especially in his letters; they are parts of the whole man, in whom we learn nevertheless to recognize what Aristotle demanded of tragedy—a certain magnitude.

Certain modifications of time-worn approaches to Coleridge have renewed the perspective, but it is no simple matter to account for what appears to be his ascending reputation. In part the answer lies in ourselves. The intellectual temper of our time is perhaps less prone, at least in the circles where Coleridge is still discussed, to the attack *ad hominem*. There is a real sense in which increase of general knowledge in our time brings not only increase of tolerant predisposed sympathy but also acceptance of realities, in this case of the fact that emotional instability is wholly compatible with very great powers of mind and imagination and moral insight. Another factor lies in the reverse situation, that in the imbalances of our time we find among Coleridge's qualities an inspiriting foresight. His relativist position in many areas, the refusal to accept "rules from without," the belief in the changeability rather than the sanctity of social institutions, the faith in education, the concept of the

need of freedom and joy for all creativity, even the delicacy of his pleas-
ures and the modernity of his sufferings and anxieties, these surprise one
—sometimes from a thicket of gangliated prose—into admiration. The
more one reads Coleridge the more one is struck by the sensitivity and the
toughness of his observations, their rootedness in explicit experience. As
pointed out elsewhere:

> When he wrote his strong plea—and one of his firmest pieces of prose—on
> behalf of Sir Robert Peel's bill to reduce the working hours of children in
> the cotton factories, he wrote from the conviction that the arguments of the
> opposition, based on the hue and cry of "free labour," were deceptive, and
> that the labor of the children was not free at all, that they were in fact slaves
> of an expanding commercial enterprise. This he knew and felt from his per-
> sonal knowledge of what freedom is and what slavery is. Slavery, he says, is
> a state of "hopelessness"; slavery to commerce, or slavery to opium are
> psychologically very much the same thing. Opium he described late in life,
> in 1832 to Green, as "the curse of my existence, my shame and my negro-
> slave humiliation and debasement." He knew what it felt like to be a Negro
> slave, or a factory child. Slavery to anything prevents the fullest integration
> of the person and blocks creative activity. Hence the cotton-children must
> be made free. It is not a question of working hours but of life itself, of re-
> leasing them from the clutches of Death-in-Life.[10]

In addition to our own increased receptivity to the conjunctions of perception that Coleridge has to offer, there have been other significant
steps in the renewed discovery of Coleridge. One has been the dissolution
of the Lakes school. Coleridge strenuously objected to the grouping of
Wordsworth, Southey, and himself, whether as poets or literary theorists;
nor did he appreciate for more than a very short time the theological,
political, and social views of the other two. The literary differences, already well-known though surrounded by confusion, appear sharper in
the notebooks and marginalia; other gulfs are made clear there also, as
well as in the work of R. J. White, David Calleo, and others, and will
be even clearer as editing progresses of works like *The Friend*, the *Lay
Sermons*, the *Biographia Literaria*, and various manuscript remains. It
has for some time been insufficient to see the three men as companion
radicals in youth and opponents alike of the Reform Bill of 1832. But
we now find that William Hone quoted Coleridge in support of liberal
views in 1817 in a journal that would never have quoted Wordsworth or
Southey in the same vein. Coleridge's relation to Wordsworth in particu-

[10] *Inquiring Spirit. A New Presentation of Coleridge from his Published and Unpublished Prose Writings*, ed. Kathleen Coburn (London: Routledge & Kegan Paul,
1950), p. 19.

lar is being viewed afresh, with distinctions perhaps to the advantage of both reputations. A tendency to see Wordsworth as the tree and Coleridge the vine (the simile is, I think, Middleton Murry's), while originating in an undoubted truth, at one time led away from some of the broader and livelier vistas of Coleridge's thought, as well as to some blurring of critical distinctions. The essay by M. H. Abrams reprinted in this volume deals with one aspect of needed clarifications in this area.

Another step in a positive direction is the increased attention to Coleridge's prose. The more it is studied the more intellectually independent of Wordsworth Coleridge is seen to be, and the more one appreciates the scale of his attention to the workings of the mind, as Professor Emmet demonstrates in her paper here on "Coleridge on the Growth of the Mind." The unpublished manuscripts when they appear will show that some of the day-dream architecture did get beyond the drafting board.

To some minds Coleridge has become not only a congenial fact of past history but an effective contemporary force. When one works closely with what he writes at his best, whether he offers a poem or a judgment, Coleridge invites the reader's participation, compels it, like his own old mariner, and with a subtle generosity based on an acute sense of the complexity of things. Poetry "calls the whole soul of man into activity," he said; poets are "gods of love that tame the chaos." Activity, creativity, in whatever area of human experience, he sees as the basis of all joy—activity as against passivity—whether in the making of a poem, a critical insight, a social reform, a philosophical reconciliation, or a religious affirmation, for these constitute life itself. Vice-versa, without joy life becomes inert and creation dies. Life must be perpetually re-created. "What we are and what we are about to become" are for him the fundamental and unending questions. He asks them of himself and of his reader, often in such penetrating and self-realizing ways that we cannot choose but hear.

Coleridge: His Life and Work

by I. A. Richards

Samuel Taylor Coleridge was born at Ottery St. Mary in Devonshire, October 21, 1772, the son of a clergyman and schoolmaster and youngest of a family of ten. His own account of his early years will be found in the 1797 letters to Poole. His father died when he was nine and about a year later he went to Christ's Hospital in London, of which his younger schoolmates Charles Lamb, in his Elia essay "Christ's Hospital Five-and-Thirty Years Ago," and Leigh Hunt, in his *Autobiography,* give vivid accounts. Memories of these days occur frequently in Coleridge's writings. (See "Frost at Midnight," "Dejection," and *Biographia Literaria,* chapter I.) He was extremely successful in the strict classical studies of the school, but the extent and energy of his other interests were still more notable. An early plunge into medical books (his brother Luke was a surgeon at London Hospital) was followed by a passionate immersion in metaphysics and theology, ranging from Plotinus to Voltaire. It is significant that he was in the sick ward for months, with jaundice and rheumatic fever, after bathing in his clothes in the New River and drying off in them.

He went up to Jesus College, Cambridge, at nineteen (October 1791). There was a year of steady reading and modest living and rheumatism. Then debts, due largely to carelessness, threw his whole being off balance. In a suicidal mood he wandered off to London and on a random impulse enlisted in the Light Dragoons (December 4, 1793) as Silas Tomkyn Comberbache. He lived up to the name by failing too frequently to stay in the saddle. He was soon given orderly duties with smallpox patients and by early April his brothers had succeeded in buying him out and he returned to Cambridge. His college behaved very reasonably to him.

In June 1794 he walked to Oxford, where he met Southey, a decisive meeting. The two at once "struck out the leading features of a pantisocracy," Coleridge inventing the name. This was a noble and philosophic project for a group emigration to America. Twelve young men with their twelve wives were to settle there as an ideal community, an "experiment of human Perfectability." Unfortunately Southey was in love with Edith Fricker, one of five daughters of a manufacturer of sugar pans whose business had vanished with the cessation of trade with America. Lovell, the earliest convert to their scheme, was engaged to another of the Fricker daughters. Why not a third, Sarah Fricker, for Coleridge? The chief impediment was a passion he had been nursing for Mary Evans, the sister of a school friend. A mild attachment to her had grown fervent in the crisis which sent him into the Dragoons. It was still painfully active throughout a walking tour in Wales and another tour, with Southey, in Somerset. These feelings did not however prevent him from becoming engaged to Sarah in the interests of Pantisocracy before returning to Cambridge. All the Fricker girls and their mother were to go. During the winter the scheme, not surprisingly, collapsed. Southey's aunt, to whom they looked to finance the emigration, had shown him the door. Worse still, Southey had proposed introducing a servant class into the community. Mary Evans had written what she thought about it all, and in a following letter had answered Coleridge's prayer, "Indulge, Mary, this my first, my last request, and restore me to *reality,* however gloomy."

The end of Pantisocracy should have put an end to his engagement. In spite of some struggles it did not. Coleridge left Cambridge, without taking his degree, before the end of the year, lingering in London till Southey came to fetch him to Bristol and Sarah. He married her in October 1795. Six weeks later Southey married his Edith, but not before a complete, though temporary, breach had occurred between the *ci-devant* Pantisocrats.

Married life began happily in the cottage at Clevedon described in "The Eolian Harp." The publisher Cottle had undertaken to buy Coleridge's verse (at a guinea and a half per hundred lines) and any prose works too. Lectures in the cause of civic liberties, anti-war pamphleteering, and some preaching as a Unitarian, led on to a venture with a periodical, *The Watchman,* addressed primarily to democrats. It failed after ten numbers, in part because Coleridge in the second number put at the head of his essay on fasts, "Wherefore my Bowels shall sound like an Harp" (Isaiah). Coleridge thought that cost him five hundred subscribers.

At this moment a group of admirers headed by Thomas Poole put up a subsidy for him of about forty pounds a year for seven years. "Reviews, the magazine and other miscellaneous literary earnings—shilling-scavenger employments," might provide another such amount. But there was an allowance of twenty pounds to be made to Mrs. Fricker, and other dependents to support, "five mouths opening and shutting as I pull the string." And in September 1796 his first son, David Hartley, was born. The search went on for some means to deal with "the two giants leagued together, whose most imperious commands I must obey, however reluctant—their names are BREAD and CHEESE."

At the end of the year he moved to a cottage at Nether Stowey near to the most faithful and helpful of all his friends, Thomas Poole, a prosperous tanner of strong democratic views. And in the spring he began to be in touch first with William Wordsworth and then also with Dorothy. They were living at Racedown (some forty miles away) and there Coleridge visited them (June 5, 1797).

The force of the attraction between Coleridge and the Wordsworths may be seen from some dates. He probably stayed at Racedown June 5 to 28, then back to Stowey and back again July 2 to fetch the Wordsworths to stay with him. On July 7 Lamb arrived for a visit. "This Lime Tree Bower My Prison" was written in Poole's garden while the Wordsworths and Lamb were out walking. "Dear Sarah" had upset some boiling milk over Coleridge's foot and he was unable to go with them. By the middle of July the Wordsworths had moved into a large vacant mansion at Alfoxden, three miles from the Nether Stowey cottage. Poole had arranged it, helpful as ever.

Soon came a visit from "Citizen Thelwall," a leading anti-Government democratic agitator. Coleridge had been disagreeing with him for some time in more and more friendly letters. His visit created local alarm. Wordsworth's coming had been bad enough, with his mysterious solitary walks toward the sea. (A French invasion, we must remember, was expected.) But now! Soon there was an agent observing and reporting on their doings, conversation, and visitors. He seems to have been a capable and sensible man, and in a conversation struck up on the road found Coleridge no friend to Jacobinism. On moving to Stowey Coleridge had written: "I have accordingly snapped my squeaking baby-trumpet of sedition, and have hung up its fragments in the chamber of Penitence." The influence of Nether Stowey worked on Thelwall too.

For Wordsworth Coleridge was soon head over heels in admiration. "Wordsworth is a very great man, the only man to whom *at all times* and *in all modes of excellence* I feel myself inferior." As with even Southey's verse before, admiration of others' work made him excessively diffident about his own, which at that date may well be thought to outweigh Wordsworth's. And, though no accountancy is possible with such deep interchanges and indebtednesses, Wordsworth seems undoubtedly the chief gainer from the strange poetic symbiosis which now began. It is arguable that as to many modes of excellence—by finding the style which Wordsworth was to advocate in the Preface to the *Lyrical Ballads,* by uttering a good half of the thoughts in that and in Wordsworth's later prose, by designing Wordsworth's major poems for him, and by discovering the philosophic seas on which they float[1]—Coleridge was Wordsworth's creator; or, since that is clearly too strong a word, that he first truly showed Wordsworth how to become his own poetic self.

As a minor example, here are Coleridge's reflections on a rivulet near Nether Stowey:

> . . . I sought for a subject, that should give equal room and freedom for description, incident, and impassioned reflections on men, nature, and society, yet supply in itself a natural connection to the parts, and unity to the whole. Such a subject I conceived myself to have found in a stream, traced from its source in the hills among the yellow-red moss and conical glass-shaped tufts of bent, to the first break or fall, where its drops become audible, and it begins to form a channel; then to the peat and turf barn, itself built of the same dark squares as it sheltered; to the first cultivated plot of ground; to the lonely cottage and its bleak garden won from the heath; to the hamlet, the villages, the market-town, the manufactories, and the seaport. My walks therefore were almost daily on the top of Quantock, and among its sloping combes. With my pencil and memorandum book in my hand, I was *making studies,* as the artists call them, and often moulding my thoughts into verse, with the objects and imagery immediately before my senses.

Biographia Literaria, Chapter X

Twenty-two years after these studies Wordsworth's Sonnet Series, "The River Duddon," realizes the design. In Sonnet XXX there could be a memory of Coleridge:

> And oft-times he—who yielding to the force
> of chance-temptation, ere his journey end,
> From chosen comrade turns, or faithful friend—
> In vain shall rue the broken intercourse.

What is certain is that Coleridge had been to Wordsworth what the Duddon may symbolize in the "After-thought" which ends the Series:

[1] As De Selincourt remarked, "It is curious that whilst [*The Prelude*] pays a beautiful tribute to Wordsworth's love for his friend, so little acknowledgement is made of his incalculable intellectual debt to him. Yet it was through Coleridge that he came first to understand himself and his poetic aims." (*Wordsworthian and Other Studies,* London and New York: Oxford University Press, 1947.)

> I thought of Thee, my partner and my guide,
> As being past away.—Vain sympathies!
> For, backward, Duddon, as I cast my eyes,
> I see what was, and is, and will abide;
> Still glides the Stream, and shall forever glide;
> The Form remains, the Function never dies;
> While we, the brave, the mighty, and the wise,
> We Men, who in our morn of youth defied
> The elements, must vanish;—be it so!
> Enough, if something from our hands have power
> To live, and act, and serve the future hour.

Serve the future hour Coleridge's designs certainly did—as often through Wordsworth's pen as his own. Meanwhile the present hour itself was asking to be served as endlessly as any other nursling. A tragedy called then "Osorio"—to become, in 1813, the moderately successful *Remorse*—was written for Sheridan and rejected by him. Work for the *Morning Post* was undertaken. Salaried posts as a Unitarian minister were considered—with much hesitation lest freedom of thought should be impeded. By January 14 he was preaching a trial sermon at Shrewsbury and almost resolved. Here is Hazlitt's well-known description of his voice:

> Mr. Coleridge rose and gave out his text, "And he went up into the mountain to pray, HIMSELF, ALONE." As he gave out this text, his voice "rose like a stream of rich distilled perfumes"; and when he came to the last two words, which he pronounced loud, deep, and distinct, it seemed to me, who was then young, as if the sounds had echoed from the bottom of the human heart, and as if that prayer might have floated in solemn silence through the universe.

> *My First Acquaintance with Poets*

The very next morning (January 15, 1798) came an offer from Josiah and Tom Wedgwood of an annuity of one-hundred-fifty pounds for life, without conditions. It was to enable him to write rather than preach, however. He accepted at once and resigned his Shrewsbury candidature.

At this point the voice of the moralizing biographer is raised. "Perhaps the worst thing possible had happened to him. He had talked long enough; sown enough wild oats. . . . It was time for him, in one way or another, to take up his share of the economic burden which is, or ought to be, the common lot of humanity." [2] From another point of

---

[2] E. K. Chambers, *Samuel Taylor Coleridge: A Biographical Study* (Oxford: The Clarendon Press, 1938), p. 90. He adds, "It is true that his first impulse was to recog-

view, this may have equally been Coleridge's narrowest escape, and the Wedgwood brothers (Tom was a philosopher and original; Josiah an administrator; and a banker brother, John, lived near Bristol and entertained Coleridge) may deserve a grateful thought from everyone who owes anything to Coleridge. This voice of his had perilous powers. He was too much a "born preacher" to become one professionally.

There followed what may reasonably be considered a productive year, in spite of what look a little like other narrow escapes—this time from bodily dangers. Wordsworth remembered "a frightful internal pain" which sometimes caused Coleridge "when they walked together in Somerset, to throw himself down and writhe like a worm upon the ground." And there was a fever caused by an inflamed tooth. Soon after his recovery he walked over to Ottery (thirty-two or more miles) and on April 18 he walked back. In the next few days he wrote "The Nightingale" and "Fears in Solitude." In February he had written "Frost at Midnight" and "France: An Ode" (earlier named "Recantation").

On May 14 a son, Berkeley, was born in the midst of a distracting embroilment with Charles Lloyd, Lamb, and Southey. Lloyd had been a most devout young disciple and for a time a paying guest-pupil in Bristol. And now (April 1798) he published a novel, *Edmund Oliver*, whose hero had a distressingly recognizable resemblance to Coleridge. "I have at all times," Edmund says, "a strange dreaminess about me which makes me indifferent to the future, if I can by any means fill the present with sensations—with that dreaminess I have gone on here from day to day: if at any time thought troubled, I have swallowed some spirits, or had recourse to my laudanum." Damaging reading—to the Wedgwoods, for example. So Coleridge spent some time, with the Wordsworths, chasing Lloyd, and more in correspondence which is often shrewd: ". . . You clothed my image with a suit of notions and feelings which could belong to nothing human." By July, however, this was in the main over and the summer, which came early that year, was in Wordsworth's memory:

> That summer when on Quantock's grassy Hills
> Far ranging, and amid her sylvan Coombs,
> Thou in delicious words, with happy heart,
> Didst speak the vision of that Ancient Man,

---

nize in full the moral obligation which it imposed upon him. 'Now I am enabled, as I have received freely, freely to give. . . .' The thought recurred to him from time to time for many years. But, unfortunately, the longer Coleridge looked at a moral obligation the more he became inclined in practice to shy away from it." The thought recurs in turning these pages: the deeper Chambers looked into Coleridge the more he became inclined to evade understanding him.

> The bright-eyed Mariner, and rueful woes
> Didst utter of the Lady Christabel.

> *The Prelude,* Book XIII,
> lines 395-400, 1805

These had been written in the late autumn of 1797, "Kubla Khan" probably in October 1797, though possibly it may have been in May 1798.

In September 1798 Coleridge, with a young Stowey admirer, John Chester, and the Wordsworths, left for Germany. There he remained till July 1799, learning German, writing affectionate letters to Sarah, plunging into German metaphysics, accumulating materials of all sorts, and planning a life of Lessing. In February the baby, Berkeley, died. The news, received some weeks later, threw Coleridge into deep ponderings of the grounds of belief: "I find it wise and human to believe, even on slight evidence, opinions, the contrary of which cannot be proved, and which promote our happiness without hampering our intellect." This may be compared, perhaps, to T. H. Huxley's assertion under a similar loss: "I know what I mean when I say I believe in the law of the inverse squares, and I will not rest my life and my hopes upon weaker convictions. I dare not if I would" (letter to Charles Kingsley).

Back at Stowey, Coleridge re-established relations, still not too cordial, with Southey; the Wordsworths had removed to Durham. Soon a false rumor of Wordsworth's ill health came and, with Cottle, he rushed in anxiety north. There, at Sockburn (October 1799) he met Sara Hutchinson, a friend of Dorothy's, and William's sister-in-law to be, and was seized with a passion which shaped ten years of his life. A later description by Coleridge's daughter Sara says, "She had fine, long, light brown hair, I think her only beauty, except a fair skin, for her features were plain and contracted, her figure dumpy, and devoid of grace and dignity. She was a plump woman, of little more than five feet." This passion probably explains why, after a walking tour with Wordsworth on which they saw Dove Cottage, Wordsworth's future home at Grasmere, he did not return to Stowey but took up work on the *Morning Post* in London (about November 27, 1799) and wrote to his wife to join him. She left after two months; but Coleridge remained, writing political articles, frequenting the theaters with dramatic reviewing in mind, reporting debates in Parliament, translating Schiller's *The Piccolomini* and *The Death of Wallenstein,* and consorting with Lamb. The great question, the Schiller job once done, was where to live. In the end he followed the Wordsworths to the Lake District; we may suppose Sara Hutchinson to have been a part of the attraction, but he was also fulfilling the promise made in lines 54-58 of "Frost at Midnight."

Greta Hall, Keswick, where Coleridge and his family took up residence July 24, 1800, was then a house with an outlook: "I question if there be a room in England which commands a view of mountains, and lakes, and woods and vales superior to that in which I am now sitting." "If impressions and ideas *constitute* our being, I shall have a tendency to become a god, so sublime and beautiful will be the series of my visual existence." For a while all this kept him up. There were many visits to the Wordsworths at Grasmere, which they returned. It was only a thirteen-mile walk over Dummail Raise. But Coleridge would sometimes add in Helvellyn or Fairfield—good mountain days. He even anticipated by more than a generation the modern taste for pure mountain adventure indulged for its own sake, making a solitary ascent (July 1802) of Scafell and down by Broad Stand into Eskdale, an expedition no tourist—as opposed to a shepherd—had ventured on before or was to repeat for another forty years. So integral may the pioneering spirit be.

In spite of this, ill health dogged him—rheumatisms which may have had as much to do with his teeth as with the weather and perhaps a good deal that would now be labeled psychosomatic. The winter of 1800-1801 saw him bedridden for weeks, and these pains drove him again to opium. As early as this the drug began to be a necessity to him. In the intervals between pain and the miraculous relief he took to yet another sort of pioneering, to experimental inquiry into sense perception. "In the course of these studies," he wrote to Poole, "I tried a multitude of little experiments on my own sensations and on my senses, and some of these (too often repeated) I have reason to believe did injury to my nervous system . . . the disgust, the loathing that followed these fits, and no doubt in part, too, the use of brandy and laudanum which they rendered necessary!"

Much of this was an offshoot of his metaphysical speculations which now became a sustained and passionate concern. It was in these two years that he renounced and extricated himself from the associationism of Hartley and the early Berkeley—the names of his sons show how much they had meant to him. Henceforth for him the mind is to be activity. The great LOCK, as he was to grow fond of calling the philosopher, had been turned; and the key, though in parts it might seem at times to have been cut and filed by Kant, was truly what he had learned long ago from Plato and Plotinus returning now in his own thought as power. The intellectual excitement of the new world he feels that he is creating for himself rings out gaily enough at times in his letters. It is a mistake to take the mood of lines 89-93 of "Dejection" and suppose this to have become constantly the habit of his soul. Metaphysics

and self-observation, so indistinguishably interfused for him hencefor-
ward, were very far from being a mere resource against spiritual agony,
"another anodyne." They were a highly positive mode of spiritual adventure. No doubt they did compensate him for some other things:

> viper thoughts that coil around my mind, Reality's dark dream!

But they were precisely his awakenings from that. By 1802 he has moved
far from his early sentiments as a preacher: "My philosophical refine-
ments and metaphysical theories lay by me in an hour of anguish, as toys
by the bedside of a child deadly sick." (Letter to Benjamin Flower, December 11, 1796). He is thinking *with* rather than thinking *of* ideas: in
these matters his opinions are turning into that kind of knowledge which
is a mode of being.

"Reality's dark dream," however, continued to be thwarting and destructive, and chiefly in scenes of domestic discord. These, perhaps, and
the contrasts with the might-have-beens that thought of the other Sara
called up, explain the stoppage for a while of Coleridge's poetry. And

> When two unequal Minds
> Meet in one House and two discordant Wills

the sight of the strong man Wordsworth, so much less in need of soothing
support and so increasingly surrounded with it, must have been less than
a help. Wordsworth's cool and condescending attitude to Coleridge's
poetry ("The Poem of my Friend has indeed great defects," he could
write of "The Ancient Mariner") and his readiness to accept even the
extremes of Coleridge's admiration as merely due may have contributed
to the dejection. Coleridge's exaltation of Wordsworth's and depreciation
of his own poetry had by now become fantastic. "If I die, and the book-
sellers will give you anything for my life, be sure to say: 'Wordsworth
descended on him like the Γνῶθι σεαυτον from heaven; by showing him
what true poetry was, he made him know that he himself was no Poet' "
(Letter of 1801 to Godwin). The humor which pervades this letter should
prevent us from taking it too tragically.

By the end of 1803 further ill health, and the continued wear and tear
of his remedy, made Coleridge seek another climate. After a tour in
Scotland and a stay in London, he sailed to Malta (April 1804) and
happened into a number of semi-official occupations there. His health
improved at first—on a holiday he made two ascents of Mount Etna—
but homesickness plagued him and it was with impatience that he awaited
a chance to be sent back overland as a King's messenger. In the end he
had to return at his own expense, via Naples and Rome, where he stayed

some months, and, after many confused adventures, sailed from Leghorn, landing in August 1806 in worse shape even than when he left England.

He lingered in London making arrangements for his first course of lectures, and writing affectionately to his wife. There had been talk of a separation since 1801 and with the failure of great efforts toward improved harmony in 1802, the idea had grown stronger. The Wordsworths encouraged it and now, after a short visit in Keswick, Coleridge resolved upon a definitive step. Meanwhile he went with young Hartley, aged ten, to stay at Coleorton, where the Wordsworths and Sara Hutchinson were wintering. On January 7 he wrote "To William Wordsworth" in response to *The Prelude*. But in many ways he was now very seriously sick in mind and body, limp in will and swollen in flesh, irritable and neglectful, at odds with most people including Wordsworth and Josiah Wedgwood (Thomas had died leaving his share of the annuity to Coleridge by will). Only a visit to Poole at Stowey for a while restored him. It was in desperate condition that he tackled his first Royal Institute Lectures (January 15, 1808). Very mixed accounts exist of these. It is probable that the strain they put upon Coleridge still further impaired his condition and increased his opium addiction. To him lecturing seemed "still too histrionic, too like a retail trader in instruction and pastime, not to be depressing." But the lectures attracted wide attention. Coleridge by now was a major celebrity.

He returned to the Lake District in August 1808. The Southeys had since 1803 been installed in Greta Hall and Coleridge took up residence with the Wordsworths, now at Allan Bank, Grasmere. Here, with his boys in the holidays, he lived till early 1810, fighting "the fatal habit of taking enormous quantities of Laudanum, and latterly, of spirits too— the latter merely to keep the former on my revolting Stomach." In the hope that he could succeed in this fight he launched *The Friend*—a series of essays "on the Principles of Political Justice, of Morality and Taste and, in the light of Principles, the work of ancient and modern English Poets" to be published in periodical form. For the business side of this venture Coleridge was hardly the right man. It is no wonder that the Wordsworths were despairful. However, as a producer of copy, Coleridge was surprisingly successful. With Sara Hutchinson as his amanuensis, he managed to keep the series going through twenty-seven numbers. But when, after the twentieth number, the collection of subscriptions had to be attempted, the picture became grim. Coleridge thought he might have lost as much as two or three hundred pounds. And in March Sara Hutchinson left Allan Bank to live with a brother in Wales. That was the end. Coleridge moved in May to Keswick—"Poor Man!—I have not the least doubt but he is the most unhappy of the two," wrote Mrs. Coleridge— and after that to London to stay with Basil Montagu, an acquaintance since Stowey days. And here (October 28, 1810) "occasioned (in *great part*) by the wicked folly of the arch-fool Montagu," occurred that "compared with the sufferings of which all the former afflictions of my life were less than flea-bites." So Coleridge felt about it a year later. Montagu in a quarrel passed on something that Wordsworth had told him warningly about Coleridge's habits. The breach thus confirmed was never more than superficially made up.

For the next six years Coleridge's personal life is an uninviting study. He resumed newspaper work for some months, gave a more successful course of lectures on Shakespeare and Milton, November 1811–January 1812, two more in 1812; revisited the Lakes for copies of *The Friend,* driving past the Wordsworths' house at Grasmere without stopping; and rewrote his play, *Osorio,* which was produced as *Remorse* at Drury Lane in January 1813 and ran for twenty nights. It brought him welcome financial relief, since war losses had compelled Josiah Wedgwood to discontinue his half of the annuity. This blow Coleridge took with dignity and understanding. Much of the next year he was in Bristol trying to help with the affairs of John Morgan, who had housed and helped him often these last years. (See the poem, "To Two Sisters.") Morgan seems to have been in prison for debt. At Bristol he gave more lectures, increasingly interrupted by opium trouble. He was making efforts to escape —with and without the help of doctors and attendants he could not help tricking. In the midst of these he wrote *On the Principles of Genial Criticism Concerning the Fine Arts.*

None of all this made money, and opium in these quantities was not cheap; and by now Hartley was due to go to college. Friends and family were concerned about this, as he knew too well: "Oh! God! It is very easy to say, Why does not Coleridge do this work or that work? I declare to God, there is nothing I would not do, consistent with my conscience, which was regular labour for a regular revenue. But to write such poetry or such philosophy as I would wish to write, or not to write at all, cannot be done amid distraction and anxiety for the day."

None the less, through a year (1815-16) with the Morgans in the country town of Calne, he busied himself in preparing an edition of his poems, with prefaces to contain "a disquisition on the powers of association and on the generic difference between the Fancy and the Imagination." *Biographia Literaria* was on the way. It is an extraordinary fact that Coleridge was able to write the best part of his most sustained prose work while in the full grasp of his malady.

Relief was at hand. In April 1816 it became only too clear again that strict measures were necessary. James Gillman, a Highgate physician, undertook them. In his devoted care, and for a time monetarily much in his debt, Coleridge spent the last eighteen years of his life. His supervision was broken only by short visits to reliable friends and a continental tour with Wordsworth in 1828. Even on his visits to the coasts for sea bathing, Gillman or Mrs. Gillman went along. How complete the cure finally became is a disputed question. But the result of control was apparent before long in production. First came *The Statesman's Manual, or the Bible the Best Guide to Political Skill and Foresight,* a "Lay Sermon" addressed to the governing classes. Then the *Biographia* could be finished off, largely with stuffing, but with Chapter XXII as well, to make up two volumes. Next came his "Treatise on Method," the introductory Essay to the *Encyclopedia Metropolitana,* editor of which he had become. He soon withdrew and made the "Treatise" over into a portion of the revised *Friend,* which was in print by the end of 1818. All this writing, moreover, did not prevent him from delivering lectures upon Shakespeare and much else (January to March 1818) and a new course on the history of philosophy (December 1818–March 1819) along with concurrent courses on literature.

These made little enough profit, however. And at this moment his publishers—the publishers of *Zapolya,* the *Lay Sermons, Sibylline Leaves, Biographia Literaria,* and *The Friend*—failed. There followed a dreary time in which numbers of Great Works had to be laid aside in favor of hack work. Rather too much of his energy went into angry complaints of critical and other ill-usage. Through 1824 he was writing *Aids to Reflection,* which earned him no money but won him a wide new group of admirers. Two years before that, an extensive circle had formed, meeting in Coleridge's parlor on Thursday evenings. Its visitors have recorded—to an extent which is itself the best witness—the wonders of the performance they came to hear.

And yet this is not the impression with which a reader of Coleridge should turn to his work. Thanks to the fascination of the phosphorescent, these sketches gain an exaggerated importance. But fifteen years divide the sage of Highgate from the author of *Biographia Literaria* and as many divide *him* from the poet of 1798 and the thinker of 1801. And it is these last, and the laborious addict of 1815, not the eloquent old man of 1830, who speak most clearly to us. It is noteworthy, moreover, that whereas his prose (and prose discourse) tended to become more relaxed and diffuse, his *poetry* (some occasional verse apart) becomes more taut and self-sustaining. Consider "Youth and Age," "Phantom and Fact,"

"Self-Knowledge," and "Epitaph." It is with these that a sketch of Coleridge's life should close.

The Work

The Coleridge legend is well established and widespread. Carlyle's first impression on meeting him states it for us: "His cardinal sin is that he wants *will*. He has no resolution. He shrinks from pain or labour in any of its shapes . . . sunk inextricably in the depths of putrescent idleness." Nobody did more than Coleridge to inculcate this view of himself. It is one of the most successful of his teachings. On this task, at least, he shrank not from labor. He began as a schoolboy and was busy with it till his last days. Friends early took it up. Eager audiences noted it down and correspondents who treasured the letters in which he voluminously developed it carried it on. His biographers all but agree over it. None the less this short account of the man and his work may well take a cool look at the legend.

In his own account of his childhood, written before he was twenty-five (referred to above) Coleridge has already said against himself most of the things which unfriendly critics have been at pains to stress in the record. "Before I was eight years old I was a *character*. Sensibility, imagination, vanity, sloth, and feelings of deep and bitter contempt for all who traversed the orbit of my understanding, were even then prominent and manifest." It should be added at once that he had an enviable number of most devoted friends, that this is written to amuse the closest of them, and that of all who traversed that prodigious orbit almost the only person for whom he expressed contempt was himself. He was joking here, in a letter to Tom Poole, a man who would well know how much to believe in this contempt. Few in fact have been freer from this "concentrated vinegar of egotism." (See *Anima Poetae,* January 1801.) CL no. 164. And it is only the rest of the picture that has become traditional. In it he is the Great Disappointment; the man who might have but didn't; the waster of unparalleled talents; the type specimen of self-frustrating genius; the procrastinator, the alibi fabricator and the idler. There is enough, factually, in his biography to account for this judgment; but do not let us forget that any remarks about his will or his idleness are diagnosis and interpretation. They may be right; but they are no more than speculation, and with the "idleness" theory at least we ought to balance its source against the facts which might support it.

The source, I have suggested, was Coleridge's own words. From his

schoolboy verses onwards (see *"Quae Nocent Docent"*) he was fond of
lamenting his lack of industry:

> Should Sloth around me throw
> Her soul-enslaving, leaden chain!

He went up to Cambridge, however, about the best-read boy of the year.
His letters early become weariful with such complainings, and with morbidly elaborate analyses of their causes. At its height, it is true, his poetry
could transform this depressant:

> And fears self-willed, that shunned the eye of Hope;
> And Hope that scarce would know itself from Fear;
> Sense of past Youth, and Manhood come in vain
> And Genius given, and Knowledge won in vain. . . . .
> That way no more! and ill beseems it me,
> Who came a welcomer in herald's guise,
> Singing of Glory, and Futurity,
> To wander back on such unhealthful road,
> Plucking the poisons of self-harm!

But as a rule his abnormal consciousness of this failing was its own
exacerbant. His demands upon himself might have been expressly cal-
culated to prevent their fulfillment. And naturally these demands
mounted with the occasion. At his lectures De Quincey remarked,
"the entire absence of his own peculiar and majestic intellect," his
failure to exhibit "that free and eloquent movement of thought which
he could command at any time in a private company." And so too with
formal essay writing. *The Friend* moved Charles Lloyd, who had been
very close to him in earlier days, to observe, almost in his master's voice:

> Coleridge has such a lamentable want of voluntary power. If he is excited
> by a remark in company, he will pour forth, in an evening, without the least
> apparent effort, what would furnish matter for a hundred essays—but the
> moment that he is to write, not from present impulse but from preordained
> deliberation, his powers fail him. He is one of those minds who, except in
> inspired moods, can do nothing—and his inspirations are all *oral*, and not
> *scriptural*. And when he is inspired he surpasses, in my opinion, all that
> could be thought or imagined of a human being.

His letters, however, and the scribblings with which he crowded the
margins of countless books, show that this "oral" theory is wrong. Coleridge certainly was a monologist of superlative scope and power; but
his random jottings often surpass even the best of his recorded talk. He

was freest then. What he wrote was for his own eyes only. The unseen audience and the need to exert his powers worthily could fade out of mind. And in his formal writing the excursions, the indulgences, the footnotes in which he runs away from his theme—the pages of which he could have doubted, as he wrote them, whether they really belonged and would in fact be used—these commonly outweigh the rest. He is most often at his best when he has turned his back, for the moment, on his many times announced, his expected and overmuch challenging goal. The chief exception is the "Essay on Method" reprinted in the third volume of *The Friend,* 1818; and even this is but a sketch towards the *magnum opus* which was always to be.

So too his best poetry is occasional or fragmentary. Apart from "The Ancient Mariner," if even that is, or could be, really finished, he has no completed poem to match his fragments. And some of the best of these come forward as metrical experiments ("A Sunset," "The Knight's Tomb"), as exercises ("A Tombless Epitaph"), as "a schoolboy poem" ("Time, Real and Imaginary") under the shelter in fact of any excuse which will free the poet from pen-fright. Uncompleted "Christabel" will serve as an example: "The reason of my not finishing 'Christabel' is not that I don't know how to do it—for I have, as I always had, the whole plan entire from beginning to end in my mind; but I fear I could not carry on with equal success the execution of the idea, an extremely subtle and difficult one" (*Table Talk,* July 6, 1833). We need not take this original entirety of the plan more seriously than Wordsworth did. But Part One (1797) had been much admired in manuscript before Coleridge's struggles to continue it in 1800 and when at last he succeeded in adding Part Two, there was a releasing circumstance:

> I tried and tried, and nothing would come of it. I desisted with a deeper dejection than I am willing to remember. The wind from the Skiddaw and Borrowdale was often as loud as wind need be—and many a walk in the clouds on the mountains did I take; but all would not do—till one day I dined out at the house of a neighbouring clergyman, and somehow or other drank so much wine, that I found some effort and dexterity requisite to balance myself on the hither side of sobriety. The next day my verse making faculties returned to me, and I proceeded successfully.

Unfortunately the use of wine had in general no such happy effect, if indeed it had any real relevance here. The secrets of inspiration are not so simple. Nor had the use of spirits or opium. This last, we should remember, was quite commonly prescribed in those days for troubles which would now send us to the dentist. As early as his first term at

Cambridge we find him referring to it as to a familiar aid. "I am not however certain, that I do not owe my rheumatism to the dampness of my rooms. Opium never used to have any disagreeable effects on me—but it has on many." Later, the remedy (with the pains) was to fasten crushingly upon him. Its effect then was to increase his self-reproaching and self-excusing beyond all endurance. We should remember that he was a sick man and that this is a symptom.

It is against this background—which should not be, for most people, very hard to imagine—a background of "such a dreadful *falling-abroad*, as it were of my whole frame," of "an utter impotence of the Volition, the faculty *instrumental* to the Will . . . (its Hands, Legs, and Feet, as it were), in the state in which you may have seen paralytic Persons, who attempting to push a step forward in one direction are violently forced round to the opposite," in which "tho' there was no prospect, no gleam of Light before, an indefinite indescribable Terror as with a scourge of ever restless, ever coiling and uncoiling serpents, drove me on from behind. The worst was, that in the *exact proportion* to the importance and urgency of any Duty was it, as of a fatal necessity, sure to be neglected: because it added to the Terror above described"—it is against such a background that we must consider the daunting amount and variety of *work* which Coleridge in cold fact actually did.

His poetry succeeds in more modes than most poets have attempted. In several, moreover, it is highly distinctive. No one else has anything like "Kubla Khan," anything like "Phantom and Fact," anything like "Constancy to an Ideal Object." As to amount, it seems more impressive now than in the years when it was being measured against the output levels of Tennyson, Browning, or Swinburne. The general impression that he dried up comes in part from his own self-upbraidings, in part from his readers' refusal to let any but Christabels count. In spite of all the celebrated weakness of his personality something in him kept him from imitating his own poetry. Few of his contemporaries or of their descendants showed equal integrity; the temptation to which this will-less man could not yield overcame them.

This poet, moreover, was a critic who, in the range of his reading, in the fertility of his comments upon writers of every degree of difference from himself, in the span of his admirations and their depth, as well as in the originative independence of his perceptions, surpasses all forerunners and, with due respect to later and better equipped "library cormorants," all successors. In scholarship, by modern standards he is of course weak. But there are aspects to this work—of being curator to the culture—on which Coleridge's poem, "Psyche," will serve as a comment.

We should not forget too that while the techniques of scholarship have advanced since Coleridge's time as much as those of medicine, current conceptions of what all this knowledge is *for* can claim no similar advances.

But this great critic was furthermore a philosopher, immersed from his teens in this very inquiry, busied his life through in maintaining, with an eloquence unmatched since, that *all* judgment of literature, all preference and choice everywhere indeed, must be grounded "in the component faculties of the human mind itself, and their comparative dignity and importance" (*Biographia Literaria*, Chapter I), and that for the highest of these faculties—call it Reason or Imagination—that on which all the rest should and can depend, the source and sanction of all else, "the rules are themselves the very powers of growth and production" (*Biographia Literaria*, Chapter XVIII). This is hard doctrine for some present-day psychologists to translate into their own languages. The faculty to which as psychologists they have sworn fealty—call it Science; Coleridge called it Understanding—is in lively revolt today, as he prophesied, against any overlord whatsoever. It claims autonomy—a claim which Reason can grant to it *within the territory of Science*. But the territory of Science is not and cannot be the globe. There are other knowledges than those which Science can order. There is Morality, there is Politics, there is Poetry, there is Religion. What authorities govern these? And what supreme Authority sustains them all, would protect them from one another, prevent their trespasses, and heal their perennial warfare? These problems, which Science has made into *world-killers* today, were Coleridge's lifelong and overwhelming questions, truly the fountain-light of all his day and master-light of all his seeing. And though he frequented the philosophers of all the ages and borrowed varied makes of lantern from them, what led him at heart was a peculiar knowledge of himself, a unique awareness of the comings forth and holdings back, of the goings on, in particular and in general, of his own mind. This speculative genius—"the most systematic thinker of our time," John Stuart Mill called him—is primarily a psychologist "by the power of imagination proceeding on the *all in each* of human nature. By *meditation* rather than by *observation?* And by the latter in consequence only of the former? As eyes, for which the former has predetermined their field of vision and to which, as to *its* organ, it communicates a microscopic power?" (*Biographia Literaria*, Chapter XVIII.) He was to say in many ways: "An idea in mind is to a Law in nature as the power of seeing is to Light" (Lecture VII, February 1818). It is true that he very often failed to apply the knowledge so gained in his dealings with others.

He was the typical Returner to the Cave, "slow in getting used to seeing in the dark" (*The Republic,* 517).

But this muser on such recondite themes was also an active if intermittent journalist-commentator, contributing through very stormy times opinion-forming articles to which he could later look back (and it may be doubted whether many commentators can) with deep satisfaction.

To have lived in vain must be a painful thought to any man, and especially so to him who has made literature his profession. I should therefore rather condole than be angry with the mind, which could attribute to no worthier feelings, than those of vanity or self-love, the satisfaction which I acknowledged myself to have enjoyed from the re-publication of my political essays (either whole or as extracts) not only in many of our own provincial papers, but in the federal journals throughout America. I regarded it as some proof of my not having laboured altogether in vain, that from the articles written by me shortly before and at the commencement of the late unhappy war with America, not only the sentiments were adopted, but in some instances the very language, in several of the Massachusetts state-papers.

Biographia Literaria, Chapter X

It was perhaps easier then than now to oppose warlike feelings. However this may be, Coleridge, we must note, was an independent in his politics. He was accused of being a turncoat. To which he could reply that he had kept true to *principles,* others only to parties or countries. We would all like to think so of ourselves. But later students, with historical perspective to help them, endorse his claim. As Harold Beeley acutely remarks, "Thus he became a Tory, and yet his essential faith was unchanged. For he demanded of Toryism what he had previously demanded of Radicalism—government according to ethical principles, the conduct of secular affairs *sub specie aeternitatis.* So far from deserting his cause, he became a missionary for it and exercised a profound influence on English Conservatism." [3] His political principles, be it noted, were no airy abstractions. They were embodied through a searching knowledge of contemporary affairs animated by a down-to-earth sense of present dangers and made practical by a rather hard-headed concern with expediency. There is nothing in the least dreamy about them. The Pantisocratic phase got rid of that. "Governments are more the effect than the cause of that which we are." There is much here that will, I think, be found highly relevant to our present problems. For example,

[3] "The Political Thought of Coleridge," in *Coleridge, Studies by Several Hands on the Hundredth Anniversary of His Death,* edited by Edmund Blunden and Earl Leslie Griggs (London: Constable, 1934), p. 161.

"A constitution equally suited to China and America, or to Russia and Great Britain, must surely be equally unfit for both, and deserve as little respect in political, as a quack's panacea in medical, practice" (*Friend* (1809-10) Essay III).

Last—but Coleridge in his later days put it first—this political realist was a theologian whose discernment and courage won him pervasive and continuing influence. This came, in part, from superior insight into the nature of persuasion, as when he exposes the "theological utilitarianism" of Paley:

> There are spiritual truths which must derive their evidence from within, which whoever rejects "neither will he believe though a man were to rise from the dead" to confirm them. . . . What then can we think of a theological theory, which adopting a scheme of prudential legality common to it with "the sty of Epicurus," as far at least as the springs of action are concerned, makes its whole religion consist in the belief of miracles?
>
> *Friend* (1818), II, ii

To many his distinction of the Understanding from the Reason offered a freedom which they recognized as veridical. What Reason beheld could be supremely trusted because "Reason is the Power of Universal and necessary Convictions, the Source and Substance of Truths above Sense, and having their evidence in themselves . . . the fountain of Ideas and the *Light* of the Conscience" (*Aids to Reflection,* "Section" CVI). To use an aphorism Coleridge himself chose from Henry More:

> The more imperious Sects having put such unhandsome vizards on Christianity, and the sincere Milk of the *Word* having been everywhere so sophisticated by the humours and inventions of men, it has driven these anxious Melancholists to seek for *a Teacher* that cannot deceive, the Voice of the *eternal* Word within them; to which, if they be faithful, they assure themselves it will be faithful to them in return. Nor would this be a groundless Presumption, if they had sought this Voice in the Reason and the Conscience, with the Scripture articulating the same.
>
> *Aids to Reflection,* §XCIV

Coleridge was not only among the first to protest, in detail and at length, against the contradictions and absurdities of supposing inerrant verbal inspiration, and against the practice, for example, of taking Bildad and Job as equally voices of the Lord; but he showed how to combine a radically historical view of the documents with a belief in their unique inspiration (*Confessions of an Inquiring Spirit,* Letter IV). In much of this he was a generation or more ahead of his time. And these were but a small portion of his theological labors. And as a make-weight, he was a copious and indefatigable letter-writer, always ready to write many pages on the obstacles to getting on with the job.

In the face of all this activity and achievement, so much self-reproach on the ground of Sloth takes on a queer air and tempts speculation. Could it be that his peculiar combination of gifts ("Never saw I his like-ness, nor probably the world can see again"—Charles Lamb; "The most wonderful man that he had ever known"—Wordsworth) *had* to set him superhuman tasks? A Jonathan Edwards—to take a not too unlike figure —can cherish an impossible enterprise life-long without knowing. But in Coleridge, until his last years, something seems to have known the impossibility as soon as he came near enough to it. It did not prevent him planning conquests from afar, but it did stop him, by one device or another, when he came to the point, and it kept him from thinking *then* and *there* that he was succeeding when he was not. He could, in brief, use his own criticism where it was most needed. The devices, the ways out, the preliminaries to the approaches to the preparations, into which this super-sanity forced him were often absurd, usually miserable, and sometimes agonizing. They could look like insanity. His unruly volition could and did martyrize him. Whether or not he saw the real causes of his troubles through the thick clouds of his excuses, there is no knowing. He comes through a raw physiological bank of them with the following: "I dare believe that in the mind of a competent Judge what I have performed will excite more surprise than what I have omitted to do, or failed in doing" (Letter of 1828 to William Sotheby). The general contrary impression is good evidence only of the hunger he had known how to arouse. "By what I *have* effected, am I to be judged by my fellowmen; what I *could* have done, is a question for my own con-science" (*Biographia Literaria,* Chapter X).

The Mariner and the Albatross

by George Whalley

I

For me, I was never so affected with any human Tale. After first
reading it, I was totally possessed with it for many days—I dislike all
the miraculous part of it, but the feelings of the man under the
operation of such scenery dragged me along like Tom Piper's magic
whistle.[1]

In these words, in a letter to Wordsworth dated January 30, 1801,
Charles Lamb spoke of Coleridge's *The Rime of the Ancient Mariner*.
Some readers continue to echo Mrs. Barbauld's complaints that the poem
is improbable and has an inadequate or distasteful moral. But these are
mental reservations: poetry of the order of *The Ancient Mariner* does
not work its magic upon the mind alone; and mental afterthoughts are
of little use in explaining, least of all in explaining away, the profound
spiritual and emotional effect of this poem. For every sympathetic reader
since Lamb has been similarly possessed and haunted by *The Ancient
Mariner*.

Lamb's criticism is remarkable in a contemporary. The incisiveness of
his comment, however, lies not so much in his sensitivity to the fascination of the poem as in his immediate recognition of human feeling as
being central in it. Lamb understood and loved Coleridge, and was
never to free himself of the fascination of the man: " 'the rogue has given
me potions to make me love him' " [2]; " 'tis enough to be within the whiff
and wind of his genius, for us not to possess our souls in quiet." [3] Unfortunately we have not the means of knowing that "provocative and
baffling personality" as Lamb did. But a close and sympathetic reading

"The Mariner and the Albatross" by George Whalley. From *University of Toronto
Quarterly*, XVI (1946-47). Reprinted, in slightly abridged form, by permission of the
author and the University of Toronto Press.

[1] *Letters of Charles and Mary Lamb*, ed. E. V. Lucas (London, 1935), I, p. 240.
[2] *Ibid.*, I, p. 185.
[3] *Ibid.*, II, p. 191.

of the *Rime* will bring us much nearer to the essential Coleridge than one would expect in a poem that is professedly "a work of pure imagination."

The Rime of the Ancient Mariner is less "a fantasticall imagination and a drowsie dreame" than "a continued allegory, and a darke conceit." There is an important letter of Coleridge's which confirms the allegorical interpretation of the poem: "I have often thought, within the last five or six years, that if ever I should feel once again the genial warmth and stir of the poetic impulse, and referred to my own experiences, I should venture on *a yet stranger and wilder Allegory than of yore*—. . . ." It is difficult to see how the missing factor in the comparative could be anything but *The Ancient Mariner;* and the opinion is confirmed by the associated idea that follows: "that I should *allegorize* myself, as a rock with it's summit just raised above the surface of some Bay or Strait in the Arctic Sea. . . ." [4] Although the early action of the poem and the killing of the albatross take place in the Antarctic Sea, the details derive from the literature of Arctic travel, as Lowes has shown and as Coleridge would certainly remember.

I wish to examine the poem (a) to show how and to what extent Coleridge's inner life is revealed in the *Rime;* and (b) to show that the albatross was for Coleridge, whether consciously or unconsciously, a symbol with profound personal significance.

I

The aesthetic and poetic qualities of *The Ancient Mariner* are impressive. . . .

Without in any way detracting from the value of *The Rime* as a poem, I wish to show that the "haunting quality" grows from our intimate experience in the poem of the most intense personal suffering, perplexity, loneliness, longing, horror, fear. This experience brings us, with Coleridge, to the fringes of madness and death, and carries us to that nightmare land that Coleridge inhabited, the realm of Life-in-Death. There is no other single poem in which we come so close to the fullness of his innermost suffering. The year after the composition of *The Ancient Mariner* he gave the self-revealing image of

> some night-wandering man whose heart was pierced
> With the remembrance of a grievous wrong,

[4] *Unpublished Letters of Samuel Taylor Coleridge,* ed. E. L. Griggs (New Haven, 1933), II, p. 262; dated (?)1820.

> Or slow distemper, or neglected love,
> (And so, poor wretch! filled all things with himself,
> And made all gentle sounds tell back the tale
> Of his own sorrow).[5]

Many years later he told how "from my very childhood I have been accustomed to *abstract* and as it were unrealize whatever of more than common interest my eyes dwelt on; and then by a sort of transference and transmission of my consciousness to identify myself with the Object—. . . ." [6] Whether or not he recognized this process at the time, Coleridge enshrined in *The Ancient Mariner* the quintessence of himself, of his suffering and dread, his sense of sin, his remorse, his powerlessness. And

> Never sadder tale was heard
> By man of woman born.[7]

For it is not only a crystallization of his personal experience up to the time of the composition of the first version, but also an appalling prophecy fulfilled to a great extent in his life and successively endorsed by his own hand as time passed.

II

Life-in-Death is a recurrent theme in Coleridge's thought. In *The Ancient Mariner* it is luridly personified:

> Her lips were red, her looks were free,
> Her locks were yellow as gold:
> Her skin was as white as leprosy,
> The Night-mare Life-in-Death was she,
> Who thicks man's blood with cold.

And when he summarizes his life in 1833 in his own epitaph, he beseeches the passer-by to

> lift one thought in prayer for S.T.C.
> That He, who many a year with toilsome breath
> Found Death in Life, may here find Life in Death.

[5] "The Nightingale: A Conversation Poem. April, 1798."
[6] *Unpublished Letters*, II, p. 262. This passage immediately precedes the passage quoted above (note 4).
[7] 1798 version. Unless otherwise indicated, quotations from the poem follow the 1834 version.

Life-in-Death meant to Coleridge a mixture of remorse and loneliness. Yet "loneliness" is perhaps too gentle and human a word; let us say "aloneness." It is precisely this combination of remorse and aloneness with which the Mariner's experience is steeped. Remorse is an emotion easy to find in the poem. It is also broadcast throughout Coleridge's letters and later poems, and requires no detailed consideration here.

The Mariner's aloneness is directly stated:

> Alone, alone, all, all alone,
> Alone on a wide wide sea!
> And never a saint took pity on
> My soul in agony.

It is thrown into relief by contrast with multiplicity:

> The many men, so beautiful!
> And they all dead did lie:
> And a thousand thousand slimy things
> Lived on; and so did I.

And it culminates in the horror of utter solitude:

> O Wedding-Guest! this soul hath been
> Alone on a wide wide sea:
> So lonely 'twas, that God himself
> Scarce seemed there to be.

The same theme recurs in smaller details. When the spirits leave the shipmates' bodies, it is with the sound of birds and "like a *lonely* flute." The "Spirit from the south pole" is a *lonesome* spirit; and, even though there is an air of self-sufficiency in the phrase "who bideth by himself," like so many solitary people—like Coleridge, like Dorothy Wordsworth —he loves birds:[8]

> He loved the bird that loved the man
> Who shot him with his bow.

When the spectre-bark has sailed away and the Mariner has snapped the spell of the dead seamen's eyes, he looks out over the ocean and feels a sense of foreboding

> Like one, that on a *lonesome* road
> Doth walk in fear and dread.

[8] For Coleridge on birds, see note 27 below.

These details have a cumulative effect in heightening the direct statement of the Mariner's desolation.

The Mariner's isolation is not "the wages of sin" so much as the state of sin.

> I looked to heaven, and tried to pray;
> But or ever a prayer had gusht,
> A wicked whisper came, and made
> My heart as dry as dust.

Or again:

> The pang, the curse, with which they died,
> Had never passed away:
> I could not draw my eyes from theirs,
> Nor turn them up to pray.

As will be shown, the same aloneness haunted Coleridge and echoes like doom through his other poems, his letters, the Notebooks. And in the passionate eloquence of his morbid remorse, he is constantly and restlessly seeking the sin at the root of the desolation: finding as alternative sins his indolence, "abstruse research," the failure of his marriage, the opium habit.

The "Moon gloss" forges a powerful link between the Mariner and Coleridge.

> In his *loneliness and fixedness* he yearneth towards the journeying *Moon,* and the stars that still sojourn, yet still move onward; and every where the *blue sky* belongs to them, and is their appointed rest, and their *native country* and their own *natural homes,* which they enter unannounced, as lords that are certainly expected and yet there is a *silent joy at their arrival.*[9]

The gloss was written some time between 1800 and 1817, and may have been under revision until the completion of the 1829 collection. It is Coleridge's personal and mature comment upon *The Ancient Mariner.* The "Moon gloss" itself contains the essence of his loneliness and homelessness, feelings which were acutely present long before the composition of *The Ancient Mariner.*

In "Frost at Midnight" (1798) Coleridge recalls the sense of isolation he felt as an orphan at Christ's Hospital:

> if the door half opened, and I snatched
> A hasty glance, and still my heart leaped up,
> For still I hoped to see the *stranger's* face,

[9] My italics.

> Townsman, or aunt, or sister more beloved. . . .
> For I was reared
> In the great city, pent 'mid cloisters dim,
> And saw nought lovely but the sky and stars.

In January, 1796, we find him writing to the Reverend T. Edwards:

I have got among all the first families in Nottingham, and am marvellously caressed, but to tell you the truth I am quite home-sick—owing to this long long absence from Bristol. I was at the *Ball,* last night—and saw the most numerous collection of handsome men and women, that I ever did in one place; but alas! the faces of strangers are but moving Portraits— . . . I feel as if I were in the long damp gallery of some Nobleman's House, amused with the beauty and variety of the Paintings, but shivering from cold, and melancholy from loneliness.

Six months before the composition of the *Rime,* we find him telling his brother that

> at times
> My soul is sad, that I have roamed through life
> Still most a stranger, most with naked heart
> At mine own home and birth-place.

And in January, 1798, he wrote: "The first sunny morning that I walk out, at Shrewsbury, will make my heart die away within me—for I shall be in a *land of Strangers!*" With the last important recrudescence of his creative genius, he was to write in 1802 a curious echo of the watersnake passage:

> All this long eve, so balmy and serene,
> Have I been gazing on the western sky,
>   And its peculiar tint of yellow green:
> And still I gaze—and with how blank an eye!
> And those thin clouds above, in flakes and bars,
> That give away their motion to the *stars;*
> Those stars, that glide behind them or between,
> Now sparkling, now bedimmed, but always seen:
> Yon crescent *Moon,* as fixed as if it grew
> In its own cloudless, starless lake of *blue,*
> *I see them all so excellently fair,*
> *I see, not feel, how beautiful they are!* [10]

It is important to notice in the "Moon gloss" the association of the Moon, the blue sky, and home. Elsewhere the same combination of symbols, sometimes with the addition of tree(s), is associated with the thought of home, friendship and love, or their absence.

---

[10] "Dejection: An Ode"; composed April 4, 1802. My italics.

Practically speaking Coleridge was homeless for the greater part of his life. Remembering the number of times he must have exhausted the patience of his hosts to the point of serious misunderstanding and even the breach of friendship, the last part of the "Moon gloss" is given pathetic personal significance by comparison with "Youth and Age" (1823-32).

> Where no hope is, life's a warning
> That only serves to make us grieve,
> When we are old:
>
> That only serves to make us grieve
> With oft and tedious taking-leave,
> *Like some poor nigh-related guest,*
> *That may not rudely be dismist;*
> *Yet hath outstayed his welcome while,*
> *And tells the jest without the smile.*

In thinking of nature as a healer, he notes (1811) the fate of the desolate man: again his thought turns to home, and the parallel with the "Moon gloss" is again striking.

> And even when all men have seemed to desert us and the friend of our heart has passed on, with one glance from his "cold disliking eye"—yet even then the *blue heaven* spreads it out and bends over us, and the little tree still shelters us under its plumage as a second cope, a *domestic firmament,* and the low creeping gale will sigh in the heath-plant and soothe us by sound of sympathy till the lulled grief lose itself in *fixed gaze* on the purple heath-blossom, till the present beauty becomes a vision of memory.[11]

And in October, 1803, he is trying to account for his aloneness. "But yet, . . . , the greater and, perhaps, nobler, certainly *all* the subtler, parts of one's nature must be *solitary*. Man exists herein to himself and to God alone—yea! in how much only to God! how much lies *below* his own consciousness!" [12]

Let us see how this sense of homelessness is imaged in the Mariner. When the ship finally reaches port he cries:

> Oh! dream of joy! is this indeed
> The light-house top I see?
> Is this the hill? is this the kirk?
> Is this mine own countree?

[11] *Anima Poetæ*, ed. E. H. Coleridge (London, 1895), p. 246. My italics.
[12] *Ibid.*, p. 31.

This utterance is charged with the deep thankfulness of the seafarer returned. In many a page of his travel books Coleridge had read of the emotions aroused by sighting the home port after a long voyage; and he is able to reproduce the feeling, mingled joy and pathos and fear, because he has experienced it imaginatively. In December, 1796, he had anticipated in a striking manner the Mariner's return: "The Sailor, who has borne cheerily a circumnavigation, may be allowed to feel a little like a coward, when within sight of his expected and wished for port." [13] Although the Mariner is returning to his "own countree," one feels sure that he does not expect anybody to be waiting for him.

> The Pilot and the Pilot's boy,
> I heard them coming fast:
> Dear Lord in Heaven! it was a joy
> The dead men could not blast.

Returned from the dead, Lazarus-fashion, he is overjoyed to see living people, to hear their voices. But there is a characteristic note of homelessness when he says

> O sweeter than the marriage-feast,
> 'Tis sweeter far to me,
> To walk together to the kirk
> With a goodly company!—
>
> To walk together to the kirk,
> And all together pray,
> While each to his great Father bends,
> Old men, and babes, and loving friends
> And youths and maidens gay!

It is an impersonal picture, pregnant with the sense of isolation. There are "loving friends" but they do not seem to be his; the "old men" are not his brothers or his father, the "youths and maidens gay" are not his children. We catch an overtone of words spoken by him on a grimmer occasion:

> O happy living things! no tongue
> Their beauty might declare:

words uttered with the same sense of isolation in which Coleridge wrote some twenty-five years later

> And I the while, the sole unbusy thing,
> Nor honey make, nor pair, nor build, nor sing.[14]

[13] *Unpublished Letters*, I, p. 63.
[14] "Work without Hope"; composed February 21, 1825.

Not only are the Mariner's spiritual and emotional experiences similar
to, if not identical with, those we know Coleridge to have suffered, but
there is rather more than a hint that the drawing of the Mariner is a
self-portrait. The Mariner's two salient characteristics are his glittering
mesmeric eye, and his passivity. The Mariner says,

> I move like night from land to land,
> I have strange power of speech.

The first line is not only a reflection of Coleridge's isolation, but also a
vivid metaphoric description of his imaginative wanderings while reading
"like a cormorant" before composing *The Ancient Mariner*. We have
Lamb's evidence for Coleridge's "strange power of speech" even at school.
"How have I seen the casual passer through the Cloisters stand still,
entranced with admiration (while he weighed the disproportion between
the *speech* and the *garb* of the young Mirandula), to hear thee unfold,
in thy deep and sweet intonations, the mysteries of Jamblichus, or
Plotinus . . . , or reciting Homer in his Greek, or Pindar—. . . ." Even
the hostile Hazlitt could write, in 1818: "That spell is broke; that time is
gone for ever; that voice is heard no more: but still the recollection comes
rushing by with thoughts of long-past years, and rings in my ears with
never-dying sound."

The Mariner's passivity is Coleridge's too; and the significance of that
word (as of "pathos," "patience," "sympathy") is rooted, in more than
the etymological sense, in suffering. In those deeply moving observations
of the night sky noted in early November, 1803,[15] all written at about two
o'clock in the morning, the elements of passivity, suffering, and the moon
meet; while finally, in a similar entry made in Malta six months later, all
combine with the longing for home and for Asra: "The glorious evening
star coasted the moon, and at length absolutely crested its upper tip. . . .
It was the most singular and at the same time beautiful sight I ever beheld. Oh, that it could have appeared the same in England, at Grasmere!"
In these entries we see a man who is waiting, capable still of feeling; and
he is driving down the intolerable suffering only by the *fixedness* with
which he gazes on the sky.[16] Sometimes there must have shaped in his
mind the blasphemy that he expunged from the *Rime* after 1798: that

---

[15] *Anima Poetæ*, pp. 43-50, 76.
[16] Cf. an amusing parallel in *Unpublished Letters*, I, p. 166: "In truth, my Glass
being opposite to the Window, I seldom shave without cutting myself. Some Mountain
or Peak is rising out of the Mist, or some slanting Column of misty Sunlight is sailing
across so that I offer up soap and blood daily, as an Eye-servant of the Goddess Nature."

"Christ would take no pity on My soul in agony." [17] And the Mariner's prayer must often have been repeated in those long nights:

> O let me be awake, my God!
> Or let me sleep alway.

At the height of the Mariner's suffering and loneliness, sleep and dream become central ideas. It is noticeable that the Mariner, like Coleridge, does not regard them as necessary concomitants. The Mariner, it is true, hears the "two voices in the air" while he is asleep; but he recognizes them as being merely voices so that the tempo of the verse does not race as it did when he sighted the spectre-bark. His prayer on entering harbor shows that the whole voyage has been, in a real and horrible sense, a dream; when he hears the Pilot approaching his pulse quickens because the dream of the voyage is broken by a breath of solid human reality. Coleridge conceived sleep to be, in its essence, dreamless. We have his own evidence for the fact that his life (like the Mariner's voyage) passed in a state of dream;[18] and that there were times, *after* the composition of *The Ancient Mariner,* when the dream, the thing imagined, was more solid and terrible than "the normal realities of life." "While I am awake, by patience, employment, effort of mind, and walking I can keep the fiend at Arm's length; but the Night is my Hell, Sleep my tormenting Angel. Three nights out of four I fall asleep, struggling to lie awake— and my frequent Night-screams have almost made me a nuisance in my own House. *Dreams with me are no Shadows, but the very Substances and foot-thick Calamities of my Life.*" [19] It is the dreams which accompany his sleep that are the torment and horror. Remove the dreams from his sleep and he would not "fall asleep, struggling to lie awake." And the Mariner's craving and prayer for sleep are paralleled by Coleridge before 1802, and are more insistently repeated after that date.

The first version of *The Ancient Mariner* was completed for publication in *Lyrical Ballads* in 1798. . . . The final version of *The Ancient Mariner* is the outcome of at least twenty years of reflection, no matter

---

[17] Cf. *ibid.,* I, p. 363: "55 days of literal horror [at sea] almost daily expecting and wishing to die"; and *ibid.,* II, p. 182: "I longed for Death with an intensity that I have never seen expressed but in the Book of Job."

[18] See the dream-epitaph, *ibid.,* I, p. 281:

> Here sleeps at length poor Col. and without Screaming,
> Who died, as he had always liv'd, a dreaming:
> Shot dead, while sleeping, by the Gout within,
> Alone, and all unknown, at E'nbro' in an Inn.

[19] *Ibid.,* I, p. 279. *Ibid.,* I, pp. 276-88, and many other letters voice the same theme.

how sporadic the reflection may have been. That can only mean that the poem continued to hold for him the personal significance with which it was charged at its creation.

In the course of revision the symbolism has been sharpened, not least of all by the gloss; the personal context has been clarified; and, most important of all, the whole poem has been confirmed in the light of his later life.

III

It is misleading to think of Coleridge's life as falling into three distinct phases: one of turbulent preparation, one of cloudless creation, and one of disappointment and broken imagination. The brief creative period, 1797-9, emerges from a mind more hopeful than in the later period; but it is essentially the same mind—restless, mercurial, morbid, remorseful, fearful. For a short time he was lifted up (though on no constant wings) by his marriage, by the birth of Hartley, by his intimacy with William and Dorothy Wordsworth. But even such "fecundating" happiness, a happiness ominously stressed in the letters of the period, was not able to change the thing that was Coleridge. The early period foreshadows the later. In 1796 he had written: "There is one Ghost that I *am* afraid of; with that I should be perpetually haunted in this cursed Acton—the hideous Ghost of departed Hope." [20] In the same year he observed that

> Such a green mountain 'twere most sweet to climb,
> E'en while the bosom ached with loneliness—. . . .[21]

In the spring of 1797 he told Cottle: "On the Saturday, the Sunday, and the ten days after my arrival at Stowey I felt a depression too dreadful to be described. . . . Wordsworth's conversation, etc., roused me somewhat; but even now I am not the man I have been—and I think never shall. A sort of calm hopelessness diffuses itself over my heart." Early in 1797 he had anticipated *The Ancient Mariner* by telling his brother George that "I have roamed through life Still most a stranger," and that "To me the Eternal Wisdom hath dispensed A different fortune and more different mind." As early as 1795 he had referred to the taking of drugs;[22]

---

[20] *Letters*, I, p. 187.
[21] "To a Young Friend."
[22] The earliest letter, of 1791 (*Unpublished Letters*, I, p. 3), is inconclusive, but is linked by E. H. Coleridge with a letter of March, 1795 (*Letters*, I, p. 173n.), where almost nightly doses of opium are mentioned. But see also Lowes, *The Road to Xanadu*, rev. ed., (Boston and New York, 1930), pp. 415, 415n., 604*i*.

and in the spring of 1798 *Kubla Khan* was conceived "in a profound sleep, at least of the external senses." All the elements of the later broken Coleridge are noticeably present by 1797. Coleridge was too intelligent and introspective a man to fail to notice them and understand, at least dimly, their import.

Before the date of the composition of *The Ancient Mariner* the sense of personal doom was present to Coleridge, even though at times, and for lengthy periods, he was able to "keep the fiend at Arm's length." It has been shown that the acute consciousness of his aloneness and homelessness was already present, foreshadowing the "Moon gloss" and the pitiful threnody "Youth and Age." The *Rime* is the projection of his own suffering, of his sense of personal danger, his passivity, his perplexity. At first he projected himself unconsciously into the poem by the intensity with which he imaginatively experienced the Mariner's situation. During the voyage from Gibraltar to Malta he had an opportunity not only to verify his "observations" of the sea, but also to know what it was to pass "55 days of literal horror almost daily expecting and wishing to die." The time in Malta was a critical, desolate period; and I believe that in Malta Coleridge realized more vividly than ever before that he trembled on the brink of inactivity, of dream, of fatal procrastination, of creative impotence. It is this realization that he projects into the 1817 version of *The Ancient Mariner*: the personal allegory is sharpened by the gloss, and the addition of important details relates the Mariner's experience more intimately with Coleridge's experience of opium.[23]

Fundamentally it is the personal quality of the poem that accounts for its vivid haunting fascination. And that effect is much heightened when we recognize the prophetic power of the poem; when we know that Coleridge himself in later life recognized the poem for a personal allegory and endorsed its prophecy by a life of wandering loneliness and suffering.

IV

The central figure of the albatross remains to be considered; for "the albatross . . . binds inseparably together the three structural principles of the poem: the voyage, and the supernatural machinery, and the unfolding cycle of the deed's results." [24] Nothing less than an intensely personal symbolism would be acceptable against the background of such intense suffering. The albatross must be much more than a stage property chosen at random or a mechanical device introduced as a motive of ac-

[23] See Bald, "Coleridge and *The Ancient Mariner*," pp. 33ff.
[24] Lowes, *The Road to Xanadu*, p. 221.

tion in the plot.[25] The albatross is the symbol of Coleridge's creative imagination, his eagle.[26]

It was Wordsworth, not Coleridge, who thought of the albatross. Whether Wordsworth or Coleridge actually stumbled upon the albatross, in Shelvocke or anywhere else, does not matter. In November 1797, the final element, around which the whole poem would crystallize, was needed. As Lowes has shown, Coleridge, in all his diverse and obscure reading before *The Ancient Mariner,* read with the falcon's eye "which habitually pierced to the secret spring of poetry beneath the crust of fact": it is as though he knew intuitively what he needed without knowing exactly what he was looking for. It would be valuable to have a verbatim record of the dialogue during that momentous walk through the Quantock Hills, rather than the retrospective and somewhat patronizing report made by Wordsworth nearly fifty years after the event.

Coleridge would notice at once that the albatross was mechanically suitable: it would fit naturally into a voyage to Antarctic regions; sailors are superstitious about birds and indeed have special superstitions about the albatross; and he may even have noticed that it was amenable to rhyming in a way that other alternatives may not have been. But apart from practical considerations of plot or versification, the albatross was exactly what Coleridge was looking for. It was a rare species of bird,[27] of exceptional size,[28] solitary, haunting a limited and strange and, for Coleridge, evocative zone, harmless yet by tradition beneficent. Some or all of these facts would, I suggest, flash through Coleridge's mind; and he

[25] Cf. *ibid.,* p. 303. Lowes emphasizes the *triviality* of the deed and suggests that Coleridge required a trivial deed to set the punishment in motion. Clarke ["Certain Symbols in *The Rime of the Ancient Mariner,*" in *Queen's Quarterly,* XI (1933), 29] dismisses the possibility of the albatross as symbol.

[26] Cf. T. S. Eliot, *The Use of Poetry and the Use of Criticism* (London, 1933), p. 69, where the eagle is used as the symbol of the creative imagination. Coleridge also seems to be using the symbol in an epigram of 1807 in reply to Poole's encouragement: "Let Eagle bid the Tortoise sunward rise—As vainly Strength speaks to a broken mind" (*Complete Poetical Works,* ed. E. H. Coleridge, II, p. 1001). Cf. Shelley's description of Coleridge as "a hooded eagle among blinking owls."

[27] Coleridge's keen interest in birds is shown by his foot-note to "This Lime-Tree Bower," and by a MS. note in a copy of Gilbert White's *Works* (quoted in *Coleridge: Select Poetry and Prose,* ed. Stephen Potter, p. 719): "I have myself made by collection [?] a better table of characters of Flight and Motion" (of birds). See also *Anima Poetæ,* pp. 178, 193, 194.

[28] The giant albatross probably would occur to Coleridge's mind. Notice Wordsworth's mention of "wingspan of 12 or 13 feet." But see Lowes, *The Road to Xanadu,* pp. 226-27 and 529, for the "feasible" species; and Bald, "Coleridge and *The Ancient Mariner,*" 6: "Saw a . . . Boy running up to the Main top with a large Leg of Mutton swung, Albatross-fashion, about his neck."

at once seized upon the albatross as the right (or, at the very lowest valuation, an adequate) symbol for his purpose.

Coleridge was a confirmed symbolist. In 1815 he wrote: "An *idea,* in the highest sense of that word, can not be conveyed but by a *symbol.*" [29] Ten years before, he had noted how

> In looking at objects of Nature while I am thinking, as at yonder moon dim-glimmering through the dewy window-pane, I seem rather to be seeking, as it were *asking* for, a symbolical language for something within me that already and for ever exists, than observing anything new. Even when that latter is the case, yet still I have always an obscure feeling as if that new phenomena were the dim awaking of a forgotten or hidden truth of my inner nature. It is still interesting as a word—a symbol. It is Λόγος the Creator, and the Evolver! [30]

The process he describes here is not a newly acquired practice, but an innate and habitual attitude of mind. *The Ancient Mariner* is what it is for the reason that Coleridge has clearly given: because in that poem he found what he was "seeking, as it were *asking* for," long before the date of the Notebook entry—"a symbolical language for something within me that already and for ever exists." Furthermore Coleridge was not the man to use words or symbols without consideration or to select them carelessly. In an entry, touched with more humility than this single sentence would suggest, he said in 1805: "Few men, I will be bold to say, put more *meaning* into their words than I, or choose them more deliberately and discriminately." [31]

That the link between the albatross and the creative imagination grows out of the inner necessity of the poem and of the man can be verified by only one passage in the *Rime.* The evidence is extremely nebulous, but, being possibly primary evidence, should not be overlooked. The shipmates' first judgment on the killing of the albatross was that the Mariner had

killed the *bird*
That made the *breeze* to blow.

Late in 1806 Coleridge connects Genius and the wind: "Though Genius, like the fire on the altar, can only be kindled from heaven, yet it will

---

[29] *Biographia Literaria,* Chap. IX.
[30] *Anima Poetæ,* p. 136; dated April 14, 1805. See also *ibid.,* p. 225: ". . . words are not mere symbols of things and thoughts, but themselves things, and . . . any harmony in the things symbolised will perforce be presented to us more easily, as well as with additional beauty, by a correspondent harmony of the symbols with each other."
[31] *Ibid.,* p. 103.

perish unless supplied with appropriate fuel to feed it; or if it meet not with the virtues whose society alone can reconcile it to earth, it will return whence it came, or, at least, lie hid as beneath embers, till some *sudden and awakening gust of regenerating Grace,* ἀναξωπυρεῖ, rekindles and reveals it anew." [32] And the symbol of the imagination, or of inspiration, is frequently, outside Coleridge's writing,[33] a bird.

Far more important is Coleridge's reply to the celebrated strictures of Mrs. Barbauld. *The Ancient Mariner,* he said, "ought to have had no more moral than the Arabian Nights' tale of the merchant's sitting down to eat dates by the side of a well, and throwing the shells aside, and lo! a geni starts up, and says he *must* kill the aforesaid merchant, *because* one of the date-shells had, it seems, put out the eye of the geni's son." [34] The tone of the retort is jocular. If the *Rime* had for Coleridge the personal significance that I believe it had, it would be difficult for him to reply other than jocularly. About seven years before the reply to Mrs. Barbauld, he tells a correspondent exactly how he reacts to a situation of that kind.

> My sentiments on the nature of all *intrusions into private Life,* and of more private *personalities* in all shapes I have given at large in the Friend, and yet more pointedly in the Literary Life. . . . These you know, but you cannot know my dear Sir! . . . how many causes accumulating thro' a long series of years, and acting perhaps on constitutional predisposition, have combined to *make me shrink from all occasions that threaten to force my thoughts back on myself personally—as soon as any thing of this sort is on the point of being talked of, I feel uneasy till I have turned the conversation,* or fairly slunk out of the room—. . . .[35]

Coleridge's facetiousness in speaking of the moral of *The Ancient Mariner* was misleading, as it was intended to be; but it both hides and contains the clue we are looking for.

The nature of the Mariner's crime is thrown into high relief by Coleridge's italics (*must, because*): and with it, the nature of Coleridge's personal "crime"—for so he regarded it in later life. The identity is then complete.

[32] *Ibid.,* p. 179. My italics. This parallel is offered with caution.

[33] But see note 29 above for an example in Coleridge's writing. *Anima Poetæ,* p. 178 is also of interest: "The moulting peacock, with only two of his long tail-feathers remaining, and those sadly in tatters, yet, proudly as ever, spreads out his ruined fan in the sun and breeze." This may be a direct observation; but, from the context, it appears likely that Coleridge is noting a personal metaphor.

[34] *Table Talk,* May 31, 1830.

[35] *Unpublished Letters,* II, p. 274. Coleridge italicized the words "personalities" and "myself." Other italics are mine.

The crime was at the same time wanton and unintentional.[36] The Mariner shoots "the *harmless* albatross," and "*inhospitably* killeth the pious bird of good omen," having no conception of the implications of his deed. The Mariner *could* have withheld his arrow, the merchant his date-shell; but neither saw any reason for doing so. Certainly the Mariner learned a sharp lesson about killing birds before the voyage was done; but that lesson was of no service to him when, in a moment of idleness or boredom, he aimed his cross-bow at the albatross. "But so it is! Experience, like the stern lanthorn of a Ship, casts it's light only on the *Wake* —on the Track already past." [37] There is the sternness and inexorability of Greek tragedy in the paradox that an act committed in ignorance of the laws governing albatrosses and genii *must* be punished in the most severe manner.

That Coleridge regarded his own suffering in precisely this light is clear from a poem written as early as 1803.

> Such punishments, I said, were due
> To natures deepliest stained with sin,—
> For aye entempesting anew
> The unfathomable hell within,
> The horror of their deeds to view,
> To know and loathe, yet wish and do!
> *Such griefs with such men well agree,*
> *But wherefore, wherefore fall on me?*

"The Pains of Sleep" is saturated with the same confusion and perplexity that the Mariner experienced. The sin from which the suffering arose was committed in the same way: "Tho' before God I dare not lift up my eyelids, and only do not despair of his Mercy because to despair would be adding crime to crime; yet to my fellow-men I may say, that I was seduced into the *accursed* Habit ignorantly." [38] Even though he may have suspected, when it was too late, what would be the outcome of his struggle with "this body that does me most grievous wrong," Coleridge did not know, when the process began, that he was killing his eagle.

[36] Bald ("Coleridge and *The Ancient Mariner*," 39ff.), in interpreting this passage, is concerned to explain the *amoral* attitude as a characteristic of opium reverie. Lamb notes the same quality without attributing it to opium.

[37] *Unpublished Letters*, II, p. 354. E. H. Coleridge (in *Coleridge: Studies by Several Hands,* ed. E. Blunden and E. L. Griggs, p. 41) notes the first appearance of this "stock sentence" as January 2, 1800.

[38] *Unpublished Letters*, II, p. 107: Coleridge is here thinking specifically of the opium habit, which he probably recognized as a symptom and not the "sin" itself. He is here replying to Cottle who considered opium to be central.

The act was wanton: yes, in the sense that it was unnecessary, that it could have been avoided. And it is that very knowledge—afterwards— that the act could, perhaps easily, have been avoided, if at the very beginning he had understood the implications of his action, that makes stark tragedy both in Coleridge's life and in the Mariner's voyage.

> O had I health and youth and were what I once was—but I played the fool and cut the throat of my own happiness, of my genius, of my utility. . . .[39]
> Well would it have been for me perhaps had I never relapsed into the same mental disease; if I had continued to pluck the flowers and reap the harvest from the cultivated surface, instead of delving in the unwholesome quick-silver mines of metaphysic lore. And if in after-time I have sought a refuge from bodily pain and mismanaged sensibility in abstruse researches, which exercised the strength and subtilty of the understanding without awakening the feelings of the heart; still there was a long and blessed interval, during which my natural faculties were allowed to expand, and my original tend-encies to develop themselves;—my fancy, and the love of nature, and the sense of beauty in forms and sounds.[40]

The interval was a good deal shorter and less blessed than he was pre-pared to remember in 1815. And there was a great deal more in the two apparently naïve verses of moral than Mrs. Barbauld could have guessed, more even than Coleridge was willing to remember when, long after their writing, he was asked for an explanation.

When the process of the atrophy of his creative imagination, fore-shadowed in *The Ancient Mariner,* was far advanced and Coleridge felt that his life was sinking "in tumult to a lifeless sea," he wrote his com-ment upon that process. The lines are some of the most desolate ever written.

> But now afflictions bow me down to earth:
> Nor care I that they rob me of my mirth;
>   But oh! each visitation
> Suspends what nature gave me at my birth,
>   My shaping spirit of Imagination.
> For not to think of what I needs must feel,
>   But to be still and patient, all I can;
> And haply by abstruse research to steal
>   From my own nature all the natural man—
>   This was my sole resource, my only plan:
> Till that which suits a part infects the whole,
> And now is almost grown the habit of my soul.[41]

[39] *Ibid.,* I, p. 403; March 17, 1808.
[40] *Biographia Literaria,* Chap. I.
[41] "Dejection: an Ode," lines 82-93; "Dejection" is itself echoed in "To William Wordsworth" (1807).

V

The Ancient Mariner, in addition to its other unique qualities, is both an unconscious projection of Coleridge's early sufferings and a vivid prophecy of the sufferings that were to follow. The poem was probably not originally intended to be a personal allegory: but that is what, in Coleridge's eyes, it became later as the prophecy was slowly, inexorably, and lingeringly fulfilled.

As far as I know *The Ancient Mariner* has never been interpreted as a personal allegory. To do so (and the evidence for it is weighty) not only gives a clue to the source of the poem's intensity but also explains beyond cavil its moral implications. *The Ancient Mariner* is, however, of primary importance *as a poem;* and no specialized interest—moral, biographical, or allegorical—can be allowed to assail the integrity to which, as a poem, it is entitled. But the interpretation I have suggested does bring the reader into intimate contact with Coleridge the man. Even to attempt to understand him will induce sympathy, and from sympathy some understanding can grow.

Carlyle's judgment of Coleridge is harsh and grossly unsympathetic: "To steal into heaven . . . is forever forbidden. High treason is the name of that attempt; and it continues to be punished as such." [42] Yet Coleridge had written:

> I dare affirm that few men have ever felt or regretted their own infirmities more deeply than myself—they have in truth *preyed* too deeply on my mind, and the hauntings of regret have injured me more than the things to be regretted.[43]

> For years the anguish of my spirit has been indescribable, the sense of my danger *staring,* but the conscience of my *guilt* worse, far far worse than all! —I have prayed with drops of agony on my Brow, trembling not only before the Justice of my Maker, but even before the Mercy of my Redeemer. "I gave thee so many Talents. What hast thou done with them?" [44]

> And as to what *people* in *general* think about me, my mind and spirit are too awfully occupied with the concerns of another Tribunal, before which I stand momently, to be much affected by it one way or other.[45]

[42] Thomas Carlyle, *The Life of John Sterling;* in *Complete Works of Thomas Carlyle* (New York, 1853), XX, p. 60.
[43] *Unpublished Letters,* II, p. 57.
[44] *Ibid.,* II, p. 107; April 26, 1814.
[45] *Ibid.,* II, p. 424; November 9, 1828.

Carlyle's judgment overlooks the quantity and quality of the work Coleridge did complete; overlooks the fact that Coleridge throughout his life was dogged by physical disease; overlooks the fact that Coleridge became a man tormented and haunted, at times beyond the capacities of desire or effort, by the knowledge that the eagle had visited him, that he had inhospitably killed "the pious bird of good omen," and that it might well have been otherwise.

The Theme
of "The Ancient Mariner"

by D. W. Harding

In *The Road to Xanadu* Livingston Lowes eschews any attempt to interpret Coleridge's work along psychoanalytic lines, and no doubt at the time he wrote (in the early 1920s) the dangers of amateur psychoanalytic interpretations were more evident than their promise. At the point where he discusses the problem explicitly he shows that Robert Graves' interpretation of "Kubla Khan," speculative and undisciplined as well as ham-fisted, founders on several errors of biographical fact which better scholarship would have avoided.

The mutual relevance of an author's personal experience and the characteristics of his writing raises questions which fortunately need not be settled as a preliminary to literary studies, even those influenced by psychological thinking. It seems entirely possible, and wise, to distinguish clearly the biographical or clinical study of the author from the literary assessment or elucidation of his writings. Each may sometimes be used to illuminate the other, though the dangers of an over-simplified view of their interrelation are alarming; but if we take the risk we ought to make it perfectly clear whether our purpose is biographical or literary.

If literary, as mine is here, the essential guiding principle is to keep close to the poem (or whatever the form of writing is) and as far as possible use only what it says, either avoiding or using with extreme caution importations from psychological theory and biography. Even the poet's other writings, though they often give useful confirmatory hints for elucidation, must take second place to the particular poem we are reading. That exists in its own right and forms our only necessary datum for literary criticism.

Yet however conscientiously we focus on the literary task we shall not escape psychological questions. Livingston Lowes's own work shows this. Most of his remarkably thorough and skillful work of scholarly detection and tracking is concentrated on the materials from which the poem was made and on the detailed thought processes of association, condensation, changed emphasis and so on that occurred in Coleridge's mind. This itself is one aspect of a psychological, as well as a literary study. But to the further psychological question of the human significance of the action of "The Ancient Mariner" he gives very cursory attention. He admits that it matters. He quotes Coleridge on the value in poetry of "the modifying colours of imagination" giving the interest of novelty to "a known and familiar landscape," and on the decision that in the "Lyrical Ballads" Coleridge's "endeavours should be directed to persons and characters supernatural, or at least romantic; yet so as to transfer from our inward nature a human interest and a semblance of truth sufficient to procure for these shadows of imagination that willing suspension of disbelief for the moment which constitutes poetic faith. . . . With this view I wrote the 'Ancient Mariner.' "

Livingston Lowes comments, ". . . if Coleridge's words mean anything, they mean that some interest deeply human, anchored in the familiar frame of things, was fundamental to his plan" and he asks "Are there truths of 'our inward nature' which do, in fact, uphold and cherish, as we read, our sense of actuality in a phantom universe, peopled with the shadows of a dream?" He discovers what he takes the human action of the poem to be, and he treats it with a succinctness that makes a remarkable contrast with his lengthy, scholarly ramblings around the fragments of Coleridge's building material. He writes:

> But the train of cause and consequence is more than a consolidating factor of the poem. It happens to be life, as every human being knows it. You do a foolish or an evil deed, and its results come home to you. And they are apt to fall on others too. You repent, and a load is lifted from your soul. But you have not thereby escaped your deed. You attain forgiveness, but cause and effect work on unmoved, and life to the end may be a continued reaping of the repented deed's results. That is not a system of ethics; it is the inexorable law of life, than which nothing is surer or more unchanging. There it stands in your experience and mine, "known and familiar" if anything on earth is so.

This summary of the action is not entirely off the target, but it is far from being a bull's-eye, and by the standards of comprehensiveness and precision reached in the less psychological parts of the book it is pitifully meager and inaccurate. Take only the obvious points: repentance without restitution or confession seldom does in fact lift a load from the soul, and it is certainly not repentance that relieves the Mariner (he had bitterly repented long before the Albatross fell off); again, although he attains forgiveness in the formal sense of being shriven, his later fate makes it evident that he has never forgiven himself; moreover his later life doesn't consist in reaping the results of the deed brought about by the continued working of cause and effect—results of that kind are strikingly absent—it consists simply in a long-drawn-out pilgrimage of repentance with recurrent bouts of acute remembrance and self-reproach.

The human experience on which Coleridge centers the poem is the depression and the sense of isolation and worthlessness which the Mariner describes in Part IV. The suffering he conveys is of a kind which is perhaps not found except in slightly pathological conditions, but which, pathological or not, has been felt by a great many people. He feels isolated to a degree that baffles expression and reduces him to the impotent, repetitive emphasis that becomes doggerel in schoolroom reading:

> Alone, alone, all, all alone,
> Alone on a wide wide sea!

At the same time he is not just physically isolated but is socially abandoned, even by those with the greatest obligations:

> And never a saint took pity on
> My soul in agony.

With this desertion the beauty of the ordinary world has been taken away:

> The many men so beautiful!
> And they all dead did lie . . .

All that is left, and especially, centrally, oneself, is disgustingly worthless:

> And a thousand thousand slimy things
> Lived on; and so did I.

With the sense of worthlessness there is also guilt. When he tried to pray

> A wicked whisper came and made
> My heart as dry as dust.

And enveloping the whole experience is the sense of sapped energy, oppressive weariness:

> For the sky and the sea, and the sea and the sky
> Lay like a load on my weary eye,
> And the dead were at my feet.

This, the central experience, comes almost at the middle of the poem. It is the nadir of depression to which the earlier stanzas sink: the rest of the poem describes what is in part recovery and in part aftermath. You need not have been a spellbound mariner in a supernatural Pacific in order to have felt this mood. Coleridge knew it well, and "Dejection" and "The Pains of Sleep" deal with closely related experiences.

A usual feature of these states of pathological misery is their apparent causelessness. The depression cannot be rationally explained; the conviction of guilt and worthlessness is out of proportion to any ordinary offence actually committed. In the story of 'The Ancient Mariner' Coleridge finds a crime which, in its symbolic implications, is sufficient to merit even his suffering. The Mariner's sin, as many have realized, was that in killing the albatross he rejected a social offering. Why he did so is left quite unexplained. It was a wanton bit of self-sufficiency. It was enough for Coleridge that this was a dreadful thing which one might do, and he did it. The Mariner wantonly obliterated something that loved him and represented in a supernatural way the possibility of affection in the world. The depth of meaning the act held for Coleridge can be gauged from the curious self-exculpation with which he ends "The Pains of Sleep." That poem is a fragment of case-history recounting three nights of bad dreams:

> Fantastic passions! maddening brawl!
> And shame and terror over all!
> Deeds to be hid which were not hid,
> Which all confused I could not know
> Whether I suffered, or I did:
> For all seem'd guilt, remorse or woe . . .

Characteristically, he assumes that these sufferings must be a punishment for something or other. Yet by the standards of waking life and reason he feels himself to be innocent. He never explicitly mentions what the supposed offense might be. But the last two lines, in which he protests his innocence, reveal implicitly what crime alone could merit such punishment:

> Such punishments, I said, were due
> To natures deepliest stained with sin . . .
> But wherefore, wherefore fall on me?
> To be beloved is all I need,
> And whom I love, I love indeed.

With those lines in mind we can judge better the force of the stanza in "The Ancient Mariner":

> The spirit that bideth by himself
> In the land of mist and snow,
> He loved the bird that loved the man
> Who shot him with his bow.

This for Coleridge was the most terrible possibility among the sins. Why, in "The Pains of Sleep," is he innocent of the fatal sin?—because he aims at nothing beyond affection and union with others, gives no allegiance to more individual interests in the outer world which might flaw his complete devotion. It is only in the light of the last two lines that the introductory section of the poem yields its meaning. Explaining that he is not accustomed to saying formal prayers before going to sleep, Coleridge continues

> But silently, by slow degrees,
> My spirit I to Love compose.
> In humble trust mine eyelids close,
> With reverential resignation . . .

And then one realizes that he is protesting against being visited with the horrible dreams *in spite of* cultivating submissive affection and so guarding against the one sin that could merit such punishments.

The Mariner committed the sin. Yet Coleridge knew that by the ordinary standards of the workaday world the act was not, after all, very terrible. Hence the ironic stanzas which show the indifference of the mariners to the real meaning of the deed. At first

> Ah wretch! said they, the bird to slay,
> That made the breeze to blow!

And then,

> 'Twas right, said they, such birds to slay,
> That bring the fog and mist.

It is not by the ordinary standards of social life that the Mariner could be condemned, any more than Coleridge felt he himself could in "The Pains of Sleep." We are to take it, I think, though the point is not made explicit, that the Mariner feels horror and guilt immediately on committing the crime; there is no suggestion that its hideousness needs demonstrating to him. His sense of guilt is there from the start. The public condemnation, the curse of his shipmates, is a later and only external confirmation of his sense of being worthless. He is cursed, by them, not for the crime he had committed but for the calamity that his action happens to have produced. The essence of the poem is a private sense of guilt, intense out of all proportion to public rational standards. The supernatural machinery of the poem allowed Coleridge to convey something of this—for the small impulsive act which presses a supernatural trigger does form an effective parallel to the hidden impulse which has such a devastating meaning for one's irrational, and partly unconscious, private standards. It is a fiction that permits the expression of real experience.

The total pattern of experience in "The Ancient Mariner" includes partial recovery from the worst depression. The offense for which the dejection and isolation were punishment was the wanton rejection of a very simple social union. One step towards recovery is suggested in "The Pains of Sleep." It is a return to a submissive sense of childlike weakness and distress:

> O'ercome with sufferings strange and wild,
> I wept as I had been a child;
> And having thus by tears subdued
> My anguish to a milder mood . . .

The Mariner's sufferings have first to reduce him to a dreadful listlessness and apathy. He contrasts his condition then with the calm activity of the Moon going about her ordinary business in the universe, accompanied by the stars which, unlike him, still have their right to be welcomed. He treats them as if they were a secure family, and, significantly, they now fill him with longing—"he yearneth":

> In his loneliness and fixedness he yearneth towards the journeying moon, and the stars that still sojourn, yet still move onward; and everywhere the blue sky belongs to them, and is their appointed rest, and their native country and their own natural homes, which they enter unannounced, as lords that are certainly expected and yet there is a silent joy at their arrival.

He has to reach complete listlessness before there is any chance of recovery. His state at the turning point makes a significant contrast to the desperate activity—the courageous snatching at hope in the direction from which he personally has decided salvation must come—which is suggested earlier by his watch for a sail and his final effort of hope:

> I bit my arm, I sucked the blood,
> And cried, A sail! a sail!

All this directed effort and expense of spirit is futile in the state of mind which Coleridge describes. Only when his individual striving has sunk to a low ebb can the recovery begin.

This naturally gives the impression, characteristic of these states of depression, that the recovery is fortuitous. It comes unpredictably and seemingly from some trivial accident. This part of the psychological experience Coleridge has paralleled in the supernatural machinery of the tale by means of the dicing between Death and Life-in-Death. To the sufferer there seems no good reason why he shouldn't simply die, since he feels that he has thrown up the sponge. Instead, chance has it that he lives on.

The fact of its being Life-in-Death who wins the Mariner shows how incomplete his recovery is going to be. Nevertheless some degree of recovery from the nadir of dejection does unpredictably occur. It begins with the momentary rekindling of simple pleasure in the things around him, at the very moment when he has touched bottom in apathy:

> Oh happy living things! no tongue
> Their beauty might declare . . .

It is the beginning of recovery because what is kindled is a recognition not only of their beauty but also of the worth of their existence and, by implication, of his own. For he had previously associated himself with them—the thousand and slimy things—in denying their right to live when the men were dead:

> He despiseth the creatures of the calm. And envieth that they should live and so many lie dead.

The earlier exclamation, in the depths of self-condemnation, "The many men, so beautiful!" is not one of simple pleasure in the things around him. He is still absorbed in his self-contempt and uses his recognition of other men's beauty only as a further lash against himself. Or, to put it differently, when he was in the depths the only beauty he would consent to see was beauty dead and spoilt; the beauty still present in the world he denied.

The moment when the worst of his load is lifted and the Albatross drops off his neck into the sea is not brought about, as Livingston Lowes would have it, by repentance. Coleridge's account of the state of acute depression, with the sense of guilt and worthlessness, is much more accurate; it emphasizes the impression of something fortuitous about the impulse that rises in him and brings him back to life:

> A spring of love gushed from my heart,
> And I blessed them unaware:
> Sure my kind saint took pity on me,
> And I blessed them unaware.

The repetition of "unaware" stresses the fortuitousness, something paralleled by the fall of the dice on the spectral bark. At this turning point in the Mariner's experience there is an unaccountable renewal of the

impulse of love towards other living things. That is enough; responsive
life has been waiting around him and the Holy Mother immediately
sends the rain and sleep he needs.

In the second stanza of "Dejection" Coleridge describes a mood in
which, like the Mariner, he watches the beauty of natural things but
fails in the vital response:

> I see them all so excellently fair,
> I see, not feel, how beautiful they are!

But the Mariner's turning towards partial recovery depends on a mood
in which the vital impulse does come. His own impulse saves him, and
this is represented as his guardian saint, whereas earlier "never a saint
took pity . . . ." It is now his guardian saint who invokes the angelic
spirits to work the ship back to port.

His returning joy in living things comes, of course, from his own
changed attitude and his willingness to look differently on the world.
Coleridge made this point also in "Dejection":

> O Lady! we receive but what we give,
> And in our life alone does nature live . . .
> Ah! from the soul itself must issue forth
> A light, a glory, a fair luminous cloud
> Enveloping the Earth—
> And from the soul itself must there be sent
> A sweet and potent voice, of his own birth,
> Of all sweet sounds the life and element!

From this one turns to "The Ancient Mariner" at a later stage in the
recovery:

> Around, around, flew each sweet sound,
> Then darted to the Sun;
> Slowly the sounds came back again,
> Now mixed, now one by one.

Still later the band of seraphs who

> stood as signals to the land,
> Each one a lovely light

can be associated with

> A light, a glory, a fair luminous cloud.

Coleridge accepts sound and light and color as the simplest adequate
expression of the beauty of the world which ebbed and flowed with his
own spirits.

In consistent development of the general theme, the Mariner's recovery leads on to reunion with the very simple and humble kinds of social life. He joins the villagers in the formal expression of atonement with each other, and with the source of love, which he sees in their religious worship. But it would be a mistake to think of this as anything like full recovery. For one thing he never again belongs to a settled community, but has to pass from land to land. For another thing there is the periodic "abreaction" and confession that he has to resort to:

> Since then, at an uncertain hour,
> That agony returns:
> And till my ghastly tale is told,
> This heart within me burns.

More important than this sign of imperfect recovery is the contrast between the submissive sociability with which he must now content himself and the buoyancy of the voyager as he first set out. Such a voyage (of the sort that fascinated Coleridge in Anson's narratives) entails a self-reliant thrusting forth into the outer world and repudiates dependence on the comfort of ordinary social ties. But the intensity of Coleridge's need for the ties of affection seems to have set up anxiety about even the degree of independent assertiveness needed for any original achievement. Where we lament his life of wasted talent, he—in one mood—feared the acclaim that even his restricted use of his powers had brought him, and he ends his own epitaph

> Mercy for praise—to be forgiven for fame
> He asked, and hoped, through Christ. Do thou the same!

The bold independence of the voyager was for Coleridge only one step from an outrageous self-sufficiency which will wantonly destroy the ties of affection. The albatross is killed, and then the penalty must be paid in remorse, dejection, and the sense of being a worthless social outcast.

My account of "The Ancient Mariner" would seem psychologically naïve and superficial to those who attach themselves more closely to one or other of the systems of depth psychology. In a Freudian study ("A dream, a vision, and a poem," *Yearbook of Psychoanalysis*, VIII, ed. S. Lorand, New York, 1952) David Beres states his aim as being "to understand the poet's fantasy in relation to his life history, to seek out the unconscious motivations of his creative art. To achieve this I propose to search in the poem, in the artist's other creations and in his life for evidence of unconscious psychic activity." In speaking of understanding "the poet's fantasy in relation to his life history" he leaves it doubtful whether he wants to understand the fantasy—a literary aim—or to understand the relation between the fantasy and the poet's life history, which would be largely a clinical and biographical undertaking. In the essay itself he shows that he does intend to enhance our understanding of the poem.

His interpretation, which is rather confusedly presented, rests on the view that Coleridge found his mother an intensely ambivalent object, and that though he said on one occasion that he had been his mother's darling he felt in the main unloved by her and experienced an unsatisfied "need that manifested itself in a search for warmth, love, and food." There is some evidence of his over-preoccupation with food in childhood; and in later life he became, in Beres' words, ". . . a man who remained in his relationship to persons a never-satisfied, ever-demanding infant," one manifestation of this characteristic being his habit of borrowing. At the conscious level the ambivalence of mother-figures was handled by the common process of splitting the good and bad aspects, with idealized women (such as Mrs. Evans, an idealized mother-image) worshipped from afar, and Mrs. Fricker, his mother-in-law, as the bad, hated mother. Examining *Christabel* along Freudian lines, Beres finds evidence there too of conflict about the mother, including unconscious murderous wishes, sexual fantasies, and the idea of a dangerous, formidably masculine mother, the "phallic mother" in Freudian terminology.

Whether or not we accept such interpretations and employ the Freudian concepts and phraseology, it is still easy enough to suppose that Coleridge was—as many people have been—in a state of rather severe conflict about his mother and the reflections of her that he found in other women. Beres is probably right in his summarizing statement that ". . . Coleridge did not permit his hostile feelings to his mother to come to the surface of his conscious mind. He repressed in his unconscious mind his conflicted ambivalent emotions about her, his crying need, his bitter frustration, and his guilt at the hate this must have engendered."

Turning to "The Ancient Mariner," Beres now concentrates on the Albatross, emphasizing that "It ate the food it ne'er had eat," and associating this with a letter in which Coleridge spoke of his reluctance to trap mice with toasted cheese, exclaiming "oh foul breach of the laws of hospitality," just as the gloss to the poem says that the Mariner "inhospitably" kills the bird. This I can accept as interesting and fairly significant. From this, however, Beres moves—perhaps skids would be the better word—to an identification of the Albatross with the mother, saying "Are not both creatures who bring protection and plenty?" He offers no further evidence from the poem. He simply repeats that the

Albatross is "an object associated with food and protection," undeterred by the fact that it was a receiver, not a giver of food. The lines in which the Albatross is referred to as "him" ("He loved the bird that loved the man Who shot him with his bow") fail to give him pause. They only confirm his view that the mother with whom Coleridge was unconsciously preoccupied was a phallic mother. He writes:

> Coleridge strengthens the concept of the phallic mother by his use of the symbolism of the snake. By its behavior and by its relation to food and protection the Albatross is the mother, but in one line in the poem is identified as "him." To Coleridge, the father was a feminine giving male; the mother a masculine, rejecting female. The Mariner at first despised the snakes; the child attempted to fight off the dangerous phallus, to deny his passive impulses; but it was a hopeless struggle. The Mariner must submit. What was ugly becomes beautiful. . . . And with submission the spell begins to break. . . .

This strikes me as a clear instance of psychological doctrines being imported into the interpretation, the facts of the poem being racked to make them fit. Coleridge's Albatross—as distinct from Beres'—is given a role much more like that of a child than a mother: it received food,

> And every day, for food or play,
> Came to the mariner's hollo!

But in fact its great significance lies in its being the only company in all that terrifying wilderness, which Coleridge describes in his gloss as "The land of ice, and of fearful sounds, where no living thing was to be seen." Its great significance was that it mitigated the isolation:

> At length did cross an Albatross:
> Thorough the fog it came;
> As if it had been a Christian soul,
> We hailed it in God's name.

In that very general sense it does possess an essential characteristic of the mother, in being a safeguard against the threat of loneliness, but it shares this characteristic with innumerable other forms of life, including children and pets who are really at the mercy of one's aggressive impulses in a way that the mother in reality is not. No doubt the value the Albatross represents is a value first experienced in the mother-child relation, but we are helped more by associating it with the mouse that the prisoner in solitary confinement comes to value for its company and the mice that Coleridge felt remorse about trapping. In objecting to an account such as Beres offers, we have to distinguish between the general psychoanalytic guesswork, which may be plausible as a clinical account of Coleridge, and the crude and inaccurate handling of the poem itself.

It seems likely enough that Coleridge's extreme susceptibility to feelings of guilt about any apparent disdain of friendliness and affection was ultimately the outcome of his relations with his mother in very early life, when he presumably experienced in specially acute form the usual problems of establishing psychological self-reliance and independence without losing the affection that originally goes with dependence. It follows that in a poem concerned with guilt arising from wanton aggression against a creature who offered love, mother-figures or -symbols are likely to be prominent. But although Beres is right in drawing attention to the mother-figures, his account is an over-simplification. He writes, ". . . the image of the mother appears as the Avenger, the Spectre-Woman, Life-in-Death, and as the forgiving "Holy Mother" who brings rain and sleep. The mother whom he restores to life brings him back to the safety of his homeland. A mother-figure forgives the crime against the mother." This summary seems inaccurate. In the first place the Avenger is the Polar Spirit; "Life-in-Death" is only the condition of guilt-ridden existence (dictated by Fate in the throw of the dice) which constitutes the punishment (though admittedly it may have been significant in Coleridge's psychopathology that this condition should be symbolized by the Mariner's becoming the property of a woman). In the second place to speak of "the forgiving 'Holy Mother'" misses the point that the Mariner never has been forgiven. We are told in the gloss "that penance long and heavy for the ancient mariner hath been accorded to the Polar Spirit." The curse of his shipmates, the public condemnation, "is finally expiated," but the far more terrible private conviction of guilt is never removed. Although he is shriven by the Hermit, the penance of repeatedly reliving the voyage and re-experiencing his guilt and horror is the perpetual penance of a man who can never forgive himself. Coleridge is engaged in a subtler experience of guilt and remorse than Beres conveys in saying "The mother whom he restores to life brings him back to the safety of his homeland." The poem itself is clinically more exact and penetrating than the elaboration that Beres offers.

Maud Bodkin (in *Archetypal Patterns in Poetry,* London, 1934) applies to "The Ancient Mariner" the ideas of Jung's psychology, especially the view that there are universal symbols and symbolic situations that recur in literature because they are part of the collective unconscious. We may reject the idea of the collective unconscious but still agree that, for other reasons, there are recurrent symbols in folklore, art, and literature that often have much the same significance, in spite of being found geo-graphically and historically far apart.

The literary question is how far it is profitable to come to a work of art with ideas drawn from other sources as to the significance of the symbols we are going to meet with. To some extent we must do this, some symbols being well-established parts of our cultural background. Voyaging into strange seas, for instance, the starting point of Coleridge's poem, has conventional implications and echoes that no one is likely to miss and that the poet would count upon in his readers. We can go a little farther, and usefully perhaps, with Maud Bodkin in noticing that wind and calm are, as she says, "symbols of the contrasted states he [Coleridge] knew so poignantly, of ecstasy and of dull inertia." It seems doubtful, though, whether we are much helped at this point by reminders of the uses to which the symbol of wind has been put in other literature; it may perhaps enrich our emotional associations to Cole-ridge's wind and calm, but on the whole the emotional value of those natural events seems to be sufficiently conveyed by the context of the poem alone without going far beyond it to wider literary contexts.

Sharper doubts arise about the use Maud Bodkin makes of her chief idea, that the poem revolves round the widespread and ancient theme of rebirth. We should all agree that rebirth, in some broad sense that includes the kind of recovery the Mariner makes, is an important part of the poem. But Maud Bodkin embarks on a rather rambling and gener-alized account of ideas and images of rebirth as they occur in everyday experience and in literature, and she draws on other pieces of literature to build up her own emotive, quasi-creative account of the rebirth theme. All this is centred on Coleridge's poem but its relation to it is left nebu-lous. To quote her summary of what she has said is not quite fair, since some of her detailed comments are useful and sharply focused on the poem, but the summary does reveal the swamp of generalities in which one may flounder through following this method. She says that the poem communicates "relations not easily detached for separate consideration from the total experience of the poem, but which we may recall in some such form as this: that the beauty of life is revealed amid the slime, that the glory of life is renewed after stagnation, that through the power of speech the values achieved by life are made immortal." The objection to this is not only that it might equally well be summarizing a poem by Patience Strong, but also that the importation into the poem of the generalized Jungian idea of rebirth has seriously distorted her under-standing of what Coleridge presents. For although the Mariner recovers from the depths of depression and the conviction that his own and every form of life is worthless, still he returns only to a guilt-haunted half-life, always in the power of the Nightmare Life-in-Death. To label this "rebirth" and mobilize around it all the other uses of the theme in literature is not to throw light on the poem but to surround it with a foggy luminosity that conceals its outlines and texture.

We can hardly read "The Ancient Mariner" now without being influenced by what is in some sense a psychological approach. If we accept the views of depth psychology we have to consider the likelihood that much of the poem has a symbolic significance that the writer was not fully aware of and certainly did not circumscribe and focus sharply as the writer of an allegory or parable does. . . . But still he must be given the credit and the responsibility for what is there in the poem and what it does to the reader. He was content, for reasons that may not have been fully conscious to him, to leave the poem as it stands, and this is the poem he wanted us to read. We are face to face with what he actually said, not with what he could have consciously described as his intentions.

The dangers of the psychological approach, of which I have given examples (some, no doubt, unwittingly), arise from a failure to give close enough attention to what precisely the poem says. Precision here includes a response to subtlety and emotional shading, and it precludes the drawing out of remote meanings from one fragment of the poem without regard to the control exercised over it by the rest. In brief any psychologizing we undertake must be controlled by the discipline of close and sensitive reading; it can never compensate for a lapse in literary vigilance.

The Nightmare World
of *The Ancient Mariner*

by Edward E. Bostetter

Probably the most influential modern interpretation of *The Rime of the Ancient Mariner* is Robert Penn Warren's essay, "A Poem of Pure Imagination: An Experiment in Reading." [1] Undoubtedly, as Mr. Pottle has recently said,[2] it is "the most elaborate and learned critique" the poem has ever received, as thoroughgoing in scholarship as it is provocative in criticism. The notes alone provide a useful guide to important critical and scholarly comments on *The Rime*, an erudite commentary on Coleridge's philosophical and critical theories, and exhaustive cross-references to pertinent essays, letters, and poems. In the essay itself Warren has cogently argued the case for a symbolic interpretation of the poem and backed it up by an elaborate and impressive analysis in terms of what he calls the primary theme of the sacramental vision or the "One Life," and the secondary theme of the imagination. It is little wonder that students of the poem, awed by so massive a reading, look upon it as a model of criticism and often appear to prefer it to the poem itself.

Yet it is in many ways a questionable interpretation. It superimposes upon the poem a rigid and consistent pattern of meaning which can only be maintained by forcing certain key episodes into conformity with the pattern and ignoring others. This practice is particularly noticeable in the interpretation of the moon-sun imagery. Warren sees the good events taking place under the aegis of the moon, the bad under that of the sun.

"The Nightmare World of *The Ancient Mariner*" by Edward E. Bostetter. From *Studies in Romanticism*, I, 4 (Summer 1962). © 1962 by the Graduate School, Boston University. Reprinted by permission of the author and *Studies in Romanticism*.

[1] *The Rime of the Ancient Mariner*, with an Essay by Robert Penn Warren (New York, 1946). Hereafter referred to as *Essay*. Reprinted in R. P. Warren, *Selected Essays* (New York, 1958).

[2] Frederick A. Pottle, "Modern Criticism of *The Ancient Mariner*," in *Essays on The Teaching of English*, ed. E. J. Gordon and E. S. Noyes (New York, 1960), p. 261.

The moon he identifies with the imagination, the sun with the understanding which is the reflective faculty that partakes of death. These
symbolic identifications, he insists, hold constant through the poem, and
he is forced into some tortuous twistings of the text, particularly in the
latter half of the poem, in order to demonstrate his contentions. Various
critics have protested the rigidity of this symbolic interpretation, but it
remained for two recent critics—J. B. Beer and Elliott B. Gose, Jr.—to
show in detail how vulnerable it is.[3] Warren had quoted extensively
from other writings of Coleridge in justification of his identifications;
these critics quote just as extensively to refute him. Specifically, they
show convincingly that Coleridge more often than not used the sun in
its traditional identification with God; and they argue persuasively for
such an identification in *The Rime.* In his zeal, Gose goes on to equate
the moon with mutable nature, and is led in his turn into an interpretation which reads almost like a parody of Warren's. Beer takes the most
convincing approach to the symbolic problem when he points out how
for Coleridge all natural phenomena were symbols of Deity and functioned ambiguously—now benignly, now malignly—as instruments of
punishment and salvation.

But both these critics—and the majority of other critics who have
written since Warren—are quite content to accept his interpretation of
the primary theme of the "sacramental vision." Yet this interpretation is
certainly as questionable as the other. In his opposition to such critics
as Griggs, who feels that no moral meaning should be sought in the
poem, and Lowes, who contends that "the 'moral' of the poem, *outside
the poem,* will not hold water," [4] Warren insists that the poem presents
symbolically a view of the world and man's relation to it which is as
valid outside the poem as within. It is a view which, Warren argues, is
"thoroughly consistent with Coleridge's basic theological and philosophical views as given to us in sober prose." As Warren interprets it,
the poem dramatizes fundamentally Christian statements of sin, punishment, repentance, and redemption. "The Mariner shoots the bird; suffers
various pains, the greatest of which is loneliness and spiritual anguish;
upon recognizing the beauty of the foul sea snakes experiences a gush of
love for them and is able to pray; is returned miraculously to his home
port, where he discovers the joy of human communion in God, and
utters the moral, 'He prayeth best who loveth best, etc.' We arrive at

    [3] J. B. Beer, *Coleridge the Visionary* (London, 1959). E. B. Gose, Jr., "Coleridge and
the Luminous Gloom," *PMLA,* LXXV (June 1960), pp. 238-44.
    [4] *The Best of Coleridge,* ed. Earl Leslie Griggs (New York, 1934), p. 687. J. L.
Lowes, *The Road to Xanadu* (Boston, 1927), p. 300.

the notion of a universal charity . . . the sense of the 'One Life' in which all creation participates and which Coleridge perhaps derived from his neo-Platonic studies and which he had already celebrated, and was to celebrate, in other and more discursive poems." [5]

The term, "One Life," appears most prominently in *The Eolian Harp,* in lines appended to the poem in 1817:

> O! the one Life within us and abroad,
> Which meets all motion and becomes its soul,
> A light in sound, a sound-like power in light,
> Rhythm in all thought, and joyance everywhere—.

Now these lines undoubtedly embody the conception of a benevolent harmonious universe in which Coleridge publicly proclaimed his belief throughout his life and which he made the cornerstone of his philosophical and critical theories. What Warren does is to define the moral tag (as it easily can be defined if lifted from context) in terms of this conception and then to superimpose the definition back upon the universe of the poem, thus apparently reconciling Christian values and the vague pantheism of eighteenth century sentimentalism. He is able to do this by interpreting the universe of the poem as one of fundamentally benevolent order and law, in which the events proceed according to a clearly demonstrable logic for the purpose of discovering to the Mariner "the sacramental view of the universe." When the Mariner in the end accepts this view, "his will is released from its state of 'utmost abstraction' and gains the state of 'immanence' in wisdom and love." [6]

But if we look at the poem with the moral tag removed (or put out of mind as much as possible), we see that the view of the universe presented is by no means so simple or so easily resolved as Warren would suggest. He has achieved the "sacramental vision" by rationalizing those portions of the poem in which the powers of the universe are presented as sternly authoritarian and punitive, and ignoring those in which they are revealed as capricious and irrational.

The universe which is jarred into revealing itself by the Mariner's act is a grim and forbidding one in which the punishment of violators is swift, severe, sustained. Insofar as it is a Christian universe, it has little or nothing in common with the necessitarian benevolence of Hartley and Priestley, on the one hand; or the idealism of Berkeley and the Neoplatonists, on the other. Its most striking affinity is with medieval Catholicism, seventeenth century Puritanism, or the lurid Calvinism of the

[5] *Essay,* p. 78.
[6] *Essay,* p. 86.

extreme Evangelicals of Coleridge's own age. The Mariner's blessing of
the snakes is like the evangelistic moment of conversion:

> A spring of love gushed from my heart,
> And I blessed them unaware.

Furthermore this act, though it reveals the Mariner as one of the Elect
and promises his ultimate salvation, does not free him from pain and
penance. He remains subject, like an Evangelical, to an unrelenting sense
of guilt, the compulsion to confession, the uncertainty as to when if ever
penance will end. We are reminded of the nightmarish experiences of
Cowper.

But the most disturbing characteristic of this universe is the caprice
that lies at the heart of it; the precise punishment of the Mariner and
his shipmates depends upon chance. The spectre crew of Death and
Life-in-Death gamble for them:

> The naked hulk alongside came
> And the twain were casting dice;
> 'The game is done! I've won! I've won!'
> Quoth she, and whistles thrice.

Now certainly these are loaded dice. As in a dream in which chance
enters, we have no doubt of the outcome, indeed we know what the outcome will be, so here we as readers accept the outcome of the throw as
inevitable. As a matter of fact, most critics including Warren are so accustomed to taking for granted the relentless logic of crime and punishment that they pass over without comment the implications of the dice
game. Surely it knocks out any attempt to impose a systematic philosophical or religious interpretation, be it necessitarian, Christian, or Pla-
tonic, upon the poem. Whether we consider it as part of the ideological
symbolism, or as the Mariner's interpretation of the fact that the men
died and he lived on (a product of his delirium, as it were), or simply
as dramatic machinery, the dice game makes chance the decisive factor
in the Mariner's punishment. It throws into question the moral and intellectual responsibilities of the rulers of the universe. To the extent
that the Mariner's act of pride and capricious sadism sets in motion
retributory forces of the same nature, the question is inevitably raised:
how responsible is he ultimately for his act of evil? How much is his
act simply the reflex of a universal pattern of action?

More or less because the dice game is ignored, the question of the
justification of the crew's death has provoked much solemn debate. Most
recent critics seem willing to accept Warren's argument that the men

have "duplicated the Mariner's own crime of pride" and "have violated the sacramental conception of the universe, by making man's convenience the measure of an act, by isolating him from Nature and the 'One Life.'"[7] But this is a specious argument which further points up the absurdity of trying to impose upon the poem a rigidly logical religious interpretation. The men are guilty of no more than the usual human frailty. True, by acquiescing they become accomplices but there is a vast difference in degree if not in kind between passive ignorant acquiescence and the Mariner's violent act. And what of the rulers of the universe? They are revealed as holding the same contempt for human life that the Mariner held for the bird's life, by finding the crew equally guilty and deserving of the same punishment as the Mariner: whether they live or die depends upon the throw of the dice. The moral conception here is primitive and savage—utterly arbitrary in its ruthlessness. Even as Warren sees it, it is the Old Testament morality of the avenging Jehovah. In suggesting that the moral implications are to be taken as relevant or meaningful beyond the limits of the poem, he seems, therefore, to be sanctioning and would have Coleridge sanction the most intolerant and merciless morality as the law of the universe—and man. Carried to its ultimate bitter implications, this morality would today find entire nations deserving of destruction because their peoples have acquiesced in the actions of their rulers.

From this point on, the sacramental vision is of a hierarchal universe. When the Mariner blesses the snakes unaware, but through a power superior to himself ("Sure my kind saint took pity on me"), he is heard by the Holy Mother who sends "the gentle sleep from Heaven" and the rain which refreshes him when he awakes. And "by the invocation of the guardian saint" the angelic spirits enter the bodies of the ship's crew. The "lonesome spirit from the south-pole," who is certainly less a Neoplatonic daemon than a kind of primitive totem-force, is subservient to the angelic forces, and is pressed into carrying the ship as far as the line. But he has power enough to demand and receive penance "long and heavy" for the Mariner. However we look at it, there is something arbitrary and less than merciful in the way in which the higher powers defer to the Polar spirit; particularly is this inconsistent with the view of the poem as a "tract on universal benevolism and the religion of nature," as Fairchild calls it.[8] Fairchild tries to draw a distinction between the hierarchal body of the poem, which he dismisses as mere dramatic ma-

[7] *Essay*, p. 85.

[8] H. N. Fairchild, *Religious Trends in English Poetry* (New York, 1949), III, pp. 292-94.

chinery, and what he calls the allegory. Even Warren, who sees the poem
as an integrated whole, glosses over the ambiguous implications of the
hierarchal action. Yet if we concede that meaning is implicit in the
poem, we have no justification for interpreting the moral other than in
terms of the total symbolic action—or indeed for deciding that part of
the poem is allegorical and part not—or for deciding that certain action
is meaningful and ignoring other action. As Warren himself says, "Insofar
as the poem is truly the poet's, insofar as it ultimately expresses him,
it involves his own view of the world, his own values." [9] We must assume,
therefore, unless we have evidence to the contrary, that the organization
and manipulation of the hierarchal action in this way rather than another reveals significant attitudes of the author.

At any rate, the arbitrary exhibition of supernatural power continues
in the sinking of the ship, and in the woeful agony that wrenches the
Mariner when he asks the Hermit to shrieve him. The Hermit is power-
less to give absolution to the Mariner, to forgive him in the name of the
Church or God. Instead, as the gloss says ominously, "the penance of
life falls upon" the Mariner from above. The conclusion of the poem is
oppressively puritanical. The Mariner passes "like night from land to
land"; he tells the Wedding-Guest that it is sweeter far than the marriage
feast with a goodly company "to walk together to the kirk" and pray;
he leaves his listener because the "little vesper bell" bids him to prayer;
and the Wedding-Guest turning from the bridegroom's door

> went like one that hath been stunned,
> And is of sense forlorn:
> A sadder and a wiser man,
> He rose the morrow morn.

Instead of the "One Life" we are confronted at the end of the poem by
the eternally alienated Mariner alienating in his turn the Wedding-
Guest, for the Guest is robbed of his happiness and the spontaneous
participation in the marriage feast (which is really the "one life") and
forced to share the disillusioned wisdom and guilt of the Mariner.[10] In

---

[9] *Essay*, p. 64.
[10] In a long footnote (p. 144, n. 136) Warren, admitting that the contrast between
marriage and religious devotion is in the poem, nevertheless argues that "in the total
poem we cannot take the fact of the contrast as being unqualified. At the level of doctrine, we do not have contrast between marriage and sacramental love, but one as
image of the other. It is no accident that the Mariner stops a light-hearted reveler on
the way to a marriage feast. What he tells the wedding-guest is that the human love,
which you take to be an occasion for merriment, must be understood in the context of
universal love and only in that context achieves its meaning. . . . In one of its aspects
the poem is a prothalamion." But in the context of the poem the marriage is pushed

the lurid light of his tale the Mariner's pious moral becomes inescapably ironic:

> He prayeth best, who loveth best
> All things both great and small;
> For the dear God who loveth us,
> He made and loveth all.

The last lines lifted from context as they generally are become the statement of a universal love and charity, of which the Mariner is the recipient and in which he shares. It implies, as we have said, the benevolent, vaguely pantheistic and egalitarian universe of the eighteenth century sentimentalists. This is the "One Life" which Warren presumably sees as prevailing throughout the poem and which the Mariner comes to recognize by way of his experience, so that in the end he "discovers the joy of human communion in God" and gains "the state of 'immanence' in wisdom and love." But by the moral principles of such a universe, the punishment of the Mariner should have been unthinkable. The God who loved man as well as bird should have been merciful and forgiving. The God of the poem, however, is a jealous God; and in context the moral tag carries the concealed threat that even the most trivial violation of his love will bring ruthless and prolonged punishment. The way to avoid conscious or unconscious sin is to withdraw from active life to humble ourselves in prayer. At best, the "love" of God is the love of the benevolent despot, the paternal tyrant, the "great Father" to whom each bends. We love not through joy and spontaneous participation in the "One Life" but through fear and enforced obedience. The little moral tag has the same ambiguous implications as Geraldine's remarks in Part I of *Christabel* which are the prelude to the enslavement of Christabel:

> All they who live in the upper sky,
> Do love you, holy Christabel!

It is because of the ambiguous and terrifying implications of the Mariner's experience that critics like Lowes have denied that the moral statement of the poem is valid outside the magic circle of the voyage and preferred simply to view the poem as a dream, a literary fairy tale,

---

into the background. The wedding-guest is prevented from attending, the Mariner's tale and the marriage end simultaneously, and the guest turns "from the bridegroom's door." If the poem had been intended as *prothalamion*, then the Mariner should have finished his tale prior to the wedding, in time for the wedding-guest to attend with his new-learned wisdom—but no! the Mariner puts his tale *in the place of* the wedding. The contrast at the level of doctrine seems to me inescapable.

or an old wives' tale. They are uncomfortably aware not only that the whole tenor of the poem runs counter to the sentimental implications of the moral tag but also that if taken seriously as philosophical or religious statement it becomes unacceptable to the modern mind. The magical world and its values are contradicted by all our knowledge and experience. In a narrower sense, this world is subversive of the Romantic world view and *its* values. It runs counter to the clichés of Romantic faith. Indeed, it seems irreconcilable with Coleridge's own religious pronouncements.

In their efforts to cope with the problem of belief, Lowes and Warren are led into opposite mistakes. Neither can bring himself to face head on the total implications of the poem; or to believe that Coleridge intended the world he had created. In order to make the poem palatable, Lowes argues that Coleridge uses the ethical background only to give the illusion of inevitable sequence to superb inconsequence, but this suggests unfortunately a kind of manipulation, a fundamental insincerity or disingenuousness. In his reaction against Lowes, Warren himself manipulates the poem by imposing a more or less orthodox sacramental pattern upon it in an effort to make it "thoroughly consistent with Coleridge's basic theological and philosophical views as given to us in sober prose." Though both Lowes and Warren recognize the dream quality in the poem, they tend for different reasons to minimize its importance as a means of resolving the dilemma of meaning. Lowes, refusing to admit that dreams reveal anything about dreamers or indeed have any relevance to waking life, uses the dream characteristics as further evidence of the poem's "inconsequence." Warren, admitting the significance of dreams to Coleridge, goes so far in the opposite direction as to see them as confirming and shoring up the sacramental vision.

But neither Lowes nor Warren takes into consideration the fact that a poem may be the expression of complex attitudes which are not necessarily consistent with the poet's formal philosophy and indeed may contradict it. The discrepancy between the way in which the poet is sometimes led by his experience, needs, and fears to look at the world, and the way in which he says or thinks he is looking at it may be great. Ordinarily the poet proceeding from the perspective of his reasoned beliefs holds the discrepancy to a minimum, as Coleridge does for example in his conversational poems. But occasionally a situation or symbol releases deeply felt and usually repressed attitudes which in turn shape and determine the symbolic action of the poem. This I think is what happens in *The Rime*. It could happen because of the dramatic structure of the poem, which provided an objective correlative dissociated from the poet, so that Coleridge felt free to indulge these attitudes.[11] The clue to the significance of the poem may lie in the subtitle Coleridge affixed in 1800: "A Poet's Reverie." "Reverie" meant for Coleridge a waking dream in which the mind though remaining aware relaxed its monitoring and allowed the imagination to roam freely in a "streamy" process of association.[12] The way in which he described the "fiendish" dreams in the notebooks indicates that they were usually reveries. With reference to *Kubla Khan,* which in a note to the Crewe manuscript he said was "composed in a sort of reverie," Miss Schneider has suggested that "Coleridge's original inclination toward daydreaming, encouraged by the use of half-stupefying doses of opium, had combined with his introspective habit of observing his own mental processes and with his interest in Hartleyan psychology to make him consciously capture and use in both his poetry and prose the content and perhaps one might say the 'technique' of the day dream." [13] She has vividly demonstrated that *Kubla Khan* expresses a perfectly meaningful attitude, similar to attitudes projected in the notebook dreams. The poem focuses on an act of power, the godlike creation of the pleasure-dome; and in the end the poet envisions himself as one who could emulate this act in his art if he could "revive within" him the symphony and song of the Abyssinian maid, and who would then be reverenced and feared by all as divinely inspired.

[11] Professor Lionel Stevenson ("'The Ancient Mariner' as a Dramatic Monologue," *The Personalist,* XXX [1949], 34-44) argues that Coleridge was "objectively depicting a mind totally unlike his own." The poem is "the monologue of a primitive seaman" who evolves in his delirium a logical train of events to account for the physical and mental tortures of thirst and exposure in which he alone is spared. But Professor Stevenson fails to consider the impressive evidence from Coleridge's letters and notebooks which George Whalley has brought together in "The Mariner and the Albatross," *University of Toronto Quarterly,* XVI (1947), 381-98. Professor Whalley perhaps goes too far in calling the poem "a personal allegory," but he is surely right in emphasizing the extent to which the Mariner's suffering, loneliness, and fears are projections of Coleridge's own feelings. The best study of the poem as revelation of Coleridge's unconscious frustrations and conflicts is by David Beres, in "A Dream, A Vision and a Poem: a Psychoanalytic Study of the Origins of *The Rime of the Ancient Mariner,*" *International Journal of Psycho-Analysis,* XXXIII, No. 2 (1951), 97-116.

[12] Coleridge in his speculations drew a distinction between "mere" dream and nightmare, which he defined in a notebook entry as "a species of Reverie, akin to Somnambulism, during which the Understanding & moral Sense are awake, tho' more or less confused." (Quoted in R. C. Bald, "Coleridge and *The Ancient Mariner,*" in *Nineteenth-Century Studies,* ed. Davis, De Vane, Bald [Ithaca, 1940], p. 35.) For Coleridge nightmare seemed to occur most often on the fringes between waking and sleeping. It is interesting that when in 1817 he named the woman of the spectre ship for the first time he called her the "Nightmare Life-in-Death." For Coleridge's views on reverie, see Bald, pp. 37-41, and Elisabeth Schneider, *Coleridge, Opium and Kubla Khan* (Chicago, 1953), pp. 81-109, 325.

[13] *Coleridge, Opium and Kubla Khan,* pp. 90-91.

In the same way, *The Rime* focuses on an act of power, a trivial act of destruction rather than a grandiose act of construction, but nevertheless god-defying and god-attracting. Thereafter the poem is the morbidly self-obsessed account of a man who through his act has become the center of universal attention. The supernatural powers who control the world concentrate upon his punishment and redemption. Two hundred men drop dead because of his act; but he is condemned—and privileged—to live on. As seen through the eyes of the Mariner, the outcome of the dice game can never be in doubt. The crew have no identity apart from him; they are not important enough to be condemned to life-in-death. The reader has no awareness of them as human beings; he watches their deaths without surprise and without feeling except as they affect the Mariner. When, dying, the men fix their eyes upon the Mariner, the effect is not only to intensify his sense of guilt but to emphasize his importance. He has become, as the wedding-guest's outcry at this point indicates, a figure to be feared in his own right.

When he blesses the water snakes, he becomes again the object of universal action. The Albatross falls. It rains. The angels and the Polar spirit are impressed into service to bring him home. And in the end, in order to perform his penance, he himself is given superhuman powers. He passes like night from land to land; he has strange powers of speech; he is apparently immortal. As Warren points out, he can be seen among other things as the *Poète Maudit,* accursed and alienated; but as such he has what Coleridge longed for all his life and achieved as poet only through writing *The Rime*—power to tell his tale and to force the world to listen. The moral is given an additional ironic twist in being presented by this figure of power and wish-fulfillment. The Mariner's act may have been a sin, but it made him important to God and men alike; in this sense he was rewarded rather than punished.

Only within the universe of the poem, however, can the Mariner's fate be seen as partial triumph. Given such a universe, the best that can be hoped for is the partial redemption from horror, the compensatory power of speech which he is granted. Like the Mariner's experience, the universe is the projection not of reasoned beliefs but of irrational fears and guilt feelings. Coleridge has created the kind of universe which his own inexplicable sins and their consequences might have suggested to him. His fear of dreadful consequences began early in life, encompassed a wide range of sinful acts, and finally focused upon his opium addiction. Even in 1798 much of his sense of impotence could have come from his efforts to break the habit. As *The Pains of Sleep* reveals, it was hard for him, consumed by so great a desire to live righteously, not to see himself as a helpless victim of forces beyond his control, forces that were part of the universal pattern of things. What he wanted to believe in and increasingly devoted his intellectual energies to asserting was a universe of order and benevolence in which man possessed freedom of will and action to mold his own destiny; what he feared was a universe in which he was at the mercy of arbitrary and unpredictable forces. *The Rime* envisions such a universe. The Mariner's act is a compulsive sin which strips away the illusion of freedom and reveals just how helpless he is.[14]

In terms of Coleridge's religious conflicts, the universe of *The Rime* is the Christian universe gone mad, rising up and reaffirming itself in the face of the philosophical heresies which he hankered after. At no time in his life was Coleridge at ease in his intellectual speculations; even in the days of greatest revolutionary fervor he sought to reconcile his republican doctrine with traditional Christian dogma, as in *Religious Musings*. His uneasiness is vividly revealed in the concluding section of *The Eolian Harp*, where ostensibly he is pacifying his wife but in reality is appeasing the Christian God

> Who with his saving mercies healèd me,
> A sinful and most miserable man.

The God who healed could as quickly punish, and Coleridge is reassuring Him that he did not mean what he said in the first part of the poem. The attitudes expressed in the wild letters to his brother George are essentially Calvinistic. In a letter in March 1798, in which he disavows his Republicanism, Coleridge melodramatically confesses,

> I believe most steadfastly in original Sin; that from our mothers' wombs our understandings are darkened; and even where our understandings are in the Light, that our organization is depraved, & our volitions imperfect;

---

[14] A lighter aspect of this matter is suggested by the intangible but important formative influence which the superstitions associated with Pixies in Ottery St. Mary brought to bear upon the mind of the young Coleridge. Professor Kathleen Coburn has called to my attention a pamphlet published on the 500th anniversary of the installation of the bell of the Church of St. Mary (R. F. Delderfield, *The Pixies Revenge*, printed by E. J. Manley, Ottery St. Mary, Devon, 1954). The pamphlet relates the various efforts of the Pixies to prevent the casting and installation of the bell, "for the ringing of a Church bell is to the little folk as Holy Water is to the Devil." It takes no Lowes to see how important the childhood associations of mischievous spirits and spells, and Mary as the agent of release from the spells and the giver of peace and sleep, were in shaping the central section of the poem. In fact, the Mariner's reference to the vesper bell takes on fresh significance in the light of these legends emphasizing the importance of the bell as a means of human communication and protection against isolation and avenging spirits. In other words, as Miss Coburn remarks, "The Mariner had been, for his sins, pixillated, as naturally to Coleridge as if he had been an Ottregian."

and we sometimes see the good without *wishing* to attain it, and oftener *wish* it without the energy that wills & performs—And for this inherent depravity, I believe, that the *Spirit* of the Gospel is the sole cure.[15]

How much this view is expressed to please George, how much it reflects Coleridge's convictions—it is certainly not in keeping with other statements of this time—is hard to say; but it reveals the state of mind which could create the universe of *The Rime*.

Just as the poem is molded and shaped by Coleridge's fears, so it makes its appeal to the irrational fears that lurk not far beneath the surface of modern consciousness. No matter how emancipated from the magical view of the universe modern man may be intellectually, he can never free himself from it emotionally or from the values associated with it. He is never quite able to eradicate the uneasy fear that it might turn out to be true. For that matter the anthropocentric conception of the universe continues to dominate western social organization and to determine social behavior. The inexorable punishment, penance, and redemption for sin is not the law of life, but most of us are afraid that it might be (and it has been to the advantage of social mores to encourage that fear). It is that fear which *The Rime* reflects and plays upon. It presents itself as the parable of the man who refuses to believe in the traditional cosmos and expresses his contempt and disbelief by an act that provokes the cosmos into reaffirming itself in its most outrageous and arbitrary form. Most of us find, I think, a curious satisfaction in having this cosmos so vividly reaffirmed; it allows us to indulge our superstitious fears quite shamelessly. We enjoy having the fear of God thrown into such thoughtless, happy souls as the wedding-guest. And finally our religious tradition conditions us to accept almost automatically the pious commonplaces by which the Mariner glosses over the terrifying implications of his experience—they are after all at the foundations of Christian faith—the commonplaces about God's love for man, bird, and beast; the preferability of spiritual love to sexual love; the happiness to be found in penance and prayer. For these commonplaces give an aura of sweet reasonableness and religious authority to an experience essentially negative and irrational; and satisfy the longing to believe that in spite of our fears the universe is ultimately benevolent and reasonable, and if we behave properly will leave us alone.

To a great extent, then, the success of the poem lies in the way it satisfies the impulse to see human fears and desires founded in and re-

---

[15] *Collected Letters of Samuel Taylor Coleridge,* ed. E. L. Griggs (Oxford, 1956), I, p. 396.

vealing universal truths. From its beginning the poem moves relentlessly toward the transformation of its action into moral statement, into an enunciation of universal law. In this connection it is interesting to recall Coleridge's famous statement of purpose in the *Biographia Literaria:* his endeavors he said were to be directed toward persons and characters supernatural, "yet so as to transfer *from our inward nature a human interest and a semblance of truth* sufficient to procure for these shadows of imagination that willing suspension of disbelief for the moment, which constitutes poetic faith" (my italics). The measure of Coleridge's success is indicated by the way in which from many critics he has procured not merely the willing suspension of disbelief, but the willing belief which constitutes religious faith. They are led into eagerly accepting the symbolic projection of our inward nature as the symbolic representation of objective reality.

The desire that a poem should mean, not be, is understandably strong among poets themselves, in spite of their present-day protestations to the contrary. They have an uneasy fear that to admit that a poem is an expression of attitudes which may not be rationally defensible is to concede some fatal weakness which robs it of greatness. The need for the poet to believe that he has been granted special moral insight is almost irresistible—otherwise of what ultimate worth is his eloquence? When he turns critic, therefore, the temptation is strong to justify poetry on moral grounds. This is the temptation to which Warren succumbs. He simply cannot believe that a poem so authoritative in vision, so powerful in symbolism as *The Rime,* is not morally meaningful beyond our fears and desires. As a result, he is led ironically into imposing the moral laws of what Coleridge called the reflective faculty upon a universe of pure imagination.

The Systolic Rhythm:
The Structure of Coleridge's
Conversation Poems

by A. Gérard

On December 31, 1796, Coleridge incidentally mentioned to Thelwall that *The Eolian Harp* was "my favourite of *my* poems" [1] and, without the slightest doubt, even in the version printed in the first edition, it is the best of the poems he had written so far. Indeed, it can be considered as the first Romantic piece to stand on its own merits as a poem. It is also the first really worthy sample of a genre which was particularly adapted to Coleridge's disposition and which Harper has termed "conversation poems": a personal effusion, a smooth outpouring of sensations, feelings and thoughts, an informal releasing of the poetic energies in Coleridge's capacious mind and soul. *The Eolian Harp* set a pattern which Coleridge was to use time and again during his *annus mirabilis* (*Reflections on having left a Place of Retirement, This Lime-tree Bower my Prison, Frost at Midnight, Fear in Solitude, The Nightingale*) and again in 1802 (*Dejection*) and in 1805 (*To a Gentleman*). Together with *This Lime-tree Bower my Prison* and *Dejection,* it ranks among the finest things, the most delicate, the most sensitive, that he ever wrote.

The Eolian Harp was first printed in 1796, in the volume *Poems on Various Subjects* and like thirty-six of the poems collected there, it was styled as an "effusion," "in defiance," Coleridge wrote in his Preface, "of Churchill's line:

'Effusion on Effusion pour away.' " [2]

"The Systolic Rhythm: The Structure of Coleridge's Conversation Poems" by A. Gérard. From *Essays in Criticism* (Oxford, July 1960). Reprinted, in slightly abridged form, by permission of *Essays in Criticism.*

[1] *Collected Letters of Samuel Taylor Coleridge,* ed. E. L. Griggs, Oxford, Clarendon Press, 1956, p. 295.

[2] *The Poetical Works of Samuel Taylor Coleridge,* ed. E. H. Coleridge, Oxford University Press, 1912, p. 1136.

The author was perfectly conscious that this kind of poetry was likely to give offense to such readers as had been bred in the traditional taste for objectivity and impersonality. Indeed, the whole of the Preface focuses round the question of egotism in a way which is alternately aggressive and defensive:

> Compositions resembling those of the present volume are not unfrequently condemned for their querulous egotism. But egotism has to be condemned then only when it offends against time and place, as in a History or an Epic Poem. To censure it in a Monody or Sonnet is almost as absurd as to dislike a circle for being round.[3]

The arguments adduced by Coleridge to justify his proclaimed egotism may sound shallow and peculiarly subjective, although one of them, at least, deserves to be quoted as it anticipates some important considerations which Wordsworth was to expound in the Preface to the second edition of the *Lyrical Ballads:*

> The communicativeness of our nature leads us to describe our own sorrows; in the endeavour to describe them, intellectual activity is exerted; and by a benevolent law of our nature, from intellectual activity a pleasure results which is gradually associated and mingles as a corrective with the painful subject of the description.[4]

As this probably did not sound quite convincing, Coleridge, in the edition of 1797, added a paragraph calling upon his own experience:

> If I could judge of others by myself, I should not hesitate to affirm, that the most interesting passages in our most interesting Poems are those, in which the Author developes [*sic*] his own feelings. The sweet voice of Cona [Ossian] never sounds so sweetly as when it speaks of itself; and I should almost suspect that man of an unkindly heart, who could read the opening of the third book of the *Paradise Lost* without peculiar emotion. By a law of our Nature, he, who labours under a strong feeling, is impelled to seek for sympathy; but a Poet's feelings are all strong. *Quicquid amet valde amat.* Akenside therefore speaks with philosophical accuracy, when he classes Love and Poetry, as producing the same effects:
>
>> "Love and the wish of Poets when their tongue
>> Would send to others' bosoms, what so charms
>> Their own."
>>
>> *Pleasures of Imagination*[5]

[3] *Ibid.,* pp. 1135-36.
[4] *Ibid.,* p. 1136. Cf. Wordsworth, (*The Poetical Works of William Wordsworth,* ed. E. de Sélincourt, Oxford, Clarendon Press, 1940-47, II, pp. 400-401).
[5] *Ibid.,* p. 1144.

This paragraph enlarges upon a characteristic observation penned down in a notebook some time in 1795 or 1796: "Poetry without egotism comparatively uninteresting." [6]

Coleridge's defense of egotism in this little-known Preface should of course be connected with the usual Romantic emphasis on feeling or emotion as the mainspring of poetry. For feelings are entirely personal and, unless the poet has that Shakespearian gift of dramatic sympathy which enables a writer to identify himself with other persons—and with this gift the English Romantics most assuredly had *not* been favored— it is only of his own emotional life that a poet is fully aware: it is therefore only his own feelings that he can convey poetically. But does this imply that he is cut off from everything that is not his own self? Does this mean that Romantic poetry is necessarily confined to subjectivism, to self-exploration and self-discovery? Twentieth century critics of Romanticism—brought up most of them in a spirit of revolt against the Romantic tradition and therefore conditioned to reserve their praise to so-called impersonal poetry—emphatically answer that it does. In a study on egotism, F. G. Steiner went so far as to assert that:

> it is precisely the dissociation between individual and universal which characterizes Romantic egotism and distinguishes it from Classical or Renaissance introspection.[7]

It is perhaps a little unfortunate that Steiner does not explain what he means by "universal," especially in view of the fact that he quotes a remark of Hazlitt to the effect that:

> Mr. Coleridge talks of himself, without being an egotist, for in him the individual is always merged in the abstract and the general.[8]

To Hazlitt, it would appear, the first Romantic upholder of egotism was himself no egotist. Clearly, the word is in need of some precise definition: for Hazlitt did not use it with the same meaning as Coleridge did. I have attempted elsewhere to draw some conclusions from a few discursive utterances of the Romantics on the subject of egotism[9] and one of those conclusions is that the term "egotism" as used in literary criticism, covers

---

[6] *The Notebooks of Samuel Taylor Coleridge,* ed. K. Coburn, London, Routledge and Kegan Paul, 1957, entry no. 62.

[7] F. G. Steiner, " 'Egoism' and 'Egotism,' " *EC,* II (1952), 449.

[8] *The Complete Works of William Hazlitt,* ed. P. P. Howe, London, Dent, 1932, XI, p. 31.

[9] A. Gérard, *L'idée romantique de la poésie en Angleterre,* Paris, Les Belles Lettres, 1955, pp. 252-56.

at least two very different concepts: it can denote an attitude of total absorption in the self, with utter and permanent disregard for the outside world of nature, humanity, and the spiritual; it can also denote interest in the self as the necessary starting-point for the poet's exploration of the universe, for his endeavor to understand his own position in relation to the world outside. It becomes then obvious that Coleridge describes himself as an egotist in the second sense, while Hazlitt states that Coleridge is no egotist in the first sense of the word—and although they seem to contradict each other, yet they are both right.

While the ego, then, is the primary source of Romantic poetry, it by no means follows that it is its essence and its aim, its center and its circumference. And if there is no denying that Romantic poetry is egotistic in its origin, it would be rash to conclude that it is altogether subjective. A more detailed analysis of the structure of *The Eolian Harp* will help to show what Romantic egotism really is, not as an abstract concept, but as a living source of inspiration.

The poem begins with an apostrophe to Coleridge's wife and a very concrete and particularized picture of the two sitting in their garden at dusk. But it soon goes beyond that initial stage of concrete immediacy. Though the first part is wholly descriptive, the description widens gradually until it encompasses not only the two young people, but also the garden itself, the sky ("clouds," "star"), the earth ("bean-fields") and the "distant" sea, so that by the end of this section, the stage is clear for the word "world." It was not the first time that Coleridge was using this image of widening perspective leading to a sort of cosmic view: such a conceit provided the main motif for his sonnet on *Life* (1789) the pattern of which is based on a simile between widening *sensory* perspective and growing *spiritual* insight.

There is another significant similarity between *Life* and *The Eolian Harp:* in the latter poem too Coleridge tries to go beyond the immediacy of sensory experience. The jasmin, the myrtle and the star appear as "emblems" of Innocence, Love, and Wisdom. The allegorizing is clumsy enough,[10] but at least it shows the poet groping for something that has clearly nothing to do with "egotism," reaching for some spiritual value which is rooted in his own experience but not limited to it.

Between the first and the second part a process of contraction takes place. After his flight into the wide expanse of nature, the poet reverts to a single definite object within his immediate experience: the lute.

[10] In the third edition of his poems (1803), Coleridge dropped ll. 5 and 8, but later changed his mind, and they remained part of the final version.

(Incidentally we must notice how skilfully the reader is prepared for the melody of the harp by the auditory imagery at the end of the first section: "a world so hush'd," "stilly murmur," "silence.") But here again the immediate datum of personal experience is only a starting-point from which the poet soon departs, not, this time, to explore the frontiers of the perceptual world, but to allow free play to his fanciful imagination.

The epithet "desultory" has significant implications: the poem's imagery also proceeds desultorily. Free association is at work in the two similes which the harp's melody calls up into the poet's mind. The first simile (harp = coy maid; wind = lover; melody = sweet upbraiding) may not sound very adequate. But then the mood is obviously playful. And it reminds us that love is very much on the poet's mind. The second simile is both more intricate and more intriguing; the perspective again widens as the poet's imagination leaves the concrete object to dream of Fairy-Land, the harp's "sequacious notes" evoking both the "witchery of sound" made by Elfins voyaging on the gales and the (personified) Melodies that float untiringly round the flowers of Fairy-Land.

The second comparison seems to fulfill with greater subtlety a purpose similar to that of the allegorizing in the first section: it dematerializes, as it were, the beauty of the harp's melody. The process is accomplished by means of comparisons with ghostly beings (Elfins) and with an abstract personification (Melodies); besides, Coleridge here uses that swift motor imagery ("footless and wild," "nor pause nor perch," "hovering," "untam'd wings") which was to become one of Shelley's favorite devices.

Different though the two similes are, they have a definite connection which becomes clear in ll. 30-31:[11] it is impossible not to *love* all things in a world *so filled*—i.e. with beauty. Moreover, the parallelism of the phrases "and the world so hush'd" (l. 10) and "in a world so fill'd" (l. 31), identical in their rhythm and similarly situated at the end of the antepenultimate line of the stanza is cleverly designed to recall the first part of the poem, and thus to clarify the meaning of "so fill'd"; Coleridge is alluding both to the objective beauty of the landscape delineated in the first part, and to the beauty of the products of his own fancy, now at its most Keatsian. The artful symmetry in the fall of the first two parts is enhanced by the note of silence on which they both end ("hush'd,"

---

[11] In the editions of 1796 and 1797, the first section ended with l. 25. In 1803, Coleridge deleted ll. 21-25 containing the second simile which has just been discussed and inserted in their place what is the first version of ll. 30-33:

> Methinks, it should have been impossible
> Not to love all things in a World like this,
> Where e'en the Breezes of the simple air
> Possess the power and spirit of Melody.

"silence," "stilly murmur," "mute still air," "music slumbering"). Nor is this silence devoid of symbolic significance: the final advice the poet will give to himself at the end of the poem is to bid his unregenerate mind keep silent.

The transition between Part II and Part III is as skilfully and unobtrusively contrived as that between Part I and Part II. The general impression of a fanciful *rêverie* built up in Part II is summed up in the word "slumbering" and the daydreaming image glides over to Part III, although in a more naturalistic key, in the picture of the poet stretched on the hillside, "musing" and looking at the world through "half-closed eye-lids."

But between Part II and Part III, a swift systolic movement of contraction has again occurred: the poet has left Fairy-Land and turns back to his own self, not as he is at the moment when the experience so far described takes place, but when he is lying on a hill slope at noon. This time, the panoramic perception is quickly suggested in a few strokes (the earth: "yonder hill"; the sky: "sunbeams"; the sea: "the main"). But the process of expansion develops in yet another direction: after the sensory apprehension of nature (Part I) and the fanciful excursion into Fairy-Land (Part II), the poet's mind now indulges in speculations of a more intellectual order.

At the same time, the harp's catalytic power to precipitate images gains in complexity. Here as in the second part, the harp is the origin of two comparisons. To begin with, the "brain" of the poet is visitated by "thoughts" and "phantasies" as the "lute" is caressed by the "gales"; "phantasies" clearly refers back to the playful and delicious images called up by the harp in Part II, while the word "thought" anticipates ll. 44-8. Anyway, ll. 39-43 supply an image of the working of free association in the passive mind. But the next simile (which comes nearer to metaphor and points to a perception of symbolic, rather than allegorical, significance), refers to the coalescence of matter and spirit: the panoramic perception of Part I has given way to the cosmic vision.

The last section of the poem, like the others, is characterized by a double process of contraction and expansion. Once more, Coleridge reverts to immediate experience and addresses Sara; and once more, he departs from his starting-point to explore wider regions—this time, the realm of Faith.

The effect of this section upon the reader is distinctly anticlimactic. The embarrassed diction (especially the double negation in ll. 50-51), the most unattractive portrait of Sara as, to borrow House's description, a rather "narrow and governessy" kind of person ("serious eye," "mild

reproof," "meek daughter"), the Sunday-school undertone of abject self-
abasement in the phrasing, provide a tame conclusion after the beautiful
image of ll. 44-8. Nevertheless, there can be no doubt, I think, that Coleridge intended this section to be climactic: he repudiates his flights of
fancy under Sara's "more serious eye"; he speaks of God and Christ, of
holiness and faith: this, clearly, should be the culmination of a pilgrimage that has led him from sensory experience, through fanciful *rêverie*
and intellectual speculation to deeper awareness of God's greatness and
the value of Faith. Whereas the sense of anticlimax that we experience
has important bearings on our understanding of Coleridge's spiritual
predicament in 1795, the realization that this last section was climactic
in intent gives us a clear view of the structure of the poem.

While the structure of Shelley's and of Keats's poetry receives the
critical attention it deserves, there seems to be among critics a widespread
feeling that the poetry of the Lake Poets is generally devoid of structure,
that it is, indeed, "the spontaneous overflow of powerful feelings" and as
such rather shapeless and, as it were, boneless! One of the very few ex-
ceptions is G. M. Harper who paid some attention to the technique of
Reflections on having left a Place of Retirement:

> the poem begins with a quiet description of the surrounding scene and,
> after a superb flight of imagination, brings the mind back to the starting-
> point, a pleasing device which we may call the "return." [12]

Harper noticed other examples of this "pleasing device" in *Frost at
Midnight* and in *Fears in Solitude*. It is rather strange that he should
not have mentioned it in connection with *The Eolian Harp*. Anyway,
this concept of the "return" over-simplifies the matter, and it should be
made clear that the structural technique of *The Eolian Harp* and a good
many other Romantic poems is far more than a "pleasing device": it casts
a most useful and pertinent light on the workings of the Romantic mind
itself.

The structure of *The Eolian Harp* is based on the simultaneous development, the interplay, and the perfect integration of three different
rhythmic processes.

The foregoing analysis has, I hope, made clear that the poem is characterized by a widening and ascending movement which carries the poet
from nature to God: from sensory perception to fanciful *rêveries,* and
thence, through intellectual speculation, to an assertion of his religious

[12] G. M. Harper, "Coleridge's Conversation Poems," *Quarterly Review,* CCXLIV
(1925), 289.

faith. But within this general framework we can observe a heartbeat rhythm of systole and diastole, contraction and expansion, in which the poet's attention is wandering to and fro between his concrete, immediate experience and the wide and many-faceted world of the non-self: from the self to the forms of nature apprehended in the panoramic perception; from the self to the poetic Fairy-Land created by Fancy; from the self to an intellectual vision of the Cosmos; from the self to humble contemplation of God.

It is the combination of these two which creates what Harper calls "the return"—only, it is not a return, for the self to which the poet finally turns back is not the same self from which he had started: it has been enriched, heightened and uplifted by the various inner and outer experiences to which it has submitted and from which it now emerges with what the poet considers to be a deeper and more accurate knowledge of the universe and of his place in it.

The reason why *The Eolian Harp* does not succeed in the end is that the diction, the thought, and the feeling fail to live up to the high level of structural integration; in other words, when we reach the highest point in the rhythmic development of the poem, the other elements break down, not, in this case, out of any insincerity on the part of the writer, but because he is caught between an exhilarating sense of oneness, which he discards, and a depressing sense of intellectual impotence, which he upholds. The poet is struggling with thoughts and feelings which are insufficiently realized and clash with each other, whereas his conscious aim is to end on an image of inward peace and harmony.

It is to a similar reason that we must ascribe the failure of *Reflections on having left a Place of Retirement.* In this poem, as Harper says, the imagination "seeks not (. . .) a metaphysical, but an ethical height." [13] Coleridge is concerned with personal happiness and humanitarian action. The widening and ascending process is obviously at work as the poem, starting from the writer's personal happiness, goes on to the panoramic perception of nature, and then to the depiction of the plight of mankind. Within this process, we can easily trace the heartbeat rhythm as, at the beginning of each section, the writer starts from his Clevedon cottage, only to mention it again at the end, after he has left it for the humanitarian reasons previously announced. While the introduction of "A wealthy son of commerce . . . , Bristowa's citizen" in the first section is ominous enough, the bombastic phraseology of the third section, contrasting with the beautifully restrained description of the second, in-

[13] *Ibid.,* p. 289.

evitably suggests that Coleridge is doing his best to work himself up into a frenzy of humanitarian feeling just as in the final section of *The Eolian Harp* he was trying hard to formulate an attitude which he believed to be right although it clashed with his deep-felt experience. The difference is that the statement contained in the *Reflections* is palpably untrue: Coleridge did not leave Clevedon in order to:

> join head, heart, and hand,
> Active and firm, to fight the bloodless fight
> Of science, freedom, and the truth in Christ.

(ll. 60-62)

but merely, as Cottle dryly tells us, to be nearer Bristol, its libraries and printing-presses.[14]

It was only in 1797, with *This Lime-tree Bower my Prison*, that Coleridge achieved the perfect blending of feeling and thought, imagery and structure, for which he was obviously groping. In this poem too the heart-beat rhythm is the fundamental pattern. It starts with Coleridge queru-lously complaining that he is obliged to stay at home as a result of Sara accidentally emptying "a skillet of boiling milk" on his foot! The process of expansion takes place as the poet's imagination follows his friends on springy heath, along the hill-top edge and up the hill, from the top of which they can rejoice ("in gladness") in the by now familiar panoramic perception ("wide Heaven," "the many-steepled tract magnificent," "the sea"). Then occurs the systolic beat as Coleridge focuses his attention on Charles Lamb: there seems to be some ground for believing that he is here identifying himself with Charles, as what is said of the latter is also true of himself:

> thou hast pined
> And hunger'd after Nature, many a year,
> In the great City pent, winning thy way
> With sad yet patient soul, through evil and pain
> And strange calamity.

(ll. 28-32)

After which, the panoramic perception briefly recalled ("glorious sun" and "clouds," "heath-flowers" and "distant groves," "blue Ocean") is transmuted into a cosmic vision of the landscape as a living thing. In the third section, Coleridge turns back to himself, noting that his mood has changed from melancholy to "delight" and his attention immediately

[14] J. Cottle, *Reminiscences of Samuel Taylor Coleridge and Robert Southey*, London, 1847, pp. 64-65.

expands to a minute description of the lime-tree bower which now appears to him as a microcosm where the presence of nature can be as intensely felt as in the "wide landscape." The poem then closes with a "return" to Coleridge himself blessing "the last rook," "black" and "creeking," in the same spirit as the Ancient Mariner blesses the "slimy water-snakes."

It may be futile to speculate about the part played by the conscious mind and the unconscious in the setting up of this pattern which often recurs in Romantic poetry. One feels inclined to believe that, while the overall movement of expansion and ascension may have been premeditated, the inner rhythm of systole and diastole probably derives from one of the deepest urges in the Romantic mind. At any rate, the structure of *The Eolian Harp* and of the other "conversation poems" illuminates the nature of Romantic egotism. Although Coleridge's Preface to the 1796 edition of his *Poems* may appear as a defense of egotism, it should be clear that this apology is no more than a tactical move designed to justify one particular aspect of his poetry. But "egotism" in the sense of a total and exclusive concentration of attention upon the self is certainly no part of the Romantic view of poetry; nor is it an important element in Romantic poetry itself. On the other hand, the architectonic framework of *The Eolian Harp* and of Coleridge's other poems that have been considered shows that, in practice as well as in theory, the ego was to the Romantics but the starting-point of their poetic meditation: it was for them what, in fact, it has been for many thinkers ever since Descartes uttered his *Cogito, ergo sum,* the basic certainty in which all else is rooted. Romanticism was concerned with the ego not in and for itself, but as an element in a complex and wide network of relationships which also embraced the fundamentals of human thought and experience: nature, man, and God. This appears not only from their explicit philosophical utterances on the subject, but also from something that is more revealing of the essential urge that drove them: the structural rhythm to which their inspiration spontaneously shaped itself.

Kubla Khan

by Elisabeth Schneider

However much it owes to Milton, Coleridge's poem has its own quite un-Miltonic individual identity of music. A particular tone is given to the whole by a predominance of *æ*- and other modified *a*-sounds that set the poem distinctly apart from any music characteristic of Milton. The sound is common in Eastern names, particularly as anglicized in Coleridge's day, and is very noticeable in *Thalaba,* where, besides the hero's own name and the staples Allah, Mohammed, Arabia, Bagdad, Babylon, Ali, the stanzas are dotted with Lobaba, Abdaldar, Dom-Daniel, Okba, Nayd, Moath, Saleah, Haruth and Maruth, Al-Maimon, Aloadin, Mohareb, Zohak, Ararat, Laila, Bahar-Danush. These names spring out from the pages as one turns them quickly, and their number might easily be doubled. Southey was conscious of their prominence and attempted, like Coleridge, to play his tune upon them. So his maiden is usually a "damsel" and she plucks fruit from the "tamarind" tree. "Camels" and "caverns" and "Paradise" and "magic" follow as automatically as a string of beads, often like a reflex motion of the voice when the mind has gone off elsewhere.

The pattern of *Kubla Khan,* however, is not confined to the *æ*-sounds. The rhyme, with all its freedom, its shiftings and *Lycidas*-like "oscillations," has elaborate hidden correspondences. The rhyme scheme of the opening seven lines, for example, is exactly repeated in the first seven lines of the second paragraph. The extraordinary elaboration, also, of the assonance keeps the music of this poem fresh through many re-readings. Even when one knows it well, it is still full of half-caught echoes, correspondences of sound felt but too complex to be anticipated or to remain tabulated in the mind even after they have been analyzed. And so they retain a subtle, secret harmony.

The most obvious of the patterns in the opening lines, apart from the ubiquity of the æ-sounds, is the alliteration that closes each of the first five lines: *"Kubla Khan," "dome decree," "river ran," "measureless to man," "sunless sea"*—a revival of the device Coleridge had practiced so conspicuously in his Spenserian-Miltonic verse of 1795. Here, however, it is only a small part of his effect and is so well subordinated to the whole pattern that one might know the poem for a long time without becoming conscious of the obvious and somewhat mechanical device.

The opening line, "In Xa'nadu' did Ku'bla Kha'n," receives its primary shape from the inclosed assonance of its four stresses, *a-u-u-a,* which swings the sound as if in a shallow curve, the symmetry being still further marked by the full rhyme of the inclosing syllables, *Xan-* and *Khan* (Coleridge undoubtedly pronounced *Khan* as it was often spelled, *Can*) and the embellishment of minor echoes, *d*'s and short *i*'s binding together the first part and *k*'s the end of the line:

Two of the next three lines are given the same outer shape by means of the same inclosing assonance, "Alph . . . ran" and "caverns . . . man"; but the extremely symmetrical swing of the first line is broken and varied afterwards.

In the first four lines only one sound stands out alone, without an echo; it is the most resounding syllable in the poem—*dome.* The word resounds naturally of itself, but its intrinsic length and weight are here increased by its isolation and its contrast against the background of the lighter vowel sounds that precede it:

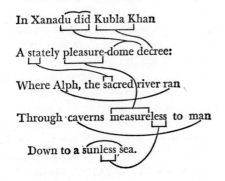

$[d\ d\ K\ K]$

$[d\ d\ c(=K)]$

The *dome* stands alone, though it is tied into the verse by its focusing of the *d*-sounds before and after. In contrast with the self-contained symmetry of the first line, the second has a freewheeling sound, for it has little internal pattern to give it a shape of its own beyond the inflectional shape determined by its meaning. Its sounds, all but *dome,* dissolve into the general fabric. The closing word, *decree,* unites in its two chief consonants the two minor alliterations of the first line, the *d*'s ("-du did") and the *k*'s ("Ku- Kha-"). *Stately* disappears into *sacred* in the next line, and *pleasure* has its full double rhyme in *measure* in the line after. This absorption of the other elements of the line lends still greater prominence to *dome.*

The tune and variations to be played upon the *æ*-sound are established by the first sentence, in which three of the five lines begin and end with stresses upon it. But this effect is overlaid or interwoven with an elaboration so intricate that one could scarcely point to its mate in English poetry if we except the more subtle harmonies of Milton and Bridges. It would be both useless and impertinent, however, to point out in detail the almost innumerable linkings of sound in *Kubla Khan.* Anyone can do it for himself who cares to, though the maziness of the design is remarkable. After the initial sentence the pattern becomes more flexible and varied. The *æ*-sounds recur, but less regularly, and often lengthen or shade into the broader *a*'s. Exactly what sounds Coleridge thought or heard when he wrote *enchanted, haunted, chaffy,* and *dance* we do not know, but it is probable that he heard at least some of them equivocally as both *hænted* and *hānted,* like the variegated *a*'s of the Eastern names. Often throughout the poem he repeats his old device of foreshadowing the terminal rhyme by a preceding echo of assonance or alliteration—"sinuous rills," "chasm which slanted," "ceaseless turmoil seething," "mazy motion," "river ran," and "measureless to man" each used a second time, "from far," "mingled measure," "loud and long." This device, used skilfully as it is here and partly concealed by the interlacing of other patterns, contributes something to the floating effect of the whole, for the assonance softens the impact of the rhyme and so lessens its tendency to bring the line to earth at the close: the terminal rhyme does not settle so heavily upon the mind when its emphasis has been partly stolen by its preceding shadow. The forward movement is made to pause and "oscillate" further at times by the considerable number of lines in which the meaning looks forward while the rhyme looks back. One finds this often elsewhere as the closed couplet of the eighteenth century broke down, but it seems to be used in *Kubla Khan* with a somewhat special effect.

To my mind, none of this bears the marks of dream-composition, though it has cooperated with Coleridge's story of a dream by contributing to the floating effect. It does not sound, either, like any other sort of fully automatic composition. The intense concentration of the act of composing does indeed bear some likeness to reverie; it is, in fact, reverie in one of Erasmus Darwin's senses, "the poet's reverie" in which the will is active though attention is detached from the outside world. But it is creative *will* that is at work and not the *wish*-fulfillment reverie of certain psychologico-aesthetic theories. That will is felt in *Kubla Khan,* I think, even though its aim may be only vaguely determined.

*   *   *

I sometimes think we overwork Coleridge's idea of "the balance or reconciliation of opposite or discordant qualities." I have to come back to it here, however, for the particular flavor of *Kubla Khan,* with its air of mystery, is describable in part through that convenient phrase. Yet the "reconciliation" does not quite occur either. It is in fact avoided. What we have instead is the very spirit of "oscillation" itself. One could scarcely find words better than those Coleridge used of *Lycidas,* "the floating or oscillation of assonance and consonance," to describe the effect not of the terminal rhymes alone but of the whole sound pattern of *Kubla Khan* and, beyond that, of its imagery, its movement, and, in the end, even its meaning. The poem is the soul of ambivalence, oscillation's very self; and that is probably its deepest meaning. In creating this effect, form and matter are intricately woven. The irregular and inexact rhymes and the varied lengths of the lines play some part. More important is the musical effect in which a smooth, rather swift forward movement is emphasized by the relation of grammatical structure to line and rhyme, yet is impeded and thrown back upon itself even from the beginning by the *æ*-inclosed line units. Like the Mariner's ship at the Equator, the verse moves "backwards and forwards half her length," or like tides rocking in a basin. In the middle of the poem the slightly stronger forward movement loses itself altogether in the floating equivocation between backward-turned trochaic and forward-leaning iambic movement. One hears the texture of Milton, whose great will and drive, even in his discursive moments, gives to all he wrote an air of power and singleness of direction, however elaborate and circuitous his form may be. But in *Kubla Khan* one hears this elaboration almost wholly deprived of such will or with only enough will to keep it afloat. Its spirit is "to care and not to care," but not in Mr. Eliot's sense.

In this forward-flowing movement counterpointed against a stationary-oscillating one, form and meaning are almost indistinguishable. The pleasure-dome is built, then it is unbuilt. The poem is about Kubla, then it is not about him. The oppositions of image are not only the obvious ones of light and darkness, sunny dome and sunless sea or caves of ice, Paradise garden and hints of hell. In the elaborate opening passage *stately, dome, decree, sacred, caverns, measureless,* and *sunless* are all rather solemn words and, except for *stately,* not cheerful-solemn but awful-solemn. Yet the dome is a pleasure-palace; the movement and music of the verse are light rather than solemn. The central statement, through the first half of the poem, is one of bright affirmation. The talk and activity are of building, the pleasure-dome and a delightful Paradise materialize. But even as the words give they take away with half-Miltonic negatives. *Pleasure* itself is rhymed with one of them—*measureless;* deprivation haunts the language. The negations recur in *sunless, ceaseless, lifeless,* a second *measureless.* The demon-lover is not in Paradise; he is an *as-if* brought in to cast his shadow. Images of awe and mystery underlie Paradise in the subterranean river and ocean, and the ancestral threat of war is heard far off. The whole poem oscillates between giving and taking away, bright affirmation and sunless negation, light flowing music that nevertheless stands still and rings the portentous sound of *dome* time after time.

The spirit of the poem, moreover, is cool and rather non-human. One feels no real warmth even in the sunny garden. And though the verse is nominally well peopled, Kubla, the wailing woman, and the Abyssinian maid are not really there, and their half-presence leaves the place less human than if the theme were a poetic scene of nature alone. Even the poet, who is half-present in the end, is dehumanized behind his mask of hair and eyes and magic circle and is only present as mirrored in the exclamations of nebulous beholders—or rather, he *would* be mirrored *if* he had built his dome and *if* there had been beholders. Nor is there any human or personal feeling in the poem; the poet's "deep delight," impersonal enough even if it were there, exists only to be denied.

Here in these interwoven oscillations dwells the magic, the "dream," and the air of mysterious meaning of *Kubla Khan.* I question whether this effect was all deliberately thought out by Coleridge, though it might have been. It is possibly half-inherent in his subject. Paradise is usually lost and always threatened, in Genesis and Milton, in the Paradise gardens of Irem, of Aloadin, of Abyssinian princes. The historical Cubla did not apparently lose his in the end, but it too was threatened with war and dissension and portents. The Paradise of Coleridge's poem was not exactly lost either. What was lost, the closing lines tell us, was the vision of an unbuilt Paradise, an unwritten poem. His Paradise in that sense was truly enough a dream. What remains is the spirit of "oscillation," perfectly poeticized, and possibly ironically commemorative of the author.

Coleridge as Critic

by Herbert Read

. . . There is an entry in the recently published *Notebooks* of Henry James in which . . . he says that he

was infinitely struck with the suggestiveness of S.T.C.'s figure—wonderful, admirable figure—for pictorial treatment. . . . There was a point, as I read, at which I seemed to see a little story—to have a quick glimpse of the possible drama. Would not such a drama necessarily be the question of the acceptance by someone—someone with something important at stake— of the general *responsibility* of rising to the height of accepting him for what he is, recognizing his rare, anomalous, magnificent, interesting, curious, tremendously suggestive character, vices and all, with all its imperfections on its head, and *not* being guilty of the pedantry, the stupidity, the want of imagination, of fighting him, deploring him in the details—failing to recognize that one *must* pay for him and that on the whole he is magnificently worth it.[1]

From that particular suggestion emerged, eventually, one of James's best stories—*The Coxon Fund*. Though our aims are so different, and have no dramatic effect in view, yet the injunctions that Henry James proposed to himself are not altogether irrelevant to our purpose. In particular, we must accept Coleridge for what he was, not merely as a person, but as an intellect, "vices and all"; and we must not be guilty of a partial portrait, of a selection of evidence designed to present a critic merely congenial—a critic of vivid perceptions, of penetrating insight— to the neglect of all that constituted the real substance and capacity of the man and his mind.

"Coleridge as Critic" by Herbert Read. From *Lectures in Criticism*, Bollingen Series XVI (New York: Pantheon Books, 1949; London: Faber and Faber Ltd., 1949), pp. 74-108. Abridged from a lecture originally contributed to a Symposium on the Great Critics held at the Johns Hopkins University, Baltimore, and delivered on April 14, 1948. ©1949 by Bollingen Foundation, Inc. Reprinted, abridged (from *Lectures*), by permission of the author, Faber and Faber Ltd., and the Bollingen Foundation.

[1] *The Notebooks of Henry James.* Ed. by F. O. Matthiessen and Kenneth B. Murdock, New York, 1947, p. 152.

The danger is a real one, and has not been avoided by writers on Coleridge. We need not, I think, take too seriously those who try to dissociate the poet and the philosopher. . . .

Admittedly there is a psychological problem; for some reason Coleridge was [after his sojourn in Germany] to find it increasingly difficult to write poetry; and in that wonderful but pathetic ode: *Dejection,* which he wrote in his thirtieth year, and in which he openly confessed the failing of his "genial spirits," he carried the psychological analysis of his mental state to a point of realistic revelation on which no external investigator is ever likely to improve. This ode must be read in its original form, first published by Professor de Selincourt in 1937, for there Coleridge reveals the real source of his affliction. . . .[2]

Writing in this same year 1802, about four months after the composition of this ode, Coleridge confessed to Southey that

> all my poetic genius (if ever I really possessed any *genius,* and it was not rather a more general aptitude of talent and quickness in imitation) is gone, and I have been fool enough to suffer deeply in my mind, regretting the loss, which I attribute to my long and exceedingly severe metaphysical investigations, and these partly to ill-health, and partly to private afflictions which rendered any subjects, immediately connected with feeling, a source of pain and disquiet to me.[3]

At first sight this might seem to confirm the theory that metaphysics destroyed the poet in Coleridge. But in another letter written only sixteen days earlier, Coleridge had said: "Metaphysics is a word that you, my dear sir, are not a great friend to, but yet you will agree with me that a great poet must be *implicité,* if not *explicité,* a profound metaphysician";[4] and there is that still more uncompromising statement in the *Biographia Literaria:* "No man was ever yet a great poet, without being at the same time a profound philosopher."[5] The greatest poetry, as we shall see when we come to discuss Coleridge's theory of poetry, is precisely that in which "the creative power and the intellectual energy wrestle as in a war embrace."

The truth of the matter is, I think, that the concentration demanded by metaphysical investigations is a better anodyne for private afflictions than poetry, for in poetry the emotions are involved. But this does not imply, and Coleridge never for a moment entertained the idea, that meta-

[2] The complete text is given by de Selincourt in his *Wordsworthian and Other Studies.* Oxford, 1947, pp. 67-76. Cf. above, pp. 30-37.

[3] *Letters* (1895), I, p. 388.

[4] *Ibid.,* p. 372.

[5] *Biographia Literaria,* ed. by Shawcross. Oxford, 1907. II, p. 19.

physics was foreign to poetry, or destructive of poetic genius. Coleridge repeatedly asserts that but for his afflictions he would have made it his business to embody his philosophy in his poetry; more exactly, to make poetry an instrument of metaphysical research.

* * *

Writing in 1840, six years after Coleridge's death, John Stuart Mill expressed the opinion that "the class of thinkers has scarcely yet arisen by whom Coleridge [as a philosopher] is to be judged. . . ."

The Transcendental Philosophy, of which Coleridge was a late but brilliant luminary, has long ago taken its due place in the historical perspective of philosophy. Certain subsequent schools, of which the most contentious have been Hegelianism, dialectical materialism, positivism, and pragmatism, have obscured for a time the originality and perennial force of that mansion of thought whose foundations were laid by Kant, whose glittering pinnacles were completed by Coleridge, Novalis, and Kierkegaard. I must speak with caution in a country where pragmatism, I am told, is still regarded as the national philosophy; but if I am not mistaken, here as well as in Europe there has been in recent years a return to a more idealistic attitude in philosophy. This is shown in the remarkable interest now shown in Kierkegaard, and in the spread of a philosophy which, in some three distinct varieties, is known as *existentialism*. It will become evident as we proceed that Coleridge, no less than Kierkegaard, comes within the range of this revivalism.

* * *

Coleridge was polymath. He took all knowledge for his province, and from the day when "the old Grey Friars re-echoed to the accents of the *inspired charity-boy*," as his schoolmate Charles Lamb called him, "the young Mirandula, waxing, even in those early years, not pale at philosophic draughts of Jamblichus or Plotinus," from that day until his death Coleridge continued to absorb knowledge from all quarters. He never lost his zest for learning, and a list of authors and works quoted in his writings would in itself fill a volume. It is never safe to assume that Coleridge had not read anything published before the year of his death. I remember my astonishment in discovering that he had read Vico's *Scienza Nuova*, long before Michelet rescued that great name from oblivion.[6] When we say that Coleridge took all knowledge for his province we must insist on the literal meaning of the phrase. It is not always remembered

---

[6] It was lent to him by an Italian lawyer called Dr. De Prati. See *Unpublished Letters*, II, p. 374. . . .

what a part the natural sciences played in his development. His main motive in going to Germany in 1798, apart from acquiring proficiency in the language, was to study chemistry and anatomy, mechanics and optics, philology and ethnology. His appetite was inordinate, his ambitions sublime. . . . At Göttingen he took courses, not only in German language and literature, but also in physiology and natural history. The study of philosophy was for a time postponed, but not forgotten; for Coleridge came back from Germany with £30 worth of "metaphysical" books, and it was these which were destined to have a decisive influence on his own philosophy.

In assessing the relative importance of these influences it is well to have some regard to Coleridge's own statements, which often betray a significant emphasis. There is no doubt that the year in Germany was a decisive watershed in his intellectual development. The impact of the systematic atmosphere of a German university—and, one might say, the impact of a nation in a state of vivid intellectual awareness—all this sufficed to make him realize that in his previous studies he had merely floundered—that his head was stored with "crude notions." What these crude notions were we know well: they were the product of a rapid and uncritical absorption of such mutually incompatible philosophies as those represented, on the one hand, by Plato and the Neoplatonists, Christian mystics like Jakob Boehme and William Law, the English divines and theologians, and, on the other hand, the much more sceptical tradition of Locke, Hume, Voltaire, Condillac, and Hartley. In the midst of these contending forces Coleridge had held on to what he called "an exclusive consciousness of God," a faith, the consequence of a deliberate act of the will, enlightened by intuition, but defiant of the logical processes of the intellect. He had held on to this rock of faith, but there is no doubt that, at the time he went to Germany, his mind was "perplexed." He remained, as he says in the *Biographia Literaria*, a zealous Unitarian; he considered the *idea* of the Trinity a fair inference from the being of God; but he had doubts about the Incarnation, the redemption by the Cross, and many other matters of doctrine. "A more thorough revolution in my philosophic principles, and a deeper insight into my own heart, were yet wanting"— such was his own analysis of the situation.[7]

It is tempting to consider how those doubts were resolved, but I must not be led astray from my main topic, which is Coleridge's critical philosophy. But Coleridge only established a critical philosophy as part of his general philosophy, and his critical activity cannot fairly be separated from his metaphysical activity—in fact, the epithet "critical," in his case

---

[7] *Biog. Lit.*, I, p. 137.

as in Kant's, is rather more important than the substantive "philosophy." The "critique" is a method of indirect affirmation. Kant felt that he could best establish the truth by criticizing the methods of reasoning, especially those used by Hume. We shall see that Coleridge made the criticism of *method* the basis of his aesthetics.

What Coleridge owed to the critical philosophy of Kant, or to the Transcendentalists as a school, cannot be established accurately. Let us realize, once and for all, that we are not dealing with the scholarly lucubrations of an academic coterie, in which priorities and credits are of some importance. Coleridge was involved in something much wider and more fundamental—in a revolution of thought such as only occurs once or twice in a millennium. Such revolutions do not come about as a result of individual efforts: the individuals are swept along in a current which they, least of all men, can control. Kant's philosophy is inconceivable without the stimulus of Hume; Fichte is inconceivable without Kant, and Schelling without Fichte. Let us rather visualize this whole movement of thought as a fleet of vessels moving towards new and uncharted seas. Kant and Fichte, Schleiermacher and Schelling; Herder and the two Schlegels; Goethe and Schiller; Tieck, Novalis and Wackenroder—so many vessels advancing in the stream of thought, flashing signals from one masthead to another, and all guided on their way by the lodestar of transcendental truth. As they proceed from some harbor in the Baltic, they are joined by solitary vessels from neighboring countries, and Coleridge is one of these, already armed and provisioned, his course set to the same destination.

Of his fellow-voyagers, Coleridge was to select two for closest alliance. We need not dismiss his obligations to the Schlegels, nor to Lessing and Schiller (Schiller in particular offers a correspondence of *aim*, as of endowments, which bring him into close sympathy). But Coleridge himself, by the warmth and fullness of his acknowledgments, gave fullest credit to Kant and Schelling. Of Kant he said that he had taken possession of him "as with the giant's hand"; that he had "at once invigorated and disciplined" his understanding; and after fifteen years' familiarity with his works, he still read them "with undiminished delight and unceasing admiration." [8] That is humble discipleship; but towards Schelling, to whom his acknowledgments were equally full, he indicated a somewhat different, and perhaps more significant relationship. "In Schel-

[8] *Biog. Lit.*, I, p. 99. Cf. *Letters*, p. 682: ". . . I reverence Kant with my whole heart and soul and believe him to be the only philosopher, for *all men* who have the power of thinking. I cannot conceive the liberal pursuit or profession, in which the service derived from a patient study of his works would not be incalculably great, both as cathartic, tonic, and directly nutritious."

ling," he said, "I first found a genial coincidence with much that I had toiled out for myself, and a powerful assistance *in what I had yet to do*." What had yet to be done was the application of Kant's dynamic philosophy to one or two spheres which had only been vaguely indicated by the master. Of his followers, with the partial exception of Fichte, only Schelling, in Coleridge's view, had succeeded in completing the system, in consolidating its victories. In what remained to be done, the application of the system to "the most awful of subjects for the most important of purposes," only Schelling's aid was of any real value.

Let me now try to recall, very briefly, the significant links between Kant and Schelling, and then we shall be in a better position to see how Coleridge added to them. A drastic simplification will be necessary.

The exceptional nature of aesthetic judgments—that is to say, of the mental experience involved whenever a distinction of inherent value or worth is made between one work of art and another—was first recognized by Leibnitz. But there it remained—an anomaly unaccounted for—until Kant, in his *Critique of Judgment,* established a connection between the formal purposiveness of nature and the creative freedom of the artist. Kant did not venture beyond the suggestion of various analogies—beauty, for example, became the *symbol* of morality, and the creative activity in art the dynamic counterpart of the teleological principle of the universe. Kant was not himself an artist; he had no inner experience of the creative activity, and his use of illustrative material is conventional and uncertain. But Schelling, whose ambition it was to complete the transcendental philosophy, though perhaps not a very good poet, was at any rate a man of sensibility, with a keen appreciation of all the arts. On the basis of this appreciative knowledge he ventured to go a step beyond Kant, to pass from mere analogies to absolute identification. Art becomes "the only true and enduring organon and document of philosophy"—"the keystone of its entire arch." He imagined, as basic to the universe, an energy, or creative impulse which, when unconscious, is manifested as nature; when conscious, as art. The objective world, which is unconscious, becomes conscious in the subjective activity of the ego—the conscious and the unconscious meet and are unified in the state of consciousness. The ideal work of art and the real world of objects are products of one and the same aesthetic activity. Art is the only permanent revelation of the nature of reality. He asks us to think of nature as a poem hidden in a secret and mysterious writing. If the secret could be revealed we should find that it was an odyssey of the human spirit; but the more we strive after its meaning, the more elusive it becomes. The senses, which are our only key, are baffled by a veil of words. It is like trying to get a glimpse

of fairyland through fleeting clouds. A painting, too, which only comes
to life when the veil between the real and the ideal world is lifted, is
merely an aperture through which are projected the forms of the world
of the imagination, which in its turn is a shimmering reflection of the
real world. For the artist nature is much the same as it is for the philosopher—the ideal world manifesting itself under continual limitations.
It is the incomplete reflection of a world that exists, not outside but
within the artist.[9] This, admittedly, is still a very metaphorical manner
of philosophizing, and a contemporary like Schiller, who had more
practical experience of the poetic activity, rightly accused Schelling of
putting the cart before the horse. Poetry, he pointed out, sets out from
the unconscious and its difficulty consists in knowing how to realize, to
make actual, the vague intimations that the poet derives from his unconscious, without at the same time sacrificing the vitality of the inspiration. The poet somehow has to manage to combine thought and sensibility, intuition and reflection.[10] Coleridge's point of departure from
Schelling is of exactly the same nature.

If we were considering Coleridge as a philosopher, rather than as a
critic, we should have to trace his relationship to Schelling in much more
detail; but enough, perhaps, has been said to establish a necessary connection. The distinction of Coleridge, which puts him head and shoulders
above every other English critic, is due to his introduction of a philosophical method of criticism. English criticism before his time, in the
hands of a Dryden, a Warton, or a Johnson, had been a criticism of
technique, of craftsmanship—sometimes presupposing some general rules,
such as that of dramatic unity, but oftener a merely mechanical, and at
best an individualistic and arbitrary activity, resulting in such per-

---

[9] Cf. *System des transcendentalen Idealismus* (1800), pp. 475-76.

[10] Schiller, like Coleridge, always referred his theories to his own practical experience as a poet. Cf. his illuminating criticism of Schelling in a letter to Goethe,
27 March 1801: "He assumes that, in the realm of nature, one should take as a
point of departure what is without consciousness, in order to attain to consciousness;
whilst, in the realm of art, one sets out from consciousness to attain the unconscious.
. . . I am afraid that these idealists do not profit much from experience; for experience
teaches that the poet's unique point of departure is in the unconscious; I would even
say that the poet should count himself lucky if he succeeds, more or less, while making use of a consciousness fully aware of its mode of operation, in recovering in the
finished work, unattenuated, the first and still obscure total-idea which he had conceived of his work. Lacking such a total-idea, obscure but powerful, anterior to all
technical apparatus, it is not possible for any poetic work to be born; and poetry, if
I am not mistaken, consists precisely in knowing how to express and communicate
this unconscious—in other words, in knowing how to embody it in an objective work
of art." The whole letter deserves careful reading, for like everything that Schiller
wrote on aesthetic theory, it is full of wise perceptions and anticipations of later
theories of art.

versities, or rather inadequacies, as Johnson's remarks on Shakespeare. Coleridge changed all that. "The science of Criticism," he himself observed,

> dates its restoration from the time when it was seen that an examination and appreciation of the end was necessarily antecedent to the formation of the rules, supplying at once the principle of the rules themselves, and of their application to the given subject. From this time we have heard little (among intelligent persons, I mean) of the wildness and irregularity of our Shakespeare. Nay, when once the end which our myriad-minded Bard had in view, and the local accidents that favoured or obstructed or in any way modified its manifestations are once thoroughly comprehended, the doubt will arise whether the judgment or the genius of the man has the stronger claim to our wonder, or rather it will be felt that the judgment was the birth and living offspring of his genius even as the symmetry of a body results from the sanity and vigour of the life as an organizing power.[11]

The "method" that Coleridge introduced into criticism is expounded in a series of brilliant essays which make up the Second Section of *The Friend,* one of the few parts of his work on which Coleridge himself looked back with any satisfaction.[12] Method is said to become natural

> 'to the mind which has become accustomed to contemplate not things only, or for their own sake alone, but likewise and chiefly the relations of things, either their relations to each other, or to the observer, or to the state and apprehension of the hearers. To enumerate and analyse these relations, with the conditions under which alone they are discoverable, is to teach the science of method.' [13]

To avoid the impression that method is merely a sterile system of classification, Coleridge illustrated its meaning from the art of Shakespeare. He sees it as "the unpremeditated and evidently habitual arrangement of . . . words, grounded on the habit of foreseeing, in each integral part, or (more plainly) in every sentence, the whole that the poet then intends to communicate." [14] Mrs. Quickly's relation of the circumstances of Sir John Falstaff's debt to her is given as Shakespeare's illustration of the want of method in the uneducated; and the habitual use of method is shown by contrast in Hamlet's account of the events which ac-

---

[11] MS. *Logic.* Cf. Snyder, *Coleridge on Logic and Learning,* Yale, 1929, p. 110.

[12] "Were it in my power, my works should be confined to the second volume of my 'Literary Life', the Essays of the third volume of the 'Friend' (Section II), with about fifty or sixty pages from the two former volumes, and some half-dozen of my poems." Letter to J. Britton, 28 Feb. 1819. Cf. Raysor, *Shakespearian Criticism,* Vol. II, p. 326.

[13] *The Friend* (4th edn., 1850), III, p. 108.

[14] *Ibid.,* p. 104.

companied his proposed transportation to England. Then, making further use of this same illustration, Coleridge shows how an "exuberance of mind . . . interferes with the forms of method; but sterility of mind, on the other hand, wanting the spring and impulse to mental action, is wholly destructive of method itself." [15] "The terms system, method, science, are mere improprieties of courtesy, when applied to a mass enlarging by endless appositions, but without a nerve that oscillates, or a pulse that throbs, in sign of growth or inward sympathy." [16] He brings this analysis down to a significant point—significant, I mean, for Coleridge's whole philosophy—the necessity, in all mental processes, for "a staple, or starting-post, in the narrator himself." Mental confusion is due to "the absence of the leading thought, which," (and here Coleridge is introducing one of the terms which have since become current in literary criticism) "borrowing a phrase from the nomenclature of legislation, I may not inaptly call the initiative." Granted a starting-post, then "things most remote and diverse in time, place, and outward circumstance, are brought into mental contiguity and succession, the more striking as the less expected." [17] But the method must not be stretched into despotism— that way lies the grotesque and the fantastical. "Confusion and formality are but the opposite poles of the same null-point." Method, true method, implies "a progressive transition," and for a transition to be continuous there must be a preconception. Thus in Shakespeare, "in all his various characters, we still feel ourselves communicating with the same nature, which is every where present as the vegetable sap in the branches, sprays, leaves, buds, blossoms, and fruits, their shapes, tastes, and odours." The excellence of Shakespeare consists in "that just proportion, that union and interpenetration, of the universal and particular, which must ever pervade all works of decided genius and true science." [18]

Coleridge reveals his debt to Kant and Schelling in all that follows, but he is everywhere giving the critical method his own application. He distinguishes between two kinds of relation—that of *law* (which is the Kantian conception of the category, of the truth originating in the mind) and that of *theory*, which is the relation of cause and effect, leading to the generalizations of science, the arrangement of the many under one point of view. Between these two relations, says Coleridge, lies method in the fine arts, which is partly a synthetical activity based on knowledge

[15] *Ibid.*, p. 112.
[16] *Ibid.*, p. 132.
[17] *Ibid.*, p. 113.
[18] *Ibid.*, p. 116.

and experience, but this activity dominated by the intuitive conceptions of the artist. Coleridge described the process by means of which this domination is achieved as "esemplastic," a word which has never taken root in our language. Whatever he might call it he always had in mind his own creative experience as a poet, and it is that fact which gives a sense of realism to all his theorizing. In this he was but following his own maxim, to the effect that in order to recognize his place in nature, man must first learn to comprehend nature in himself, and its laws in the grounds of his own existence. In this spirit Coleridge becomes the first psychologist in criticism—he was, indeed, the first literary critic to make use of the very word "psychology."

This psychological analysis of the workings of the poetic process in himself, and, so far as external examination could yield the facts, of the same process in his friend Wordsworth, led Coleridge to formulate what I would call the romantic principle in art. To this principle he gave several formulations, but the substance of them does not vary. From Schelling he had got the idea that art was "a dim analogue of creation"; but creation itself was the process to be rendered a little less dim. In the separate tasks assigned to himself and Wordsworth in the composition of the *Lyrical Ballads,* while Wordsworth was to "consider the influences of fancy and imagination as they are manifested in poetry," Coleridge's task was "to investigate the seminal principle" itself. Wordworth was to sketch "the branches with their *poetic* fruitage"; Coleridge "to add the trunk, and even the roots as far as they lift themselves above the ground, and are visible to the naked eye of our common consciousness." [19]

Professor Raysor, whose editorial work on Coleridge has put us all under a great debt, has described Coleridge's theory of the imagination as "eccentric" and "unfortunate"; and Coleridge himself as "a mediocre philosopher." [20] I do not know from what more positive standpoint Professor Raysor is criticizing the critic and philosopher to whom he has given such loving care; but from my own standpoint I must dissent from these strictures. Its terminology apart, I believe that Coleridge's theory of the imagination has been proved essentially sound by later and more scientific researches; and as for his philosophy, I would now like to suggest that in this sphere, too, Coleridge, so far from being mediocre, anticipated in many important respects the point of view to which the philosophy of our own time is busily returning.

[19] *Biog. Lit.,* I, p. 64.
[20] *Shakespearian Criticism,* pp. xxxiiin, xlviiin.

Coleridge was convinced that the imagination, in its highest potency, was something "essentially *vital*." [21] He also felt that its source was in the unconscious—"there is in genius itself," he said, "an unconscious activity; nay, that is *the* genius in the man of genius." [22] What Coleridge meant by the unconscious, and what Schelling meant by it, is not in doubt; they both make frequent references to the unconscious activity of the dream, and they were both directly influenced by Mesmer, from whose pioneer work on hypnosis developed, in good time, the whole theory of a dynamic unconscious that Freud made the basis of his doctrine and practice of psychoanalysis. For Coleridge, as for Schelling, the unconscious was a reality of immense psychological significance.

The distinction between reason and understanding was, of course, of ancient origin; and Plato had been aware of the irrational sources of inspiration. But Fichte was perhaps the first philosopher to elaborate a threefold principle of knowledge. On the basis of Fichte's analysis, Schelling distinguished three "potencies." Again, I must stop on the threshold of metaphysics, but I think it can be stated, quite simply, that these three potencies of Schelling's represent, first, an irrational non-ego; second, rational consciousness; and finally, a development of rational consciousness into a higher form of subjective consciousness. It has already been pointed out by an American scholar, Dr. Bolman, of Columbia, that Schelling's use of the three potencies in psychic life corresponds to Freud's threefold description of personality in terms of the id, the ego, and the super-ego.[23]

Now let us turn to Coleridge's theory of the imagination. He begins by telling us what the transcendental philosophy demands—first, that two forces should be conceived which contradict each other by their essential nature; secondly, that these forces should be assumed to be both alike infinite, both alike indestructible. "The problem will then be to discover the result or product of two such forces, as distinguished from the result of those forces which are finite. . . ." The next step is

> to elevate the thesis from notional to actual, by contemplating intuitively this one power with its two inherent indestructible yet counteracting forces, and the results or generations to which their interpenetration gives existence, in the living principle and in the process of our own self-consciousness. By what instrument this is possible the solution itself will discover, at the same time that it will reveal to and for whom it is possible.[24]

[21] *Biog. Lit.*, I, p. 202.

[22] *Miscellaneous Criticism*, p. 210.

[23] Frederick de Wolfe Bolman, Jr., in his edition of Schelling's *The Ages of the World*, Columbia University Press, 1942, p. 166n.

[24] *Biog. Lit.*, I, pp. 197-98.

The one power that issues from the interpenetration of these two assumed forces, Coleridge adds, is "inexhaustibly re-ebullient"—it cannot be neutralized, but must issue as a tertium quid, in finite generation. "This tertium quid can be no other than an interpenetration of the counteracting powers, partaking of both." [25]

Having delivered this flight into "High German Transcendentalism," Coleridge breaks off to interpose in his *Biographia Literaria* that "very judicious letter" from a friend "whose practical judgment I have ample reason to estimate and revere," namely himself; a letter in which he anticipates with humor and modesty the objections of those who, like Professor Raysor, regret his meddling in metaphysics—of the many, as he says, to whose minds his speculations on the esemplastic power will be utterly unintelligible. He then gives, in summary form, his famous definition of the Imagination, in its threefold potency—namely:

the *primary* imagination, the living Power and Prime Agent of all human Perception;
the *secondary* imagination, an echo of the primary, co-existing with the conscious will, yet still identical with the primary in the *kind* of its agency, and differing only in *degree,* and in the *mode* of its operation;
and finally the *fancy,* no other than a mode of memory emancipated from the order of time and place, blended with and modified by that empirical phenomenon of the will, which we express by the word *choice.*

These summary definitions are amplified and illustrated throughout the whole of Coleridge's literary criticism, and it is my contention that that criticism derives its penetrative power from the use of the systematic method he had established by his philosophical speculations. I have already mentioned the famous illustration of Shakespeare's poetic use of method; illustrations of Coleridge's own critical use of method abound in his lectures and miscellaneous writings. One example will suffice—the blinding sword that he drives between the talents of Beaumont and Fletcher and the genius of Shakespeare. "What had a grammatical and logical consistency for the ear," he said,

what could be put together and represented to the eye, these poets [Beaumont and Fletcher] took from the ear and eye, unchecked by any intuition of an inward impossibility, just as a man might fit together a quarter of an orange, a quarter of an apple, and the like of a lemon and a pomegranate, and make it look like one round diverse coloured fruit. But nature, who works from within by evolution and assimilation according to a law, cannot do it. Nor could Shakespeare, for he too worked in the spirit of nature,

[25] *Ibid.,* p. 198.

by evolving the germ within by the imaginative power according to an idea—for as the power of seeing is to light, so is an idea in mind to a law in nature. They are correlatives that suppose each other.[26]

This, let me say in parenthesis, is one more statement of what I have called the romantic principle—the idea that the imagination is a shaping power, an energy which fuses, melts, and recombines the elements of perception, and bodies them forth in a unity or synthesis which is the work of art. Coleridge everywhere insists on the difference between "form as proceeding" and "shape as super-induced"—"the latter is either the death or the imprisonment of the thing;—the former is its self-witnessing and self-effected sphere of agency." [27] And this, of course, is the precise difference between classical and romantic art.[28]

But Coleridge, in his lecture on Beaumont and Fletcher, went on to make a further distinction which he regarded as of the utmost importance—

> Shakespeare shaped his characters out of the nature within; but we cannot so safely say, out of *his own* nature, as an *individual person*. No! this latter is itself but a *natura naturata*, an effect, a product, not a *power*. It was Shakespeare's prerogative to have the universal which is potentially in each *particular*, opened out to him in the *homo generalis*, not as an abstraction of observation from a variety of men, but as a substance capable of endless modifications, of which his own personal existence was but one, and to use *this one* as the eye that beheld the other, and as the tongue that could convey the discovery.[29]

Here again Coleridge is anticipating the hypotheses of modern psychology, for what seems to be suggested in this passage is some conception such as that of a *collective unconscious,* a deep store of phyletic experience to which the poet has direct access, and of which he is the inspired exponent. Inspiration, however, is no arbitrary process; nor is beauty a copy of the mere externals of nature. The artist must master the essence, the *natura naturans,*

> which presupposes a bond between nature in the highest sense and the soul of man. . . . Man's mind is the very focus of the rays of intellect which are

[26] *Misc. Crit.,* pp. 42-43.
[27] "On Poesy or Art," *Biog. Lit.,* II, p. 262.
[28] But one should recognize that some so-called classical art is, in the sense of Coleridge's distinction, romantic (Euripides, for example; even Racine), and that some so-called romantic art is classical (much of Goethe, for example; even Wordsworth). The real distinction is between academic art and personal art; between "tradition and the individual talent."
[29] *Misc. Crit.,* pp. 43-44.

scattered throughout the images of nature. Now so to place these images, totalized, and fitted to the limits of the human mind, as to elicit from, and to super-induce upon, the forms themselves the moral reflexions to which they approximate, to make the external internal, the internal external, to make nature thought, and thought nature—this is the mystery of genius in the Fine Arts.[30]

The process might be illustrated in Coleridge's all too brief references to the function of language in poetry. Coleridge realized, long before the theory of Einfühlung or Empathy had been formulated, that "to know is to resemble." The artist

must imitate that which is within the thing, that which is active through form and figure, and discourses to us by symbols—the *Natur-geist,* or spirit of nature, as we unconsciously imitate those we love, for so only can he hope to produce any work truly natural in the object and truly human in the effect. The idea which puts the form together cannot itself be the form. It is above form, and is its essence, the universal in the individual, or the individuality itself—the glance and the exponent of the indwelling power.[31]

Following up this notion there is a passage on language in one of Coleridge's unpublished Notebooks which runs:

A man of Genius using a rich and expressive language (the Greek, German, or English) is an excellent instance and illustration of the ever individualizing process and dynamic Being, of Ideas. What a magnificent History of acts of individual minds, sanctioned by the collective Mind of the Country, a Language is—This Hint well deserves to be evolved and expounded in a more auspicious moment. *Qy* whether words as the already organized Materials of the higher Organic Life . . . may not after a given period, become *effete?* How rightly shall we conceive this marvellous Result, a Language?— A chaos grinding itself into compatibility. But this would give only the Negative attributes.[32]

Coleridge was never to find an auspicious moment to evolve and expand this hint, though in his criticism of Wordsworth's poetry he distinguishes between "words used as the *arbiterary marks* of thought, our smooth market-coin of intercourse," and words which convey pictures, "either borrowed from *one* outward object to enliven and particularize some *other;* or used allegorically to body forth the inward state of the person speaking; or such as are at least the exponents of his peculiar

---

[30] "On Poesy or Art," *Biog. Lit.,* II, 257-58.
[31] *Ibid.,* p. 259.
[32] This notebook [when this essay was written] was in the possession of the Coleridge family. The extract quoted here is printed in Snyder, *Coleridge on Logic and Learning,* p. 138. [Now in the British Museum—ED.]

turn and unusual extent of faculty." [33] There are other hints scattered throughout his criticism which show Coleridge's interest in the stylistic manipulation of words, but obviously he had a profounder conception of the function of language. This conception I find well expressed by a modern philosophical critic, Jean-Paul Sartre:

> For the poet, language is a structure of the external world. The speaker is *in a situation* in language; he is invested with words. They are prolongations of his meanings, his pincers, his antennae, his eyeglasses. He maneuvers them from within; he feels them as if they were his body; he is surrounded by a verbal body which he is hardly aware of and which extends his action upon the world. The poet is outside of language. He sees words inside out as if he did not share the human condition, and as if he were first meeting the word as a barrier as he comes toward men. Instead of first knowing things by their name, it seems that first he has a silent contact with them, since, turning toward that other species of thing which for him is the word, touching them, testing them, palping them, he discovers in them a slight luminosity of their own and particular affinities with the earth, the sky, the water, and all created things.[34]

This is an observation that Schelling, no less than Coleridge, would have found very sympathetic, and perhaps it is to be expected that a modern existentialist should speak the same language as one of the earliest exponents of existentialist philosophy. I realize that it may cause some surprise to hear Coleridge described as an existentialist, but I think it would not be difficult to justify the label. The origins of existentialism are usually traced to Kierkegaard; but a much better case can be made out for Schelling, as Dr. Bolman has already pointed out.[35] No doubt Coleridge was here again in debt to Schelling, but there is an actuality and

---

[33] *Biog. Lit.*, II, p. 98.

[34] From *Qu'est-ce que la littérature?*, 1947, trans. by Bernard Frechtman in *Partisan Review*, Nov.-Dec., 1947, p. 570. As for the "testing" and "palping" of words, cf. the following passage from the manuscript *Logic*:

> In disciplining the mind one of the first rules should be, to lose no opportunity of tracing words to their origin; one good consequence of which will be, that he will be able to use the *language* of sight without being enslaved by its affections. He will at least secure himself from the delusive notion, that what is not *imageable* is likewise not *conceivable*. To emancipate the mind from the despotism of the eye is the first step towards its emancipation from the influences and intrusions of the senses, sensations and passions generally. Thus most effectively is the power of abstraction to be called forth, strengthened and familiarized, and it is this power of abstraction that chiefly distinguishes the human understanding from that of the higher animals—and in the different degree in which this power is developed, the superiority of man over man chiefly consists.

Cf. Snyder, *op. cit.*, pp. 126-27.

[35] *Op. cit.*, pp. 8n, 56n, 198n.

eloquence in his statement of the problem which suggests that he had discovered it for himself. Take, for example, the following passage from *The Friend:*

> Hast thou ever raised thy mind to the consideration of existence, in and by itself, as the mere act of existing? Hast thou ever said to thyself thoughtfully, It is! Heedless in that moment, whether it were a man before thee, or a flower, or a grain of sand,—without reference, in short, to this or that particular mode or form of existence? If thou hast indeed attained to this, thou wilt have felt the presence of a mystery, which must have fixed thy spirit in awe and wonder. The very words,—There is nothing! or,—There was a time, when there was nothing! are self-contradictory. There is that within us which repels the proposition with as full and instantaneous a light, as if it bore evidence against the fact in the right of its own eternity.
>
> Not to be, then, is impossible: to be, incomprehensible. If thou has mastered this intuition of absolute existence, thou wilt have learnt likewise, that it was this, and no other, which in the earlier ages seized the nobler minds, the elect among men, with a sort of sacred horror. This it was that first caused them to feel within themselves a something ineffably greater than their own individual nature. . . .[36]

I cannot pursue these metaphysical speculations of Coleridge's much further; I must content myself with pointing out that, writing before Kierkegaard was born, Coleridge had already formulated the terms of an existentialist philosophy—the *Angst* or sacred horror of nothingness, the Abyss or "chasm, which the moral being only . . . can fill up," the life in the idea which "may be awakened, but cannot be given," the divine impulse, "that the godlike alone can awaken." [37]

Once again we have come to the frontiers of philosophy, but once again I must affirm that philosophy directed the course and determined the ends of Coleridge's criticism. It had been very tempting—it still is tempting—to assign to art a teleological function. Schelling, in his earlier works, had not hesitated to do this—to make art the copula or connecting link between transcendental being and human consciousness—only in the work of art could man make an objective representation of the nature of the supreme reality. But that, as Coleridge and indeed Schelling himself were quick to perceive, would lead to an identification of the moral and the aesthetic. I personally believe that that identification is still possible, but for Coleridge, as later for Kierkegaard, there was inherent in the human situation an ineluctable Either/Or. For Coleridge

---

[36] *The Friend,* III, p. 192.

[37] . . . Essay XI of the third volume of *The Friend* (p. 202) illustrates in still further detail the existential nature of Coleridge's philosophy.

a "standpoint," or a "starting-post" as he called it, was a psychological necessity—a knot must be tied in the thread before we can sew, as Kierkegaard expressed it; and Coleridge, at an early age, had made his standpoint the Christian revelation. He had a horror of any kind of self-consistent system—that seemed to him merely a dialectical trick, a mechanical top spinning in nothingness, not touching the human heart. "The inevitable result of all consequent reasoning," he said,

> in which the reason refuses to acknowledge a higher or deeper ground than it can itself supply, and weens to possess within itself the centre of its own system, is—and from Zeno the Eleatic to Spinosa, and from Spinosa to the Schellings, Okens and their adherents, of the present day, ever has been—pantheism under one or other of its modes, the least repulsive of which differs from the rest, not in its consequences, which are one and the same in all, and in all alike are practically atheistic, but only as it may express the striving of the philosopher himself to hide these consequences from his own mind.[38]

These religious considerations were decisive, but they were linked in Coleridge's mind with aesthetic considerations. He had come to realize, from his investigations into the nature of dramatic poetry, that all dramatic effect was dependent on a tragic sense of life. "To the idea of life," he wrote in his essay on "Poesy or Art," "victory or strife is necessary; as virtue consists not simply in the absence of vices, but in the overcoming of them. So it is in beauty." [39] The wisdom in nature gave unity and perfection—the thought and the product were one; but since there is no reflex act, no element of consciousness of existence, so there could be no moral responsibility. But in man there is reflection, there is freedom, there is choice. This not only makes man "the head of visible creation"; it requires him to impose upon the images of nature the categories of moral reflection—to make thought nature, and nature thought.

At this point we must stop, for there Coleridge stopped. He had discovered that "existence is its own predicate"; that the dialectic intellect is "utterly incapable of communicating insight or conviction concerning the existence or possibility of the world, as different from Deity." But he did not trace out the consequences of this discovery for his philosophy of art. It was left for Kierkegaard to pronounce the absolute Either/Or—*either* the aesthetical *or* the ethical. The final beauty, for Coleridge and Schelling no less than for Kierkegaard, was the beauty of holiness; but it was left to Kierkegaard to point out, eloquently, loquaciously, that beauty

---

[38] *The Friend*, III, p. 204.
[39] *Biog. Lit.*, II, p. 262-63.

in man (as distinct from beauty in the work of art) requires a certain perspective, movement, history; and in such a condition of "immanent teleology," as he called it, we have "passed beyond the spheres of nature and of art and are in the sphere of freedom, of the ethical." [40]

Coleridge's critical activity debouched (I can think of no more appropriate word to describe the physical effect) into this ethical realm, and as we are on this occasion restricted to his aesthetical realm, we must now take leave of him. I have given regrettably little account of the *variety* of Coleridge's criticism—of the brilliance and range of his perceptiveness. But those are incidental features of his work which must be appreciated extensively—without the intermediation of a secondary critic. I have confined myself to general aspects of Coleridge's criticism, because only in that way can we realize the greatness of his achievement. He made criticism into a science, and using his own experiences and those of his fellow poets as material for his research, revealed to the world for the first time some part of the mystery of genius and of the universal and eternal significance of art.

[40] Cf. *Either/Or*, trans. W. Lowrie, Princeton, 1944, II, p. 229.

Idea and Symbol:
Some Hints from Coleridge

by L. C. Knights

In *The Statesman's Manual* Coleridge gives an account of symbols and the symbolic process that is well known to all students of his thought.

> The histories and political economy of the present and preceding century partake in the general contagion of its mechanic philosophy, and are the product of an unenlivened generalizing understanding. In the Scriptures they are the living educts of the imagination; of that reconciling and mediatory power, which, incorporating the reason in images of the sense, and organizing (as it were) the flux of the senses by the permanence and self-circling energies of the reason, gives birth to a system of symbols, harmonious in themselves, and consubstantial with the truths of which they are the conductors. . . . An allegory is but a translation of abstract notions into a picture-language, which is itself nothing but an abstraction from objects of the senses. . . . On the other hand a symbol . . . is characterized by the translucence of the special in the individual, or of the general in the especial, or of the universal in the general. Above all by the translucence of the eternal through and in the temporal. It always partakes of the reality which it renders intelligible; and while it enunciates the whole, abides itself as a living part in that unity, of which it is the representative.[1]

This account follows an eloquent passage on the seminal power of ideas —ideas which, as Coleridge is at pains to insist, can be "suggested and awakened" but, unlike the conceptions of the understanding, cannot be

[1] *Political Tracts of Wordsworth, Coleridge, Shelley,* edited, with an Introduction, by R. J. White, pp. 24-25.

adequately expressed by words[2]—and it is plain that for Coleridge the function of symbols is to handle meanings that cannot be conceptually grasped. "An IDEA, in the *highest* sense of that word, cannot be conveyed but by a *symbol*." [3]

Now it seems to me that there is very much that is useful in those passages, especially perhaps the association of symbols with what Coleridge calls the "self-circling energies of the reason." This however is something to which I shall return. The question that I wish to take up first is how one may be said to take meanings in any way that is not loosely subjective from symbols that, by definition, are not susceptible of the clarity and distinctness proper to the understanding. There is no need to make a mystery of this. Certainly there are some symbols, of the kind that Jung calls archetypal, that seem to draw their power from sources well beyond the power of direct conscious inspection; and if I think that the invocation of archetypes can sometimes make literary criticism too easy (curiously enough, more shallow instead of more profound), I am also prepared to agree that images of this kind are sometimes to be found in great literature, and that we need to recognize their "archetypal" quality. But in clarifying our sense of how verbal symbols have meaning we can go a very long way indeed before we need invoke these entirely unanalyzable psychic entities. In literature, at all events—and I think the same applies to religious writing—the meaning of anything that we recognize as a symbol is determined by a context. To be more exact, there are two overlapping contexts within which meaning takes place: there is the context from which the symbol emerges—namely the work within which it occurs, and the yet wider context of meanings which the artist draws on in making his work; and there is the context into which it enters—namely the moving and developing life of the person responding. Neither of these is a simple notion, but if we examine them we may find a way of giving some account of the way symbols work, and of distinguishing various degrees of power.

The given context is, in the first place, what is made by the writer; indeed it is obvious that in discussions of this kind it is only for convenience that we can refer to "a symbol" as a sort of extractable unit in any work of imaginative literature. The symbol in Blake's poem is not "a tiger," it is

> Tyger! Tyger! burning bright
> In the forests of the night,

---

[2] See, for example, *On the Constitution of Church and State According to the Idea of Each*, ed. H. N. Coleridge (1839), p. 176.

[3] *Biographia Literaria*, ed. J. Shawcross, Vol. I, p. 100.

—and so on through all six stanzas. Blake's symbolic tiger is Blake's poem.[4] That is obvious enough, but we may as well remind ourselves that with symbols, as with every other aspect of a literary work, everything depends on the artist's genius; it is that alone, in its specific working, that can make his symbols nodal points of meaning. And even if we confine our attention to works of considerable stature there are distinctions to be made: good intentions are not enough; and we can properly distinguish between, on the one hand, the generative "life" symbols of *Macbeth,* or the significance taken on by the White Whale in *Moby Dick,* and, on the other, the comparatively inert, worked-out symbolism of *The Golden Bowl.*

But although the writer makes his own immediate context (and this indeed is of fundamental importance), beyond the work itself, entering into it and in part determining it, is a far wider context. T. S. Eliot has reminded us that a great writer is not only a master of language, he is also its servant, and language, in Coleridge's words, is "the embodied and articulated spirit of the Race," "a magnificent History of acts of individual minds, sanctioned by the collective Mind of the Country" [5]; in using language creatively the writer invokes—in part deliberately, in part intuitively and unconsciously—the accumulated thought and experience that has shaped it.[6] It is the same with the writer's more or less

[4] As Martin Foss says of metaphor in his remarkable book, *Symbol and Metaphor* (p. 61), "Metaphor is a process of tension and energy, manifested in the process of language, not in the single word." Particular works of art, moreover, may have a symbolic quality or aspect, whether or not, in any instance, we find it convenient to isolate the more obvious focal points of symbolic meaning. In a discussion of symbolism in the American novel, Marius Bewley writes: ". . . the excessive claims made for symbolism today have a tendency to blind us to those subtle, but more modest, achievements of symbolic technique where the method itself is working quietly hand in hand with the materials and pressures of external reality, and where the symbolic process is not defined by the operation of some one overwhelming symbol such as Moby Dick, but is a quality of imagery and organization in the texture of the prose, gradually gathering towards a concentration of effect that is, in fact, a symbol although it may not overtly present itself as one." (*The Eccentric Design: Form in the Classic American Novel,* p. 106.)

[5] T. S. Eliot, *Selected Prose,* ed. John Hayward (Pelican), p. 100; Coleridge, *Aids to Reflection,* ed. Thomas Fenby (1896), p. 212; autograph notebook, quoted by A. D. Snyder. *Coleridge on Logic and Learning,* p. 138. ("A man of genius using a rich and expressive language [the Greek, German, or English] is an excellent instance and illustration of the ever individualizing process of dynamic Being of Ideas. What a magnificent History of acts of individual minds, sanctioned by the collective Mind of the Country, a Language is.")

[6] As Professor Vinaver says of Racine's language in a passage that is very relevant in the present connection, "Words have poetic life only in so far as they condense their own history." (*Racine and Poetic Tragedy,* trans. P. Mansell Jones, p. 78.) See Owen Barfield, *Poetic Diction.* It is hardly necessary to add that the writer's genius also shows itself in *keeping out* irrelevant or incongruous associations.

deliberate use of symbols of recognized significance and power. These very obviously have a context, and what makes for success in any instance is not only the particular operation of the artist's genius but the availability of a tradition. I speak with diffidence here, but I take it that what is weak in *Moby Dick*—among so much that is strong—may be partly explained by the absence of a coherent body of symbols and a tradition of symbolic thinking such as were available to Dante in the thirteenth century.[7] When there is a rich tradition of that kind the meanings of a writer who uses the symbols necessarily include a reference to the tradition, which is itself part of the relevant context, even though clearly enough it cannot do the writer's work for him.

All this is familiar ground. What needs to be brought out however is that "context" even as so far used—the context within which the writer defines his symbols—is not, from the reader's point of view, something simply given, fixed, static, and belonging solely to a past which he picks over to glean information. As with all aspects of literature, for the defining context to be effective there is necessary not only the art of the writer but also the collaborative activity of the reader. As Professor Walsh puts it:

> Words are not formulae. Scientific symbols are engaged almost exclusively in pointing beyond themselves, they neither require nor reward involvement, they are thoroughly bleached of everything but reference. Words as symbols, on the other hand, always contain more than reference; what they point to is also in part embodied in and enacted by them, and they compel in consequence some degree of involvement.[8]

In other words there is a *forward-looking* element—the ability to assimilate and use—in the very act of understanding what any particular symbol may mean. And although this is true of the understanding of *any* expression, whether symbolic or not—for all understanding involves the power to use and deploy in fresh circumstances what is communicated [9]

---

[7] For the break with an older tradition, as well as the persistence and renewal of some forms of symbolic thinking in nineteenth century America, see Charles Feidelson, Jr., *Symbolism and American Literature*. H. Flanders Dunbar deals at length with the inherited tradition of the age of Dante in *Symbolism in Medieval Thought and its Consummation in the Divine Comedy*. In *A Reading of George Herbert*, Rosemond Tuve deals with the availability of a tradition of symbolic thinking in the early seventeenth century.

[8] William Walsh, "Theory of Language and Practice in Education, and T. S. Eliot," *The Use of Imagination: Educational Thought and the Literary Mind*, p. 238. See also p. 242.

[9] This point is put effectively by Professor H. H. Price in *Thinking and Experience* (pp. 230-231)—a book, it should be said here, which illuminates many aspects of image-thinking.

—the mere range of reference of "symbolic" writing ensures that the activity of understanding shall be correspondingly strong and ranging.

The fact is however that our response to expressive or imaginative symbols goes far beyond "understanding," if by that we mean some kind of detached knowledge in which the reader is not essentially involved. Poetry for example can be regarded as a rather complicated language game of which the rules can be learned by an acute mind. But to read poetry in this way is obviously to denature it: our response to even the simplest lyric is something very different from the response, "Why, yes, I see how it works," or even, "How interesting!" As Maritain says,

> The fact remains, in any case, that not only those who glancing at a work expect from it a mere pleasurable mirroring of their own customary feelings, habits of thought, and trite perceptiveness simply live in barbarous parts, but also that a mere external contemplation of a work, appreciating its qualities even with trained intelligence and aesthetic discernment, but from the outside, remains on the threshold of poetry. We must listen to the interiority of the work and to the poetic sense, be open to what it conveys, let ourselves be attracted by the magnetic ring of which Plato spoke. And this requires a sort of previous, tentative *consent*—to the work and to the intentions of the poet—without which we cannot be taken into the confidence of the poem.[10]

This seems to me true of all art, but it applies with especial force to those powerful nuclei of meanings for which we find ourselves using the word "symbol." A symbol, I have said, takes its meaning from a context: but—as it were—overlapping with the given context is the context of each individual's developing life experience, and the full meaning—the generative power—only exists in so far as this too is in some way—powerfully or subtly—affected.

That, I suppose, is most obvious with regard to the symbols and symbolic events of religion. Certainly these can be studied, as material for psychology, anthropology, the history of religions, and so on. But as operative symbols they only exist for the kind of knowledge that is also an involvement.[11]

Erich Auerbach, in the first chapter of his book, *Mimesis*, makes an impressive contrast between an episode in the *Odyssey* and the Old Testa-

---

[10] Jacques Maritain, *Creative Intuition in Art and Poetry*, p. 308.

[11] There are of course degrees of involvement. Full commitment to the major symbols of any religion involves a profession of belief. But it is also clear that very many religious symbols are operative outside the bounds of the religion to which in a special sense they belong.

ment story of the sacrifice of Isaac (*Genesis* 22).[12] His point is that in the Homeric narrative there is no "background," only "foreground": "What [Homer] narrates is for the time being the only present, and fills both the stage and the reader's mind completely" (p. 4). "Such a problematic psychological situation [as that of Abraham commanded to sacrifice Isaac] is impossible for any of the Homeric heroes, whose destiny is clearly defined and who wake every morning as though it were the first day of their lives" (p. 12). In the Biblical story, on the other hand (and in this it is characteristic of the Old Testament narratives), we are conscious of a history that presses on the present moment, much that is of the greatest importance is left unsaid, depths of meaning are implied; "the whole . . . remains mysterious and 'fraught with background' " (pp. 11-12). This applies to the separate personages as well as to events.

> God is always so represented in the Bible, for he is not comprehensible in his presence, as is Zeus; it is always only "something" of him that appears, he always extends into depths. But even the human beings in the Biblical stories have greater depths of time, fate and consciousness than do the human beings in Homer; although they are nearly always caught up in an event engaging all their faculties, they are not so entirely immersed in its present that they do not remain continually conscious of what has happened to them earlier and elsewhere; their thoughts and feelings have more layers, are more entangled. Abraham's actions are explained not only by what is happening to him at the moment, nor yet only by his character . . . , but by his previous history; he remembers, he is constantly conscious of, what God has promised him and what God has already accomplished for him—his soul is torn between desperate rebellion and hopeful expectation; his silent obedience is multilayered, has background.
>
> (p. 12)

A consequence of this is that whereas "Homer can be analyzed . . . but he cannot be interpreted" (p. 13), the Abraham-Isaac story *demands* interpretation. "Since so much in the story is dark and incomplete, and since the reader knows that God is a hidden God, his effort to interpret it constantly finds something new to feed upon" (p. 15). Moreover, the Biblical narrative claims "absolute authority." "Far from seeking . . . merely to make us forget our own reality for a few hours, it seeks to overcome our reality: we are to fit our own life into its world, feel ourselves to be elements in its structure of universal history" (p. 15).

This is a bald summary of an essay of which the impressiveness lies

---

[12] Erich Auerbach, *Mimesis: The Representation of Reality in Western Literature,* trans. Willard R. Trask (Princeton University Press, 1953), Chapter I, "Odysseus' Scar."

largely in the detailed analysis, but it may be held to establish a point of the greatest importance in the present connection. The sacrifice of Isaac is a symbol in the Coleridgean sense—it "partakes of the reality which it renders intelligible"; whilst remaining a moving story, firmly anchored to the actual, it "demands" interpretation—demands it, that is, by the very manner of its telling, by the kind of claim it makes on the reader, and for the sake of the meaning that we sense within it. And interpretation obviously is something very different from the skillful manipulation of other events around the story which may illuminate it: it is essentially an inward process in which we can only hope for under-standing to the extent that our own experience—at different levels of consciousness—is brought to a focus in the symbolic structure: self and story are mutually illuminating.[13] Paul Tillich, speaking of religious language, but with an awareness of similar processes in poetry and the other arts, says:

> Every symbol opens up a level of reality for which non-symbolic speaking is inadequate. . . . But in order to do this, something else must be opened up—namely, levels of the soul, levels of our interior reality. And they must correspond to the levels in exterior reality which are opened up by a sym-bol. So every symbol is two-edged. It opens up reality and it opens up the soul.[14]

George Herbert put the same idea, perhaps more simply, when, in a poem addressed to the Bible, he wrote:

> Such are thy secrets, which my life makes good,
>   And comments on thee: for in ev'ry thing
>   Thy words do finde me out, & parallels bring,
> And in another make me understood.[15]

[13] "Self" of course includes subconscious drives. For the psychoanalytic implications of the story and its relevance to relationships within the family, see *Isaac and Oedipus,* by Erich Wellesch.

[14] Paul Tillich, *Theology of Culture,* "The Nature of Religious Language," pp. 56-7. Cf. Ronald W. Hepburn, "Poetry and Religious Belief," in *Metaphysical Beliefs,* ed. A. C. MacIntyre, p. 142: "The power of meditative verse such as Herbert's is largely due to its making the reader feel that the Biblical types are not only being restated but also that their creative life is still producing new enrichment of its own materials, new startling transformations of the familiar, the seemingly 'tamed' and archaic. He feels also that he is *participating* in the life of the symbols; his own life is caught up in theirs; he is not the mere spectator of an exegetical exercise." And Coleridge: "This, then, is the prerogative of the Bible; this is the privilege of its believing stu-dents. With them the principle of knowledge is likewise a spring and principle of action." (*The Statesman's Manual,* in White, *Political Tracts of Wordsworth etc.,* p. 19.)

[15] "The H. Scriptures, ii."

The truth of this, as applied to the symbols of religion, would, I think, be generally admitted. What seems to be less generally recognized is that it applies also to the symbols of the poets. It is the principle of involvement, of some degree of personal commitment, *that makes symbols.* It is easy to be misunderstood on this point, and I should like to make it clear that I do not regard a tensed desire for self-improvement as a suitable attitude in which to read poetry; neither do I regard a life devoted to literature as a series of moral crises. I am referring to the supple and subtle life of the mind when it is wholly engaged in an imaginative act. "The whole soul of man" which the poet "brings into activity" [16] includes not only perception, feeling, and judgement, but motions of assent which, if too slight to be regarded as conscious will, are nevertheless the ground from which emerges an orientation to life as a whole.

Three short examples may help us here.

You never Enjoy the World aright, till the Sea it self floweth in your Veins, till you are Clothed with the Heavens, and Crowned with the Stars. . . .
(Traherne, *Centuries of Meditation,* I, 29)

Man is all symmetrie,
Full of proportions, one limbe to another,
And all to all the world besides:
Each part may call the furthest, brother:
For head with foot hath private amitie,
And both with moons and tides.
(George Herbert, "Man")

. . . when you do dance, I wish you
A wave o' the sea, that you might ever do
Nothing but that; move still, still so,
And own no other function . . .
(Shakespeare, *The Winter's Tale,* IV, iv)

I am not sure what an intelligent scientist who read little poetry would make of these. The Shakespeare might pass as a graceful compliment to a girl. The Herbert might be found interesting as an expression of something no longer believed in—for example, the notion that different parts of the body were affected by the motion of moon and stars and planets. The Traherne would probably be regarded as, at most, vaguely "poetical." Well of course Florizel's lines to Perdita are a graceful compliment. What more they are the poetry enforces. Not only is the rhythm of the waves evoked, together with the speaker's responsive delight, in

---

[16] *Biographia Literaria,* ed. Shawcross, Vol. II, p. 12.

the firm and delicate rhythm of the lines; the action of the human dancer is related—by something more than an illustrative analogy—to the impersonal movement of the sea. Once that is recognized the still living import of the lines from Herbert and Traherne—so far from mere quaintness or mere "poetry"—comes into view. What all three passages have in common is not only a deep responsiveness to the great natural rhythms; implicit in the Herbert and Traherne, virtually explicit in the Shakespeare, is a sense of the impersonal depths of the personality. None of these poets could have written as he did unless he had felt that the conscious ego rests on, draws its strength from, something greater than itself. No one can "understand" their lines unless he meets them with a corresponding recognition that is also an affirmation. It may well not appear as a conscious affirmation—indeed anything approaching that would run the risk of slipping over into sentimentality: it may only appear as delight. But it is only when the roots of the will are touched that the meaning of the sea symbolism appears. Even so delicate and slight an attunement as we make in responding to the rhythm of George Herbert's lines—

> For head with foot hath private amitie,
> And both with moons and tides—

belongs to the same world—the world of action and relationship and commitment—as that in which we make and enact our being. And so, as Henry James said in a different connection,

> among our innumerable acts, are no arbitrary, no senseless separations. The more we are capable of acting the less gropingly we plead such differences; whereby, with any capability, we recognize betimes that to "put" things is very exactly and responsibly and interminably to do them. Our expression of them, and the terms on which we understand that, belong as nearly to our conduct and our life as every other feature of our freedom.[17]

I think that instances of the kind just given could be multiplied, and that examination of them would likewise lead us to a position diametrically opposed to that implied in an assertion Susanne Langer once made, "Art . . . has no consequences.[18] For the symbol, at all events, to have consequences is an integral part of the meaning. For Coleridge (since we are still working within the field of his promptings) the apprehension of a symbol is clearly an imaginative act; and if there is one attribute above all others, that, throughout his critical writings, Coleridge assigns

---

[17] Preface to *The Golden Bowl*, p. xxviii.
[18] *Philosophy in a New Key* (Mentor Books), p. 214.

to the imagination it is that of a transforming *energy* of the mind. To the other union of opposites in the symbol—the "translucence" of the special in the individual, of the whole in the part, of the eternal in the temporal—we may add the active involvement of the self—the whole self—in the self-forgetful act of contemplation. "Yet consider," Coleridge said, "that like can only be known by like: that as truth is the correlative of being, so is the act of being the great organ of truth: that in natural no less than in moral science, *quantum sumus, scimus.*" [19]

I hope that this has helped to make sense of my earlier statement that the meaning of a literary symbol emerges from two interlocking contexts, that of the created work (including the more or less that it brings into play from tradition) and that of the reader's own life in the very process of living. Because of this the symbol is both "tied" and "free." It is tied by the artist's power to integrate all elements of meaning in a closely articulated structure: you can't make Blake's sick rose or Dante's *selva oscura* mean just anything you choose. It is free because the meaning has not been given once for all, it develops and takes on substance as it "opens up" "levels of our interior reality" and becomes incorporated in our being. Like the Coleridgean idea (and we have seen how closely Coleridge associated idea and symbol) it is "living, productive, partakes of infinity . . . and contains an endless power of semination." [20] What we have to do with, therefore, is no paraphrasable meaning but a direction of the personality as a whole.[21] It is the capacity of symbols (both individual symbols and whole imaginative works in their symbolic aspect) to foster a life-direction that explains our sense of the very great importance of the kind of enquiry undertaken in this Symposium. What is in

[19] *The Statesman's Manual*, p. 39. On the relation between idea and symbol, reason and imagination, in Coleridge, see D. G. James, "The Thought of Coleridge," in *The Major English Romantic Poets*, ed. Clarence D. Thorpe, Carlos Baker, and Bennett Weaver.

[20] See *The Statesman's Manual*, pp. 21-22.

[21] We must of course guard against the implication that this is only—or even usually—a matter of conscious will. The direction springs from a preparedness to live one's life in a certain way, and this includes an openness to promptings from below the threshold of consciousness. "One must be able to *let things happen*. I have learned from the East what it means by the phrase 'Wu wei': namely not-doing, letting be, which is quite different from doing nothing. Some Occidentals, also, have known what this not-doing means; for instance, Meister Eckhardt, who speaks of 'sich lassen,' to let oneself be." (Jung, *The Integration of the Personality*, English edition, 1940, pp. 31-2.

question is nothing less than a fundamental quality of human life—man's capacity for growth and renewal in response to the transforming energies stored in structures of the imagination.

For out of olde feldes, as men seyth,
Cometh al this newe corn from yer to yere.

Perhaps it should be added that to seek the meaning of a symbol in **a**
direction, a state of being, rather than in any analyzable propositions,
however subtle, is not to express a preference for "floating and obscure
generalities." [22] When Coleridge spoke of "ideas which may indeed be
suggested and awakened, but cannot, like the images of sense and the
conceptions of the understanding, be adequately expressed by words," [23]
he was not turning his back on his lifelong plea for habits of mental
accuracy and verbal precision; he was merely reminding us that our
habits of thought must be adequate to the material with which they
profess to deal.

[22] Coleridge, *Essays on his Own Times,* Vol. II, p. 543.
[23] *Church and State,* p. 176.

The Marriage of Night and Day:
Notes on Coleridge and Romanticism

by Yasunari Takahashi

"Marriage" seems to be one of the most important metaphors in Romantic poetry. It is, aesthetically paraphrased, the "reconciliation of opposites" which, while it constitutes perhaps the ideal of art in all ages, is a doctrine particularly dear to the Romantics with their endless endeavors to fuse subject and object, reason and imagination, the conscious and the unconscious, light and darkness. For instance, their poetic principle, based on the concept of "symbol" as something indivisibly fused and non-intellectual, is fundamentally different from, say, the Metaphysical poetics of yoking together the heterogeneous ideas which, like Donne's lovers and compass, remain "separate" to the last.

The moonlight in which is steeped Coleridge's poetic world is a perfect symbol for such fusion, embodying as it does the devoutly wished end, "le jour nocturne" and "la nuit diurne" as Schelling (quoted by Albert Béguin) finely puts it.

The Romantic "marriage," however, was in constant danger of becoming unbalanced in the form of the inevitable ascendancy of imagination over reason, the inner over the outer, the unconscious over the conscious, the nocturnal over the diurnal. Kubla Khan's pleasure dome is certainly a "miracle of rare device" uniting the "sunny" dome and the "caves of ice," but the garden as a whole contains many threatening elements. Kubla, the Mariner, Geraldine—all Coleridge's major characters are those who deeply partake of the nocturnal side ("Nachtseite" of Schubert, "Night-side" of Coleridge) of existence.

In spite of his own professed belief in "organic nature," Coleridge can sometimes utter Sade-like sentences: "The Earth is not a Goddess in petticoats, but the Devil in a strait waistcoat." The fate of the Mariner

"The Marriage of Night and Day: Notes on Coleridge and Romanticism" by Yasunari Takahashi. From *English Quarterly*, I, 4 (Apollon-sha Kyoto, Japan, Summer 1964). Reprinted in the author's synopsis form by his permission.

is decided (partly at least) not by any providence but by "un coup de dée" on the spectre-ship—a Mallarméan contingency which resists a facile reading of a "sacramental vision" or a "universal Benevolism" into the poem.

Coleridge shares that Romantic desire to merge with Night, Sea, and Death, which is manifest for instance in Keats's *Ode to a Nightingale* and is carried to an almost absurdly sublime extreme by Wagner in the *Liebstod* of *Tristan und Isolde*. But he was *saved* from this extreme by his existentialistic awareness, his insistence on the relationship between "consciousness" and "conscience," his search for reason and logic even in the subconscious and the imaginative. Or (depending upon one's point of view) he was *prevented* from an adventurous plunge into the nocturnal depths by his guilt-stricken conscience, his domestic unhappiness, and other causes.

Whichever the case may be, his insights into Night coupled with his efforts to combine it with Day allow him to claim a unique place in the history of European as well as English Romanticism. Even his failures make him all the more fascinating and familiar to us.

Wordsworth and Coleridge
on Diction and Figures

by M. H. Abrams

The typical neoclassic theory of poetry was a rhetorical theory, in the basic sense that it conceived poetry, like rhetoric, to be an art of achieving effects on an audience, and looked upon the various elements of a poem chiefly as so many means toward that end. Accordingly neoclassic critics usually treated diction as a topic common both to rhetoric and to poetry and differentiated the treatment in the two provinces largely in terms of whether the primary effect in view was to persuade or to please (and sometimes to instruct) the auditor.

We can think of Wordsworth's Preface to the *Lyrical Ballads* as related to this antecedent theory in two important ways. The root principle of the Preface was the statement, twice uttered, that poetry is the overflow of powerful feelings; and feelings, of course, are most readily conceived to flow over into words. But Wordsworth also said, "poetry is the *spontaneous* overflow of powerful feelings"; and this spontaneity, although it may follow upon prior thought and practice, and may be an attribute of "emotion recollected in tranquillity," is not compatible with the artful manipulation of words to the deliberate end of affecting the reader. From our present point of view, therefore, Wordsworth's Preface is notable first, because it made the topic of diction, rather than plot, character, or design, the central and engrossing subject of critical inquiry, and secondly, because it sheared away the rhetorical frame in which this topic had been traditionally treated. Commentators have always remarked that Wordsworth, in his Preface, attacked the neoclassic use of diction in poetry. It is worth making the point that Wordsworth

"Wordsworth and Coleridge on Diction and Figures" by M. H. Abrams. From *English Institute Essays 1952* (New York: Columbia University Press, 1954). © 1954 by Columbia University Press. Reprinted, in abridged form, by permission of the author and the publisher.

also attacked the poetic theory on which this use of diction was commonly justified, and that he did so by the drastic expedient of subverting its premises.

*   *   *

In the *Biographia Literaria* Coleridge tells us that he agrees with Wordsworth's attack against the "falsity" in the modern poetic style, attributable to the use of figures and metaphors which have been "stripped of their justifying reasons" and "converted into mere artifices of connection or ornament." He disagrees, however, with certain parts of the reasoning on which Wordsworth based his attack, and in particular with Wordsworth's thesis that the proper model for the diction of poetry is the language (in Coleridge's words) "which actually constitutes the natural conversation of men under the influence of natural feelings." [1] The dialectical machinery by which Coleridge attempted to come to terms with Wordsworth on this fundamental issue is too elaborate to reconstruct here in detail, but for our purpose two aspects of Coleridge's argument need to be emphasized.

1) The most revealing clues to Coleridge's standpoint and intention in his debate with Wordsworth are to be found in a sequence of letters written in 1802, in which he voiced his growing doubts about Wordsworth's recently published theories, which had not been allayed by their subsequent discussions of the subject. Although Wordsworth's Preface was "half a child of my own brain," he told Southey,

> I rather suspect that somewhere or other there is a radical difference in our theoretical opinions respecting poetry; this I shall endeavour to go to the bottom of, and, acting the arbitrator between the old school and the new school, hope to lay down some plain and perspicuous, though not superficial canons of criticism respecting poetry.[2]

In this passage Coleridge announced his awareness that Wordsworth's Preface was no less a revolution against the older poetic theory than against the older poetic practice. He announced also—and this, I think, has been overlooked at the expense of misinterpreting Coleridge's own theory—his own intention to act "the *arbitrator* between the old school and the new school." The "canons of criticism" which Coleridge promised to lay down, it seems plain, were conceived in accordance with his ruling principle of method, that truth lies in the reconciliation of op-

---

[1] *Biographia Literaria*, ed. J. Shawcross, Oxford, 1907, II, pp. 28-9.
[2] *Letters*, ed. E. H. Coleridge, Boston and New York, 1895, I, pp. 386-87; see also I, pp. 374-75.

posing doctrinal systems,[3] and were intended to save the valid elements in both the traditional and the innovative theories of poetry and poetic diction.

When Coleridge made good his promise some fifteen years later in the *Biographia,* he demonstrated his belief that Wordsworth, in the zeal of his opposition, had thrown out the baby with the bath, by setting out to rescue the elements of earlier theory which he thought indispensable for a criticism adequate to its tasks. This part of Coleridge's enterprise centered on his treatment of what he called a "poem," in distinction from what he called "poetry." You will notice that his definition of a poem is quite in accord with the old rhetorical pattern, making it out to be the disposition of various means, including diction, to the end of effecting pleasure in the reader.

> A poem is that species of composition, which is opposed to works of science, by proposing for its *immediate* object pleasure, not truth; and from all other species . . . it is discriminated by proposing to itself such delight from the *whole,* as is compatible with a distinct gratification from each component *part.*

With this concept Coleridge incorporated a number of traditional terms and distinctions which Wordsworth had either minimized or renounced. For example he differentiated the subject matter from the form of a poem; he distinguished between thoughts and feelings, and between these mental elements and the diction in which they are conveyed; he even discriminated various conventional levels of diction and style. In this context of discussion unity is conceived according to the old principle of decorum, or what Coleridge calls "appropriateness" among the poetic parts, while failures of unity are denoted by such terms as "incongruity" or "disproportion." [4] By this mode of reasoning Coleridge retained the seemingly indispensable conception, of which there is almost no hint in Wordsworth's Preface, that while we can make predications about poetry in general, we must also recognize that there are diverse kinds of poems, each a unity of its relevant subjects, thoughts, feelings, words, and imagery, and each achieving its own effect and a discriminable kind of aesthetic pleasure.

Most persistently Coleridge set himself to prove that Wordsworth's opposition of nature and spontaneity to art was untenable because at odds with many observable facts of a poem and of poetic composition.

---

[3] See, e.g., *Biographia,* I, pp. 169-170; *Anima Poetae,* Boston and New York, 1895, pp. 142-43.
[4] E.g., *Biographia,* II, pp. 10, 14, 69-73, 97-8, 109, 115.

Poetry, he says, as "Mr. Wordsworth truly affirms, does always imply
PASSION," and all figures of speech (including, as Coleridge says elsewhere,
even puns and conceits) must indeed be grounded in a state of emotion.[5]
Coleridge's point, however, is that the feelingful language and figures of a
poet must differ from the spontaneous and feelingful language spoken
sometimes by men in real life, in that the poet, after all, sets himself to the
artificial act of composing a *poem*, which is a conventional, metrical medium for producing foreseen effects. The "natural language of excitement," Coleridge says, is therefore altered by the fact that the elements of
a poem are "formed into metre *artificially*, by a *voluntary* act, with the
design and for the purpose of blending *delight* with emotion."

> There must be . . . an interpretation of passion and of will, of *spon-*
> *taneous* impulse and of *voluntary* purpose. Again, this union can be mani-
> fested only in a frequency of forms and figures of speech (originally the
> offspring of passion, but now the adopted children of power) greater than
> would be desired or endured, where the emotion is not voluntarily en-
> couraged and kept up for the sake of that pleasure.[6]

2) So much for Coleridge's retention of certain neoclassic concepts
of poetry and diction. But it is obvious that Coleridge also moves on a
quite different level of theory and that this additional element is what
marks the *Biographia Literaria* as a great innovative document in the
history of English criticism. On the very first page Coleridge announced
as one principal object of the book "a settlement of the long continued
controversy concerning the true nature of poetic diction." This enterprise, then, helped set off that philosophical chain reaction which led
Coleridge through a critical review of the entire history of philosophy,
from Aristotle through Hartley to Kant and Schelling. The terminus of
this review (which Coleridge eventually reached, but only with the help
of a pseudonymous letter to himself advising him to postpone the philosophical details for treatment elsewhere) is to be "the deduction of the
Imagination, and with it the principles of production and of genial criticism in the fine arts." His view of the imagination Coleridge summarized
in a triple parallel intended to be exhaustive of all forms of creation,
cosmic, epistemological, and poetic. In each instance creation is conceived
as a productive conflict or tension of opposites, resulting in a synthesis
in which the opposing parts are reconciled in a new whole. At the top
of this parallel is the divine archetype—"the eternal act of creation in

---

[5] *Ibid.*, II, p. 56; see also *Letters*, I, p. 374, and *Shakespearean Criticism*, ed. T. M.
Raysor, Cambridge, Mass., 1930, II, pp. 102-103.

[6] *Biographia*, II, p. 50.

the infinite I AM." This act is repeated in the "primary imagination," or creative process which constitutes all human perception of the sensible universe; and it is repeated once more—through the dissolution of the images of this perception and their fusion or reconciliation into a new unity with diverse aspects of human thought and feeling—in the act of recreation by the "secondary imagination" of the poet of genius. In the fourteenth chapter of the *Biographia* Coleridge finally brings this cumulative concept to bear on his original problem, the nature of poetic diction, by his definition of "poetry" as distinguished from a "poem." For in Coleridge's description the essential factor in producing poetry— regarded as the product of "the whole soul of man" in activity—is explicitly the operation of the secondary imagination, which fuses or reconciles "opposite or discordant qualities" (the hallmark of any kind of creation) into an organized whole.[7]

What Coleridge has done by this long train of reasoning is to supplement the rhetorical view of poetry as an art of adapting diverse means to given aesthetic ends by a profoundly different mode of dealing with the subject—one which calls into play a total philosophy of the universe and of mind. The supreme imaginative passages—the poetry of a poem—are no longer regarded as the disposition and adjustment of words, nor, in Wordsworth's fashion, as the simply "natural" correlates of passion. They are regarded as acts of the mind in which the universe of sense is created anew and made into a whole compounded of subject and object ("the idea, with the image"), by a process blending both "the natural and the artificial." And the unity which in the rhetorical discussion of a "poem" had been an appropriateness or just matching of discernible parts becomes in "poetry" a unity by organic synthesis, in which the parts lose their identity by the nature of their relation to the other parts and to the whole—becomes, in a phrase Coleridge uses elsewhere, a "higher third," in which the parts are *alter et idem,* different though the same.

In this new region of discourse Coleridge is able to reconsider the question of figures of speech, whether valid or invalid, from the standpoint of the operation of the powers and elements of mind on the objects and images of sense. For example, the typical "rhetorical caprices" of eighteenth century poetic diction he now describes as "the native

[7] *Ibid.*, I, pp. 180, 185, 202; II, p. 12. An antecedent of Coleridge's distinction between "poem" and "poetry" may have been the ancient distinction between *poema* and *poesis*—between the poem and the poetic art. Behind his exposition of the role of imagination in producing "poetry," of course, was the concept of the "creative imagination," as this had developed in the preceding century from Addison and Vico through Friedrich Schelling.

produce neither of the fancy nor of the imagination," but "the juxta-position and *apparent* reconciliation of widely different or incompatible things," and therefore "a species of *wit, a* pure work of the *will.*" And all of Coleridge's specific examples of fancy and imagination, it should be noted, are what in the rhetorical mode are classified as figures of speech. Thus, Shakespeare's metaphors in the lines

> Full gently now she takes him by the hand,
> A lily prison'd in a gaol of snow,
> Or ivory in an alabaster band,

are a product of fancy, in that the images—although in contrast to the ornaments of bad poetic diction they have one or more entirely relevant points "of likeness distinguished"—remain discernibly the "fixities and definities" of perceptual memory. Shakespeare's simile, however,

> Look! how a bright star shooteth from the sky,
> So glides he in the night from Venus' eye

is a proof of imagination in that one image or feeling is made "by a sort of *fusion to force many into one,*" so that the component parts are lost in the new whole. And at its supreme level in Shakespeare the imagina-tion demonstrates itself in the passage of sustained prosopopoeia uttered by King Lear on the heath, "where the deep anguish of a father spreads the feeling of ingratitude and cruelty over the very elements of heaven." [8]

It has seemed to various commentators remarkable, perhaps a sign of Coleridge's veiled animosity to Wordsworth, that while approving Words-worth's objective in reforming the diction of contemporary poetry, he should have drawn up such heavy philosophical artillery against the arguments by which Wordsworth had tried to achieve the objective. But to Coleridge it helped very little to be right in intention if one were wrong in principle. To him more than to almost any critic principles were important, and not only in judging but also in writing poetry, for as he said, "in energetic minds, truth soon changes by domestication into power; and from directing in the discrimination and appraisal of the product, becomes influencive in the production." [9] In Wordsworth's writ-ings Coleridge thought he detected proofs that inadequate theory was producing bad poetry by a first-rate poet. This was to him a matter of

---

[8] *Biographia,* II, p. 68; *Shakespearean Criticism,* I, pp. 212-13; also *Biographia,* II, pp. 16-18. Contrast Beattie's use of Lear's speech on the heath to demonstrate that tropes and figures "are often more *natural,* and more *imitative,* than proper words," on the ground that prosopopoeia is among "the most passionate of all the figures." (*On Poetry and Music,* pp. 245-46.)

[9] *Biographia,* I, p. 62.

supreme concern, because he believed that Wordsworth was the one man capable of producing the "FIRST GENUINE PHILOSOPHICAL POEM," and still more because Wordsworth's early poetry, by its special excellence, had been the instance on which Coleridge had shaped the keystone of his own system of poetic criticism.

In recounting the development of his theory of poetry and poetic diction in the early chapters of the *Biographia Literaria,* Coleridge cites three milestones in his progress. The first of these was the instruction of the Reverend James Bowyer, a hard headed, heavyhanded, and on the whole quite eighteenth century rationalist, not unlike Dr. Johnson. Bowyer taught Coleridge to judge poetic thoughts and diction by the criteria of "truth," "plain sense," and "universal logic"; to recognize that the "fitness" of the words in a poem is subject to a causal logic "as severe as that of science"; and on grounds of "sound sense" not to say "lyre" when he meant pen and ink, or "Muse" when he meant the nurse's daughter, or "Pierian spring" when he meant the cloister pump. The second important stage, which occurred in 1789, was Coleridge's discovery of the newly published sonnets of William Lisle Bowles, which, departing from the fashion represented by Erasmus Darwin, demonstrated in practice the very combination of "natural thoughts with natural diction" for which the Reverend Mr. Bowyer had prepared him in theory. Coleridge's utter intoxication with Bowles's poems, which seem to us so undistinguished, is a commonplace of literary history. In the course of the following decade, however, Coleridge's enthusiasm waned, and the reasons for his disenchantment are pertinent to our topic.

Speaking summarily, one may characterize Bowles's poems as a transfer to the sonnet form of a major neoclassic invention, the topographical, or meditative-descriptive, poem. Dr. Johnson defined the type as the poetical description of a particular landscape, "with the addition of such embellishments as may be supplied by historical retrospection or incidental meditation." [10] The essential rhetorical tactic of such a poem was to ornament or, in Johnson's terms, to "embellish" an element in the external scene with a relevant thought or reminiscence suggested to the observer; one of its most characteristic figures, accordingly, was the presentation of a parallel, explicit or implied, between ethos and perceptual object. Denham's "Cooper's Hill," the prototype of the genre, also presented an instance of its central trope, which, in its perfect poise between natural phenomenon and moral analogue, bewitched the sensibilities of eighteenth century readers and worked its way into the substance and cadence of thousands of later couplets.

[10] Johnson, "Life of Denham," in his *Lives of the English Poets,* I, p. 77.

> O could I flow like thee, and make thy stream
> My great example, as it is my theme!
> Though deep, yet clear; though gentle, yet not dull;
> Strong without rage, without o'erflowing full.

A century and one half later Bowles's many rivers—the Itchin, the Cherwell, the Wainsbeck, the Tweed—still flow recognizably in the rhetorical manner of Denham's Thames. The "incidental meditation" in Bowles has become almost invariably pensive and self-pitying, and is managed without allegiance to the fashion of wit-writing which had showed itself in the ingenious particularity of Denham's match between river-vehicle and moral-tenor. We still detect, however, as the element on which the poem usually turns, the meditative-descriptive parallel. A sonnet begins:

> Evening! as slow thy placid shades descend,
> Veiling with gentlest hush the landscape still,

and ends

> Alas for man! that Hope's fair views the while
> Should smile like you, and perish as they smile.

Coleridge spelled out the reasons for his dissatisfaction with Bowles's poetry in a letter written in 1802, not many weeks after he had expressed his dissatisfaction with Wordsworth's theory of diction. He objected to Bowles's "perpetual trick of moralizing everything," by connecting natural appearances, "by dim analogies, with the moral world." Nature, Coleridge insisted, "has her proper interest"; and

> a poet's heart and intellect should be *combined,* intimately combined and unified with the great appearances of nature, and not merely held in solution and loose mixture with them, in the shape of formal similes. . . . The truth is, Bowles has indeed the *sensibility* of a poet, but he has not the *passion* of a great poet.

From this perception Coleridge went on, after referring to the difference between Greek and Hebrew religious poetry, to make his first formal distinction between fancy and imagination; a distinction which was still free from the immense conceptual elaboration he was later to derive from German metaphysics, yet contained in germ the substance of what he was to say.

> At best, it is but fancy, or the aggregating faculty of the mind, not imagination or the *modifying* and *coadunating* faculty. This the Hebrew poets appear to me to have possessed beyond all others, and next to them the

English. In the Hebrew poets each thing has a life of its own, and yet they are all our life.[11]

The grounds of Coleridge's objection to Bowles's procedure are clarified if we recall that this was the very time Coleridge was turning away from Hartley's associationism to a philosophy positing a more intimate relation between subject and object, mind and nature. Rhetorically speaking, Bowles's characteristic yoking of subject and object in parallel is a kind of simile, or "loose mixture," which Coleridge says is well enough in its way: "I do not mean to exclude these formal similes; there are moods of mind in which they are natural . . . but they are not [the poet's] highest and most appropriate moods." The device, as he might have put it later, is proper to a poem, but it is not poetry. In terms of mental powers and operations, Bowles's links between external scene and moral reflection are analyzable as associations by contiguity in past experience (as W. K. Wimsatt has pointed out in his illuminating article on "The Structure of Romantic Nature Imagery"),[12] or as associations by similarity in form, function, or feeling. Accordingly, Coleridge attributes this poetic mode to the "fancy," or purely associative process of poetic invention: "the faculty of bringing together images dissimilar in the main by some one point or more of likeness distinguished." [13] What Bowles lacks is the higher power of imagination, which acts not by yoking, but by "coadunating" passion, intellect, and the images of nature —or man's life and the life in nature—into a new whole.

What had given Coleridge this new perspective point, which served to reduce Bowles's poetic stature so drastically, was his exposure to Wordsworth's poetry; and this experience, as Coleridge describes it in the *Biographia,* marked the third and final stage in the development of his theory of poetry. In 1796 he heard Wordsworth recite a manuscript poem (part of which was later published as "The Female Vagrant"), and he says, "I shall hardly forget the sudden effect produced on my mind." Coleridge sets out to define the special qualities of this poem, and his procedure is revealing. His initial description is entirely in rhetorical terms, and by this description Coleridge merely demonstrates that Wordsworth's poem exhibits the same naturalness and mutual appropriateness of the component parts—thoughts, diction, and images, elements of mind and of nature—that he had found earlier in Bowles. "There was here," he tells us, "no mark of strained thought, or forced diction, no crowd or turbulence of imagery," while "manly reflection, and human associations

[11] *Letters,* I, pp. 403-406.
[12] In *The Age of Johnson,* New Haven, 1949, p. 294.
[13] *Shakespearean Criticism,* I, p. 212; se also *Biographia,* II, p. 16.

had given both variety, and an additional interest to natural objects."
The "style" of Wordsworth's poem had no peculiarity except such "as
was not separable from the thought and manner," and even Wordsworth's use of phrases taken from ordinary speech was authorized by
suitability to the Spenserian stanza, "which always, more or less, recalls
to the reader's mind Spenser's own style."

But when everything which can be said in this rhetorical mode has
been said, something remains unaccounted for; and this is the element,
Coleridge says, that "made so unusual an impression on my feelings
immediately, and subsequently on my judgment." For Wordsworth's
poem is not only a poem, but also poetry; and to explain this aspect
Coleridge moves into a different province of terms and concepts, based
on the modifying activity of mind which reconciles the opposites and
disparates of all experience, mental and material.

> It was the union of deep feeling with profound thought; the fine balance
> of truth in observing, with the imaginative faculty in modifying the ob-
> jects observed. . . . To find no contradiction in the union of old and new;
> to contemplate the ANCIENT of days and all his works with feelings as fresh,
> as if all had then sprang forth at the first creative fiat. . . . To combine the
> child's sense of wonder and novelty with the appearances, which every day
> for perhaps forty years had rendered familiar . . . this is the character
> and privilege of genius, and one of the marks which distinguish genius from
> talents.

This excellence, Coleridge tells us, "which constitutes the character of
[Wordsworth's] mind, I no sooner felt, than I sought to understand."
And the end of his seeking, he goes on to say, was the discovery "that
fancy and imagination were two distinct and widely different faculties,"
as different as Otway's "Lutes, lobsters, seas of milk, and ships of amber"
is from King Lear's "apostrophe to the elements." [14]

Coleridge, then, the greatest of the romantic critics, owes his eminence
in no small degree to the fact that he was a deliberate moderator between the old and the new and that he retained control of the analytic
tools of earlier criticism at the same time that he assimilated the inno-
vations of German aesthetic philosophy. The powers of this double critical vision, by which poetic passages can be regarded both as rhetorical
structures and as products of the soul of man, are demonstrated in the
two chapters of the *Biographia* (the twentieth and twenty-second) which
Coleridge devotes to a detailed critique of Wordsworth's poetry. Here
Coleridge, having shown what, using the antique distinction, he calls the

[14] *Biographia*, I, 58-62.

characteristic "defects" and "beauties" of Wordsworth's poetry, climaxes his *examen* with the proof that in power of imagination Wordsworth "stands nearest of all modern writers to Shakespeare and Milton; and yet in a kind perfectly unborrowed and his own."

The passages from Wordsworth which Coleridge selects for special attention and praise are all densely figurative. It is noteworthy that the figure most conspicuously represented is that of personification, which assimilates man to nature in a peculiarly intimate way, and of which the abuse by eighteenth century poets, in the absence of justifying reasons, had moved both Wordsworth and Coleridge to the highest indignation. Coleridge even cites one example of the personification of abstractions in Wordsworth's poem the "Yew Trees,"

> beneath whose sable roofs . . .
>   ghostly shapes
> May meet at noontide—FEAR and trembling HOPE
> SILENCE and FORESIGHT—DEATH, the Skeleton,
> And TIME, the shadow . . .

He gives several examples of Wordsworth's personification of inanimate objects, such as that in "The Blind Highland Boy," where, as Coleridge observes, Wordsworth brings all the "circumstances of a sea-loch before the mind, as the actions of a living and acting power." Finally, Coleridge instances Wordsworth's most characteristic and unexampled kind of personification—it is no less a depersonification—in which, before the poet's fixed and visionary stare, single and solitary human figures transform themselves into something which is both less and more than human. In the passage Coleridge quotes, Wordsworth's old leech gatherer, after a sequence of prior metamorphoses, is modified into an archetypal figure haunting the imagination of the race.

> While he was talking thus, the lonely place,
> The old man's shape, and speech, all troubled me:
> In my mind's eye I seemed to see him pace
> About the weary moors continually,
> Wandering about alone and silently.[15]

According to the rationale underlying the *Biographia Literaria,* such achievements occur in the form of a poem, which is an artful, verbal medium adapted to the achievement of certain ends. They can therefore be analyzed, as Wordsworth's own published theory could not be, as modes of diction, partly literal and partly metaphorical, appropriate to

[15] *Ibid.,* II, 79, 84, 124-125.

the subject, thought, and feeling expressed, to the diction of the rest of the poem, and to the aesthetic effects intended. But these achievements are also, to Coleridge's way of thinking, instances of the poetry in a poem; so that a merely rhetorical analysis, while pertinent, must be supplemented by reference to the powers of the human mind, at once spontaneous and controlled, ordered and self-ordering, to remake and humanize the world of sense. What to the traditional view had been a matter of the kinds and sanctions of figures of speech are now viewed also as the works of the esemplastic imagination of man; and for these Coleridge makes the towering claim that they are the nearest analogue in the finite world to "the eternal act of creation in the infinite I AM."

Coleridge on Milton's Satan

by Benjamin T. Sankey, Jr.

Coleridge's remarks on *Paradise Lost,* although surprisingly orthodox for a Romantic reader, provide what is probably the most interesting interpretation of Milton's Satan to come out of the Romantic period:

> The character of Satan is pride and sensual indulgence, finding in self the sole motive of action. It is the character so often seen *in little* on the political stage. It exhibits all the restlessness, temerity, and cunning which have marked the mighty hunters of mankind from Nimrod to Napoleon. The common fascination of men is, that these great men, as they are called, must act from some great motive. Milton has carefully marked in his Satan the intense selfishness, the alcohol of egotism, which would rather reign in hell than serve in heaven. To place this lust of self in opposition to denial of self or duty, and to show what exertions it would make, and what pains endure to accomplish its end, is Milton's particular object in the character of Satan. But around this character he has thrown a singularity of daring, a grandeur of sufferance, and a ruined splendour, which constitute the very height of poetic sublimity.[1]

In interpreting Satan, Coleridge was able to make use of theories which he had worked out in dealing with two other problems: (a) the philosophical problem of determining the relationship between *noumenal* and *phenomenal* worlds, and (b) the political problem of interpreting the character of Bonaparte and his relationship to the ideals of the French Revolution.

The distinction which Coleridge made between the world of *phenomena* and the world of *noumena* was central to his thought. In borrowing this distinction from Kant he appears to have copied the strategy of Jacobi, whose motives for adopting Kant's terminology were essentially

"Coleridge on Milton's Satan" by Benjamin T. Sankey, Jr. From *Philological Quarterly,* XLI, 2 (1962). © 1962 by the University of Iowa. Reprinted by permission of the author and the University of Iowa Press.

[1] Lecture X of the 1818 series, in *Coleridge's Miscellaneous Criticism,* ed. T. M. Raysor (London, 1936), p. 163.

anti-philosophical. This may not be fair to Coleridge, but in any case he resembled Jacobi in emphasizing the negative results of Kant's criticism of the human understanding. Thus, although the understanding is perfectly capable of arriving at certainty in the physical sciences, it is incapable of knowing anything at all about *noumena;* and man, as a moral agent, has to do with the *noumenal* world. Kant's approach to this problem involved the practical reason, which functioned by means of postulates. Both Jacobi and Coleridge, however, preferred to believe that the reason (i.e., rational intuition) not only postulates ethical and religious principles but discovers or apprehends them; this may account for Coleridge's insistence that his own doctrines were first suggested by English thinkers of the seventeenth century, and that Kant's philosophy had served him only as confirmation of these doctrines. In any case, Coleridge felt that what was ordinarily called "faith" ought to be called "reason," and he objected to any theory which opposed the truths of reason to those of faith.

The dominant philosophies of the eighteenth century, however, had emphasized the possibility of treating ethical matters in a more or less empirical manner. In order to do so, one had only to assume that human motives were analogous to physical causes. It followed that a knowledge of human motives could form the basis for a knowledge of all aspects of human behavior. And—if one treated the subject from a normative rather than a descriptive point of view—one could argue that all human actions were "right," since they were all determined by the strongest motive. The traditional opposition of reason and the passions would then be abolished, since reason could do no more than discover effective means to realize the ends determined by passion. Maynard Keynes quotes an interesting illustration of the practical consequences of this doctrine from a book entitled *Easy Lessons on Money Matters for the Use of Young People* (12th ed., 1850):

> It is curious to observe how, through the wise and beneficent arrangement of Providence, men thus do the greatest service to the public, when they are thinking of nothing but their own gain.

This, I suppose, was the standard treatment of money matters by one kind of utilitarian; and Coleridge's philosophy may best be understood as an attack upon this position. Coleridge believed that the only way to attack the position was to assert that human actions are not determined by motives derived from the phenomenal world (where man is essentially a selfish, "economic man"). As a moral agent man must be free, and he must have access to truths better than those supplied by the external world. Both of these requirements are satisfied by the doctrine of separate *phenomenal* and *noumenal* worlds.

For Coleridge, however, the "economic man" was not simply an economist's fiction. The ideal of rational selfishness had been advocated for so long that the purely selfish man had become a practical possibility: Coleridge saw Napoleon as the embodiment of this possibility. During the Spanish campaign, Coleridge became preoccupied with the question of the source of Napoleon's power. As a man with evil motives Napoleon *ought* to be weak; but for some reason he is not. Coleridge reasoned that it was precisely his *total* selfishness that accounted for his strength. The ordinary villain is occasionally torn by conflict; Napoleon knows no conflict because his motives are totally selfish. Writing in the *Courier* (1809), Coleridge indulged in a long discussion of his own ethical doctrines, then turned to the character of Napoleon:

> The preceding observations are by no means digressive. For to the complete defence of the Spanish contest, which is the theme and object of this and the preceding Letters, it is indispensable, that man should have clear conceptions of what the main power of a remorseless tyrant, such as Bonaparte, consists in. This cannot lie in vice as vice, for all injustice is in itself feebleness and disproportion; but, as I have elsewhere observed, the abandonment of all principle of right enables the soul to choose and act upon a principle of wrong, and to subordinate to this one principle all the various vices of human nature. Hence too the means of accomplishing a given end are multiplied incalculably, because all means are considered as lawful. He, who has once said with his whole heart, Evil, be thou my good! has removed a world of obstacles by the very decision, that he will have no obstacles but those of force and brute matter.[2]

Thus, in order to understand a man like Napoleon, one must understand the way in which philosophical principles are translated into human actions. Coleridge believed that moral choice may best be described in philosophical terms, and that consequently the philosophical outlook of a given person or nation may serve to explain a great many other things. In adopting what he believed to be a selfish and sensual philosophy, the French (in his opinion) had prepared the way for the excesses of the Revolution and had made possible the diabolic figure of Napoleon. But the philosophy dominant in eighteenth century France was not essentially new; it was simply a new (although peculiarly malignant) form taken by an attitude which was as old as the human race. Napoleon, in embodying the ideals of this philosophy, was simply the latest representative of the archetypal "mighty hunter."

[1] *Essays on his Own Times,* ed. Sara Coleridge (London, 1850), p. 659.

In order to perceive the significance of historical events, one had to be familiar with such archetypes. And, for precisely this reason, history as it was written during the eighteenth century by men like Hume was completely unsatisfactory. Mere accuracy could not give value to a study of history by a writer whose conception of human nature was superficial. This explains the importance of the Bible for Coleridge's philosophy of history: he thought of it as a source book for the study of the influence of character upon history. His own commentary on the Bible, *The States-man's Manual* (1816), was an attempt to demonstrate its value as such a source book.

Great works of imaginative literature possessed a similar value, and it was for this reason that Coleridge considered great literature to be philosophical. In Appendix B to *The Statesman's Manual* Coleridge has occasion to refer to Milton's characterization of Satan:

> But in its utmost abstraction and consequent state of reprobation, the will becomes Satanic pride and rebellious self-idolatry in the relations of spirit to itself, and remorseless despotism relatively to others; the more hopeless as the more obdurate by its subjugation of sensual impulses, by its superiority to toil and pain and pleasure; in short, by the fearful resolve to find in itself alone the one absolute motive of action, under which all other motives from within and from without must be either subordinated or crushed. *This is the character which Milton has so philosophically as well as sublimely embodied in the Satan of his Paradise Lost.* Alas! too often has it been embodied in real life. Too often has it given a dark and savage grandeur to the historic page. And wherever it has appeared, under whatever circumstances of time and country, the same ingredients have gone to its composition; and it has been identified by the same attributes. Hope in which there is no cheerfulness; stedfastness within and immovable resolve, with outward restlessness and whirlwing activity; violence with guile; temerity with cunning; and, as the result of all, interminableness of object with perfect indifference of means; these are the qualities that have constituted the commanding genius; these are the marks, that have characterized the masters of mischief, the liberticides, and mighty hunters of mankind, from Nimrod to Bonaparte.[3]

A great deal has been said on the subject of Coleridge's philosophy and its relation to his criticism: Dr. Leavis and others hold that Coleridge's theories simply get in the way. But it ought to be clear that Cole-

[3] I use the edition *On the Constitution of the Church and State* and *Lay Sermons,* ed. H. N. Coleridge (London, 1839), pp. 262-63. Appendix B to *The Statesman's Manual* appears in R. J. White's edition of the *Political Tracts of Wordsworth, Coleridge and Shelley* (Cambridge, 1953), and the passage in question may be found on page 34. Italics are mine.

ridge's interpretation of Milton's Satan would have been impossible had Coleridge not been preoccupied with metaphysical and ethical problems. His interpretation, of course, may not be entirely "correct"—it does not agree precisely with what modern scholarship has taught us about Milton's intentions. But it is both sympathetic and suggestive, and it certainly comes closer to the original Satan than the interpretations of Blake and Shelley do.

Coleridge's Economic Views
on Postwar Depression: 1817

by William F. Kennedy

Coleridge's most serious attempt to analyze economic conditions was made in the second lay sermon published in 1817 and "addressed to the higher and middle classes on the existing distresses and discontents." He divided his treatment of the economic crisis of the postwar depression into two parts: the short-run factors, or "the immediate occasions of the existing distress," and the long-run factors, or "its true seat and sources." The latter he regarded as of far greater importance, because permanent improvement could not be attained unless the problem was dealt with at the true seat and sources of distress. Attention to the immediate occasions of distress would provide only temporary relief. Nevertheless, Coleridge felt temporary relief should be provided, for he was confident that the state could do many things to deal effectively with existing distresses.

An entirely new light has been thrown on the economic and social thought of Coleridge by the recent discovery by Kathleen Coburn that Coleridge in his youth had read and taken notes on Sir James Steuart's *Inquiry into the Principles of Political Oeconomy*. So far as I know this important source of ideas for Coleridge has not been previously noted; and so excellent and so recent a commentary on the two lay sermons as R. J. White's fails to mention it. Coleridge, in keeping with his general practice, did not hint at the influence of Steuart's ideas on his own, so it is easy to see why this discovery was so long delayed.

Young Coleridge adopted Steuart rather than Adam Smith as his chief economic mentor, not because he found any superiority in economic analysis in the former, but because he found Steuart's political and philosophical predilections more congenial to his own. For one thing,

"Coleridge's Economic Views on Postwar Depression: 1817" (originally Chapter V: "Existing Distress: Its Immediate Occasions") by William F. Kennedy. From *Humanist Versus Economist* (Berkeley: University of California Press, 1958). Reprinted (with footnotes omitted) by permission of the author and the publisher.

Steuart started with an organic view of society, holding that "the best way of binding a free society together, is by multiplying reciprocal obligations, and creating a general dependence between all its members." For another thing, Steuart's nationalistic sympathies appealed to Coleridge's sense of patriotism in a way that Smithian internationalism could not, and furthermore, gave support to the Coleridgean concepts of God, King, and Country. Coleridge had a bent for the historical and pragmatic and thus was sympathetic toward Steuart's contentions that overly abstract theory was misleading and that economics should consider all attendant circumstances. Miss Coburn points out that Steuart's work "possibly confirmed his abandonment of pantisocracy, because of its scepticism as to the validity of economic systems and of universal descriptions of social forces." The attractions of Steuart for Coleridge were not economic, but this did not mean that the economic thought of Steuart would fail to impress Coleridge. Numerous points of this influence will be revealed throughout the subsequent discussion of the economic thought of Coleridge.

Coleridge, writing in 1817, noted that preceding this depression there had been a twenty-year boom stimulated by the war and characterized by high wages, agricultural prosperity, growth of cities and of capital improvements, and an increase in population by two million. The war did not

> die away into a long-expected peace but was brought to a sudden end, which, accompanied by a lack of insight into the true effects and influences of taxation, . . . became now a real misfortune. . . . Retrenchment could no longer proceed by cautious and calculated steps; but was compelled to hurry forward, like one who crossing the sands at too late an hour finds himself threatened by the inrush of the tide.

The difficulty lay in a deficiency of total demand.

> The great customer at home wants less, and our customers abroad are able to buy less. . . . They cannot but occasion much distress, much obstruction, and these again in their reaction are sure to be more than doubled by the still greater and universal alarm, and by the consequent check of confidence and enterprise, which they never fail to produce."

Reductions in government expenditures would not help in this situation despite the assertions of demagogues who were blaming the hardships of all classes on the amounts paid by government for pensions and sinecures. Low wages and want of employment of the workingman could not be blamed on "the circumstance, that a sum (the whole of which, as far as it is raised by taxation, cannot take a yearly penny from him) was dispersed and returned into the general circulation by annuitants of the Treasury instead of annuitants of the Bank. . . ." Retrenchment had supporters beyond Cobbett and his radicals, and among them was Ricardo, who, in 1817, insisted on the economic wisdom of retrenchment. In answer to the arguments on the favorable economic effects of retrenchment, Coleridge replied: "The Government is employed already in retrenchments; but he who expects immediate relief from these, or who does not even know that if they do anything at all, they must for a time tend to aggravate the distress, cannot have studied the operation of public expenditure."

Coleridge saw that the trouble was a deficiency of demand, but he did not propose that the deficiency be met by an excess of government expenditures over revenues. His solution was to maintain the high level of both taxes and expenditures. During the war there had been a high level of economic activity and also a high level of taxes and expenditures. This high level of economic activity could only be maintained by retaining this proportionately high level of both taxes and expenditures, for it was better to have fifteen left after paying taxes of five than to have less than ten after having paid but two and a half.

The observation that a high level of economic activity was associated with a high level of taxes and expenditures led Coleridge to confuse the effects of public expenditures and taxes. He opposed tax reduction in the postwar period as a disturbance of the balance, whereas he was really opposed to the curtailment of government spending. He also attributed to taxation the stimulation to income which actually is caused by spending.

Coleridge's recognition of the possibility of a general deficiency in demand and of the need for government action to maintain a balance between supply and demand may well have stemmed from Steuart. Steuart said:

> When we say that the balance between work and demand is to be sustained in equilibrio, as far as possible, we mean that the quantity supplied should be in proportion to the quantity *demanded,* that is, *wanted.* While the balance stands justly poised, prices are found in the adequate proportion of the real expense of making the goods, with a small addition for profit to the manufacturer and merchant.

At equilibrio the balance "gently vibrates" under double competition. The statesman must intervene in each industry to keep the gentle vibrations, and not let "demand" or "work" overturn the balance. For example, if supply becomes too great the statesman must diminish workmen by making some of them soldiers, or "by employing them in public works." This adds to demand, and then the number of workmen must be "gently increased."

We return to Coleridge by summarizing his analysis and recommendations for the postwar period. He held that the postwar depression was due to a general deficiency in demand and that the popular policy of rapid retrenchment was exactly opposite to what should be done. He advocated continuance of high levels of both government spending and taxation. This program was provocative to Ricardian economists and drew fire from two of them, John Stuart Mill and Thomas De Quincey.

Mill in his essay, which in other respects was highly favorable to Coleridge, commented that on political economy he wrote "like an arrant driveler" and that "it would have been well for his reputation, had he never meddled with the subject." De Quincey's study of Coleridge on political economy made three points: first, Coleridge was ignorant of every principle of political economy and was too proud to attempt to learn anything from anyone else; secondly, his criticism of the Malthusian principle of population was ineffective; and finally, his ideas on taxation were vulgar errors long ago refuted even by Necker, the "rickety old Charlatan." Only the last point concerns us here.

Mill and De Quincey held that Coleridge's ideas on taxation, national debt, and saving were heretical in that they denied Say's Law, one of the subjects of great controversy at the time and one on which all, with the single important exception of Malthus, were united in the depression of 1815-1820. But now the tables have been turned. Say's Law is no longer the universally accepted standard for judging soundness of economic opinion on saving, taxes, and national debt, and Coleridge's thought cannot be dismissed by appealing to the dogmatism of his contemporaries.

There are curious parallels in the economic thought Coleridge and Malthus brought to bear on the problems of the post-Napoleonic War depression. Both Coleridge and Malthus attributed the depression to a general deficiency in demand. Ricardo denied this on the basis of Say's Law, and the argument between Ricardo and Malthus centered on the effects of saving. Malthus held that not everything saved is invested. The conversion of revenue into capital, or saving, as Malthus used the terms, implied an increase in money-capital or in the holding of cash as a first step, whereas Ricardo interpreted the conversion of revenue into capital as a single process extending to the spending of the capital for investment goods. These differences on the meaning of capital were brought out in one of Ricardo's comments on Malthus: "Does adding to capital in any case slacken consumption?" Near the end of their lengthy debate on this question of savings Ricardo concluded that Malthus always came up with the wrong answer: "Mr. Malthus never appears to remember that to save is to spend, as surely, as what he exclusively calls spending."

Coleridge believed that there could be too much conversion of revenue into capital or saving, and taxation helped to meet the difficulty inasmuch as it checked the "indolence of the wealthy" by transferring property to the industrious and enterprising. His discussion of saving and capital does not go beyond the insight that there could be "indolence of the wealthy," a failure to convert savings into investment spending. For this he should be credited with a correct insight, but not with a useful analytical achievement.

Malthus and Coleridge shared common ground, too, on what should be done to make good the general deficiency in demand. Both men turned to fiscal policy, and interestingly enough independently arrived at valuable insights and identical errors.

The main point of Coleridge and Malthus was that the popular policy of rapid retrenchment of government expenditures made worse the existing deficiency of demand. (Ricardo, of course, was arguing for retrenchment of government expenditures, even those required as payment of either principal or interest on the national debt.)

The error that Coleridge and Malthus shared was opposition to tax reduction in the postwar period. Neither saw that the government could supply the deficiency in demand by a deficit between its expenditures and revenues, and that expenditures remaining the same, taxes should be reduced and deficits incurred.

Coleridge was outright in his opposition to the removal of the Property Tax, which was a progressive income tax with exemption of the first £60 of income. Malthus also opposed this reduction in taxes and pointed out that many persons saved a part of their returned Property Tax, and "This saving is quite natural and proper, and forms no just argument against the removal of the tax; but still it contributes to explain the cause of the diminished demand for commodities, compared with their supply since the war." Ricardo's comment was: "If Mr. Malthus's reasoning be correct it forms an irresistible argument against the removal of the tax. Can any conclusion be more at variance with the premises?" On the scores of consistency and clear expression Coleridge rates higher than Malthus on this issue.

It might be said, in extenuation of the error of Coleridge and Malthus, that when they spoke of tax reduction they had particular reference to the single important tax cut of their time, the abolition of the Property

Tax. It would have been consistent with their theories of the relation of saving to income for them to oppose the abolition of the most progressive tax of the time so that taxes burdening the consumption of necessities could first be removed. But they did not take this position. Neither thought that the incidence of particular taxes was of any practical significance in the depression. Both argued that there should be no concern with the level of taxes as long as the demand for labor was deficient. Malthus, for example, wrote in 1820, ". . . since seventeen millions of taxes have been taken off from the people, we have experienced the greatest degree of distress, both among capitalists and labourers." He held, too, that heavy taxes were not one of "the immediate sources of our present distresses."

Several things explain why Coleridge and Malthus persisted in their error. A fundamental cause was the primitivity of the analytical apparatus at this time. Ricardo and Malthus, after several years of excellent debate conducted by personal meetings and voluminous correspondence, were unable to set the problem in an analytical framework that would reveal the error.

The crudity of available economic data added to the difficulties of arriving at truth. The tasks of these men would have been considerably lightened by the use of anything like modern data on incidence of taxes, propensity to consume, income, employment, and production. For example, Malthus and Coleridge apparently assumed that the difference between the taxpayers' propensity to consume and the tax beneficiaries' propensity to consume was so great that the transfer of the wartime level of taxes from one class to the other would add an amount to total spending sufficient to overcome the deficiency in demand. If they had had better data on income distribution, consumption, and the incidence of taxes, they might have seen that they were too sanguine in their expectations of what a budget balanced at a high level could provide in the way of stimulation. The only tax with a notable degree of progression was the Property Tax and it yielded about £15,000,000 out of gross revenues of about £83,000,000 in 1815. For the rest, taxes largely fell on consumption, and the burden on the mass of the people was a heavy one.

Finally, the moral standards of Malthus and Coleridge blinded them to a fiscal theory that would deliberately uphold an unbalanced budget in times of peace. They tended to apply their moral standards of individual responsibility, which both held dear, to public morality. This moral tone is best seen in Malthus near the end of his *Principles of Political Economy*. Alleviation of human suffering, a moral good, required a large amount of government expenditures, which in turn required high taxes.

But high taxes, he felt, were not beyond reproach; hence, ". . . to state these facts is not to favour taxes; but to give one of the strongest reasons against them; namely, that they are not only a great evil on their first imposition, but that the attempt to get rid of them afterwards, is often attended with fresh suffering."

Although this moralistic influence was strong on both men, it did not bind them at every point in their thought. Regarding the implications of his theory on thrift, Malthus pointed out that the private virtue was not always a public benefit. He pointed out, too, the value of government expenditures in meeting the deficiency in demand, but, as has been noted above, found it necessary to give this idea its proper moral tone. Strangely, the professional economist, Malthus, was concerned to state the moralistic position, and the professional moralist, Coleridge, was equally concerned to state the economic position. Of these two, it was Coleridge who most forthrightly stated that when there is a general deficiency in demand, publicly spent money is as good as privately spent. He did this in a long footnote in the *Lay Sermon* where he showed by an hypothetical example that the cessation of government expenditures in depression had exactly the same economic effects on income and employment as the closing down of a factory by a private owner.

Many points in Coleridge's theory of taxation can be traced to Steuart. Steuart defended high levels of taxation in England by showing that other countries with low taxes had made little progress. Nothing, he pointed out, "can be concluded in favour of the progress of industry, from an abolition of taxes." Furthermore, taxes were the means by which the statesman did all the good he was capable of: helping industry, removing abuses, colonizing, improving land, and providing for defense.

> In proportion, therefore, as taxes draw money into circulation, which otherwise would not have entered into it at that time, they encourage industry; not by taking the money from individuals, but by throwing it into the hands of the state, which spends it; and which thereby throws it directly into the hands of the industrious, or of the luxurious who employ them.

To the objection that the people from whom taxes are taken would have spent it as well as the state, "the answer is, that it might be so, or not: whereas when the state gets it, it will be spent undoubtedly."

On national debt policy both Coleridge and Malthus opposed current proposals, such as Ricardo's, for immediate elimination or rapid reduction in the debt. Coleridge gave a fuller treatment to problems of national debt than Malthus. He condemned the popular view that represents the nation in debt "as the same both in kind and consequences, as an individual tradesman on the brink of bankruptcy!" This analogy is inapplicable to "a nation indebted to itself." A large national debt, which we owe to ourselves, is a factor of political stability rather than otherwise, for none of the classes has the least interest in permitting a national bankruptcy.

Coleridge, writing in 1818, showed that the growth in the national debt during the war promoted growth in national income and improved economic well-being despite temporary and local distresses always occasioned by war. This growth in national debt had injurious effects on "the literature, the morals, and religious principles of this country," but its purely political and economic advantages were many. Politically, it "wedded in indissoluble union all the interests of the state." Economically it led to a rapid rise in prices which forced all to join in common industry and add to the national produce, and furthermore, it provided a base for ample credit for those interested in expanding production.

Growth in national debt was justified politically and economically in a national emergency such as war, but the state of affairs it promoted was injurious to religion and morals in that it led to an inordinate pursuit of gain. Coleridge therefore opposed deficit spending and consequent increases in national debt in normal times; however, he was not in favor of getting rid of the national debt. He repudiated Hume's thesis that there was a certain mathematical point of safety beyond which the debt should not be permitted to go.

Malthus was in fundamental agreement on these policies of debt management. He opposed "sudden diminution" of the debt in 1820, and he believed that the emphasis should be "especially to discourage the growth of it in future." Malthus preserved a more balanced view than Coleridge, and pointed out that service of the debt was a burden on production. This had more importance than Coleridge granted it, for service of the national debt probably represented about 10 per cent of national income.

Coleridge's attitude toward the national debt was conditioned by his lack of concern with the high level of taxation which brings it into being. This idea has already been traced to Steuart. Another point he might have found in the same source is that a debt internally owned cannot cause national bankruptcy. "To say that a *nation* must become bankrupt to itself, is a proposition which I think implies a contradiction."

Steuart made a recommendation on debt policy to which Coleridge did not allude. In this he was correct because it was applicable to a situation of excessive, rather than deficient, demand. Steuart proposed to raise taxes when expenditures dropped at the end of the war in order to accumulate a surplus to be used to pay off the debt. These funds would "regorge" or pile up in creditors' holdings, and creditors would be forced to ask the government to stop paying off the debt, in return for which they would accept a lower rate of interest. This was a scheme to reduce the burden of the debt by lowering the interest rate. This method, as Steuart observed, was more promising of results than the current practice of the government in depending upon its powers of persuasion to get the creditors to reconsider their bargain and voluntarily accept a lower rate.

A modern appraisal of Coleridge's views on the postwar depression must assign them more merit than accorded by his contemporary critics Mill and De Quincey. His views on government spending, taxation, and the national debt were similar to those held by Malthus, and were prior in publication. Coleridge's views, as they related to the depression, appeared in the *Lay Sermon* in 1817, although some of the ideas on taxes and debt were evident in a more general discussion that appeared in an essay in *The Friend* in 1810. Malthus published his comments on the depression in the concluding section of his *Principles* in 1820. One might hazard a guess that Malthus did not read the *Lay Sermon,* since Coleridge is not mentioned in his extensive correspondence with Ricardo on these topics. Even if Malthus had read Coleridge he would not have been under moral obligation to attribute ideas published in 1820 to Coleridge because he had discussed most of these ideas in his correspondence with Ricardo as early as 1814.

The publication of Keynes's *General Theory* has enhanced the merits of both Malthus and Coleridge, but the historian of economic thought should draw a line of distinction between the two on the basis of analytical achievement. Malthus succeeded in some measure in fitting his views into a consistent theoretical construction. Coleridge did not even attempt this. All the theoretical content of his explanation can be found in Steuart, and there is no evidence that Coleridge tried to improve it.

In dealing with public policy, Coleridge was superior to either Malthus or Ricardo in that he had a more philosophical and sophisticated political theory. Malthus favored public works to alleviate human suffering, but this was thought out in moral rather than political terms. Coleridge developed a logical theory of state intervention in which the state could do useful things for society not attainable by unguided self-interest. This contrasts with Ricardo's political preconceptions in advocating "annihilation of the debt" by a capital levy or by repudiation,—that is, "by refusing to pay the stockholder either principal or interest." Public credit would be destroyed by this act of repudiation but Ricardo was neither illogical nor short-sighted in his recommendation. Given his political theory, there was no need for public credit. His preconception was that the scope of state action was a narrow one that could be amply provided for by a modest level of taxes. Economic progress was best promoted by private capital accumulation, and the accumulation had to be protected against loss through removal to other countries by keeping the burden of taxes at a comparatively low level.

An interesting commentary on the narrowness of Ricardo's views on the economic functions of the state lies in the fact that the name of Ricardo is not mentioned once in Lionel Robbins's excellent analysis of the ideas of the classical economists on this question. Inclusion of Ricardo's views would have disrupted the pattern of liberal thought of the other classical economists which Robbins developed so clearly; yet exclusion of Ricardo from a serious study of the classical economists leaves a gap not easily overlooked.

Coleridge's Historical Thought

by Robert O. Preyer

I

Coleridge's thought was dualistic. There was the world of facts, of things seen as members of classes rather than in their ineluctable reality, of phenomena treated as catalogable and manageable. This was the workaday world of ordinary logic, defined by scientific laws, described by abstractions. Over against this was the poetic world which had been familiar to him from his earliest youth: the world of emotion, value, and culture, of unique moments, felt-truths, and "concrete universals." This world, unverifiable by scientific reasoning, he described in his poetry, affirmed in his religion, and searched for in history.

Most students are familiar with the romantic conception of two faculties of mind, reason and understanding, which correspond to these two kinds of experience. By reason man was said to penetrate beyond the truth of appearance and attain a knowledge of the Idea (which Coleridge defined as "that conception of a thing which is not abstracted from a particular state, form, or mode, in which the thing may happen to exist at this or that time; nor yet generalized from any number or succession of such forms and modes; but which is given by the knowledge of its ultimate aim").[1] Coleridge insisted that Ideas had an historical as well as a metaphysical existence. They belonged to human minds, participating in and explaining the actions of men. In this sense they were "the most real of all realities." [2] His use of the term comes out clearly in the following account of the "idea of moral freedom":

Speak to a young Liberal, fresh from Edinburgh or Hackney or the hospitals, of free-will as implied in free agency, he will perhaps confess with

---

"Coleridge's Historical Thought" by Robert O. Preyer. From *Bentham, Coleridge, and the Science of History* (West Germany: Verlag Heinrich Pöppinghaus, 1958), where it appears as Chapter II. Reprinted by permission of the author.

[1] *On the Constitution of the Church and State According to the Idea of Each, Lay Sermons*, Pickering edition, London, 1839, p. xi.

[2] *Ibid.*, p. 18.

a smile that he is a necessitarian,—proceed to assure his hearers that the liberty of the will is an impossible conception, a contradiction in terms . . . Converse on the same subject with a plain, simple-minded, yet reflecting, neighbour, and he may say . . . "I know it well enough if you do not ask me." But alike with both the supposed parties . . . if we attend to their actions, their feelings, and even to their words, we shall be in ill luck, if ten minutes pass without having full and satisfactory proof that the idea of men's moral freedom possesses, and modifies their whole practical being, in all they say, in all they feel, in all they do and are done to . . . We speak, and have a right to speak, of the idea itself as actually existing, that is, as a principle existing in the only way a principle can exist,—in the minds and consciousness of the persons. . . ."[3]

Coleridge, then, contended that Ideas belong to individual minds and govern instinctive behavior. It is in this sense that they were "the most real of all realities." ". . . This knowledge or sense," he continued,

may very well exist, aye, and powerfully influence a man's thoughts and actions, without his being distinctly conscious of the same, much more without his being competent to express it in definite words . . . it is the privilege of the few to possess an idea: of the generality of men, it might be more truly affirmed that they are possessed by it.[4]

These Ideas constituted the basic reality which the historian is in search of: for Coleridge wished to show that history was not a natural process governed by abstract laws but rather a process governed by the consciousness of laws, that is, by Ideas.

He defended this view with two arguments. First, that the historian's knowledge of the past differs from the scientist's knowledge of nature; second, that every historical narrative presupposes the existence of ideas.

If history records the thoughts and actions of individuals and societies then it seemed obvious that the methodology of history differed from that of the natural sciences. To argue the question in its simplest terms, the historian can know what it is like to be George III; he cannot know *in the same way* what it is like to be a natural object. As Dilthey was to point out at the end of the century, history belongs (with law, economics, literary criticism, and sociology) to a group of studies called "sciences of mind" (*Geisteswissenschaft*) which differed from the natural sciences in that their subject matter could be "lived through" (*erlebt*) or known from within. The first task of the historian, it followed, was to identify himself imaginatively with the age which he studied. He should

[3] *Ibid.,* pp. 17, 19.
[4] *Ibid.,* p. 12.

consult ". . . contemporary historians, memorialists, and pamphleteers," sources ". . . which the Dignity of History has excluded from the volumes of our modern compilers, by the courtesy of the age called historians." [5] The facts must be experienced in an immediate way. For the act of historical thinking consisted in the re-creation of the ideas and emotions that had lived in the minds of earlier peoples.

This view of historical thinking had immediate practical consequences. To begin with, it challenged the rationalist notion that historical "objectivity" was much the same thing as scientific "impartiality." James Mill, for example, had declared (in the Preface to *The History of British India*) that previous historians of India, *because* they were acquainted with the language and peoples of that land were biased and untrustworthy. Mill, who lacked these credentials, was the better historian for that reason: disinterested, judicial, and above party feeling. What the historian chiefly required—". . . the most profound knowledge of the laws of human nature, which is the end, as well as the instrument, of everything" [6] he possessed. It never crossed his mind that the historian, if he is truly to possess his knowledge of the past or of different cultures, must enter mental worlds very different from his own and find there at least some of the criteria by which he judges.

For Coleridge this judicial attitude was radically "unhistorical." "The histories of highest note in the present age," he wrote, "present a shadow-fight of Things and Quantities. . . . (They) partake in the general contagion of mechanic philosophy, and are the *product* of an unenlivened generalizing Understanding." He appealed for a history comparable to that found in the Scriptures—free from "the hollowness of abstractions," presenting "the history of men" and balancing "the important influence of individual minds with the previous state of national morals and manners." [7]

Coleridge stated his opposition to the prevailing modes of historical thought in various ways. We may summarize his favorite observations as follows. The historian must be imaginative and sympathetic rather than judicial, for his subject, ultimately, is the human consciousness in its past manifestations. He should reflect that the needs and aspirations

---

[5] *Biographia Literaria,* ed. J. Shawcross, London, 1949, I, pp. 147-48.

[6] James Mill, *The History of British India,* second edition, London, 1820, I, p. xviii. On the same page Mill quotes with approval Gibbon's remark, "Aux yeux d'un philosophie, les faits composent la partie la moins interessante de l'histoire. C'est la connaissance de l'homme; la morale, et la politique qu'il y trouve, qui la relevant dans son esprit."

[7] *Lay Sermons,* p. 228.

of every age are likely to differ. Therefore past events could not be considered in abstraction from the feelings and thoughts which motivated them. He must ask of every institution, what need did it satisfy, what purpose did it seek to realize? The past could not be "known" by the application of arbitrary modern standards of reason and utility.

We may now turn to the second argument by which Coleridge defended the proposition that history is a process governed by the presence of ideas. It is this: to organize historical facts into a significant narrative, one must rely upon the presence of ideas. Coleridge reasoned that, broadly speaking, all human actions tend to realize purposes and ideas. If we grant that a single purpose or idea is generally expressed by a series of actions, then the historian is justified in speaking of the "internal" and "intrinsic" relationships which existed between the members of the series. Coleridge cites, as an example, those actions—"sometimes with, sometimes without, not seldom, perhaps, against the intention of the individual actor" [8]—which tended to realize the idea of the British Constitution. These actions were not undertaken as parts of a deliberate plan. Nevertheless, they were intrinsically related: the later actions being conditioned by the earlier, and the earlier ones by the fact that later actions were envisaged—a situation peculiar to human actions and not to be found in the natural world.

At first sight this theory appears to be wildly metaphysical. Actually it conforms very closely to the observed practice of historians. Even a rationalist historian like Mill "explains" an event by saying it was a part of a larger movement going on at the time. For purposes of narration, historians are forced to act as though there are intrinsic connections between events and the purposes which they tend to realize. Coleridge was one of the first writers to make this fact explicit.

II

With his next step, however, Coleridge moved off into the regions we associate with the philosophy of history. If there existed connections between events and the larger purposes which they realized, then it was possible to draw an analogy between historical development and the growth of the human personality. As the individual passes from infancy to old age his substantial identity may be said to persist through the different stages of his growth and development, and it is natural to think

---

[8] *Church and State*, p. 33.

of the "personality" of the individual as the "Idea" which is being realized through these changes. Since the state was taken to be the basic unit of historical study by all historical students whether rationalist or otherwise, it was plausible for Coleridge to see in the events of its past a development through various stages of growth which resembled very closely that of the human organism. Every state, like every individual, developed its own unique personality; the stages of development through which it passed were similar and comparable. Now no man of sense would judge the conduct of a child by standards appropriate to the mature man; and Coleridge felt himself to be on safe ground when he expanded this bit of common sense to read, "In the education of the mind of the race as in that of the individual, each different age and purpose requires different objects and different means; though all dictated by the same principle [i.e., growth], tending toward the same end [realization of the Idea— Personality], and forming consecutive parts of the same method [that of life itself, or the design of Providence]." [9] The diversity of history was not without a transcendental unity—a unity of process.

The adoption of this philosophic point of view would have immediate practical consequences for the historian. By a comparative study of similar stages in the development of various nations, the historian might discover the nature of the problems common to them all, and the relative success of past attempts to come to grips with them. This was the sense in which a science of history seemed possible to Coleridge and his followers; and we can see at once that it is distinct from the rationalist attempts to construct a science of history. Where the rationalist relied upon the uniformity of human nature to insure a uniform progress as the basis of his narration, the Coleridgeans relied upon the diversity of human nature which exhibited many forms of progress, spiritual as well as material. Where a writer like Hume reduced all change to a succession of mere diversities, Coleridge arrived at the notion of a substantial identity which persisted through all stages of growth and constantly realized itself in new configurations. He was thus able to reconcile (in theory at least) the conflicting emotions which beset every historian when he regards the past: he opened the way for the expression of an intense delight in the variousness and detail of the past and at the same time he relieved their consciences by pointing out that the unifying "ideas" which gave this diversity its practical meaning could be realized only through this delight in the flavor of the past.

[9] "The Friend," in *The Complete Works of Samuel Taylor Coleridge,* ed. Shedd, New York, 1853, II, p. 454.

III

It remained for others to work out a coherent comparative study of historical ages—Coleridge scarcely touched the subject. What really interested him was the possibility of exhibiting the presence of spirit in the course of history.

In *The Constitution of the Church and State in Accordance with the Idea of Each* (1829), he set about this task in earnest. The epigraph, taken from *Troilus and Cressida,* defined the subject:

> There is a mystery in the soul of state,
> Which hath an operation more divine
> Than our mere chroniclers dare meddle with

Coleridge did not think of himself as a mere chronicler (or a mere historian for that matter); he was determined to set forth the workings of that spiritual mystery.

Coleridge begins by stating that the idea of the British Constitution consists in a balance between the conservative "landed interest" and the innovating "personal interest" (made up of business and professional classes). "I am not," he declared,

> giving an historical account of the legislative body; nor can I be supposed to assert that such was the earliest mode or form in which the national council was constructed. My assertion is simply this, that its formation has advanced in this direction. The line of evolution, however sinuous, has still tended to this point, sometimes with, sometimes without, not seldom, perhaps against, the intention of the individual actors, but always as if a power, greater and better than the men themselves, had intended it for them.[10]

This then is "the idea of the constitution of the State." But the picture is not yet complete. The historian must take into account "a more enlarged sense of the term [state], namely, the constitution of the nation." [11] The "nation" includes not only the interest of permanence and progression but also a third—that of maintaining and advancing the moral cultivation of the people. Without this third interest (which Coleridge most ineptly called "the national church") neither permanence nor progression could continue to exist. It is here that Coleridge brings in

[10] *Church and State,* p. 33.
[11] *Ibid.,* pp. 33-4.

the ethical and spiritual to supplement the utilitarian estimate of government.

Specifically, this third interest had two functions: ". . . to secure to the subjects of the realm, generally, the hope, the chance, of bettering their own and their children's condition"; "to develop in every native of the country those faculties, and to provide . . . that knowledge and those attainments, which are necessary to qualify him for a member of the State, the free subject of a civilized realm." [12]

In an extraordinary passage, too long to be quoted in full, Coleridge explained that the permanence and progression of the nation depended "on a continuing and progressive civilization. But civilization is itself but a mixed good . . . [where it] . . . is not grounded in cultivation, in the harmonious development of those qualities and faculties that characterize our humanity. We must be men in order to be citizens." It was the duty of the Clergy, the members of the third estate or interest, to see to the cultivation of the people. A small number were to "remain at the fountain heads of the humanities" while the rest were to be "distributed" throughout the country ". . . to diffuse through the whole community and to every native entitled to its laws and rights that quantity and quality of knowledge which was indispensable both for the understanding of those rights, and for the performance of duties correspondent . . .".

The object of the first two estates was to reconcile law with liberty; that of the third estate was "to secure and improve the civilization, without which the nation could be neither permanent nor progressive." [13]

We may pause now to observe what this theory of the three estates meant for the writing of history and the extent to which the theory may be said to be founded on historical fact.

Taking the second question first, it is clear that Coleridge's notion of the composition of the Permanent and Progressive interest is grossly unhistorical. To begin with, there never has been a stationary party of permanence in England: what the historian observes is the conflict among groups who want to move in different ways. Furthermore, history does not support the contention that there is a basic quarrel between landlords and entrepreneurs. On the whole it would be safer to say that industrial workers and tenant farmers have more in common with each other than with their respective bosses and vice versa. Again, it is a tremendous oversimplification to assume that all men will vote according to their economic status or for that matter to say that manufacturers and professional people are always progressive and farmers and land-

[12] *Ibid.,* p. 76.
[13] *Ibid.,* pp. 45-7.

owners conservative. To cut the matter short, we may say that the political theory of Coleridge is one which cannot be verified on historical grounds. As a historian, Coleridge falls far more deeply into oversimplifications than the rationalists whom he chastises for this same failing. The idea of the constitution is based on a fanciful or ideal version of the history of England.

But when we turn to the larger question of the relevance of Coleridge's theory of the three estates for historiography, our conclusions will be far from negative. Henry Hallam's *Constitutional History* (which appeared at this time) was far superior in its account of the actual representation of interests in the state; but Coleridge's essay, with its emphasis on the cultural and spiritual aspect of the state, added a whole new dimension to the writing of history. The order of facts which Hume piled together under the title of "Miscellaneous Transactions" became the center of Coleridge's investigation. The nation, as he defined it, was a moral organism as well as a utilitarian arrangement. Since the end of the nation was the cultivation as well as the civilization of its members, it possessed a moral right to those things necessary to the adequate fulfillment of its functions: as Coleridge noted in a passage quoted above, every right entailed a corresponding duty. Since the self-realization of individuals was a direct concern of the nation, then *ipso facto* the nation was an ethical concept.

Now it was just such ideas as these which the idealists of the German *Historismus* were concurrently introducing into the study of the past; and we may say that Coleridge and his admirers were responsible for preparing an English audience for this new form of historical writing. But we cannot simply dismiss Coleridge as an interesting but eccentric native precursor of a continental historical outlook. His importance for the writing of history was far greater than this. We must conclude our discussion therefore by pointing to the peculiarly English, we might say Anglican, twist he gave to Continental speculation.

Coleridge had contended that the state was concerned with "interests," that is, with classes and institutions rather than individuals. The individual as a moral and religious person, was, he declared, above the competence of the state; the law knew nothing of moral guilt. He never lost sight of the fact that the state was a utilitarian power mechanism only *indirectly* implicated in the spiritual and cultural well-being of its citizens. (For this reason he carefully separated "civilization" and "the state" from their spiritual manifestations, "cultivation" and "the nation.") But the German idealists had not made this distinction. The nation-state was taken to be the embodiment and expression of the spiritual life of the

Volk (as opposed to the individual). It had a right and even an obligation to make absolute demands on its citizens, demands superior to those of individual conscience. The state was deified—and so was the power it exercised.

Coleridge, to his credit, was not taken in by these views. He insisted on the organic and spiritual aspects of the state without retreating a step from the traditional Protestant (and English) emphasis on the freedom of the individual.[14]

It was this insistence which distinguished (and continues to distinguish) British idealism from the absolute idealism of the Germans.

[14] See *Lay Sermons*, pp. 229-34 for a discussion of free will and necessity.

Coleridge
on the Growth of the Mind

by Dorothy M. Emmet

Coleridge has long provided matter for reflection for literary critics; in recent years we have had studies of him from writers as varied as Mr. Richards, Mr. Read, and Professor Willey. So it may well be asked whether there is anything left for a mere philosopher without any pretence to literary criticism to say. My excuse for joining in the discussion is, first, that I find myself fascinated by Coleridge: he makes me think about things I want to be thinking about; secondly, that I do not think we have yet understood the relation between the poet and the philosopher in him; and thirdly, I believe that out of the rubbing together of these two sides there came insights which may well be important, not only in helping us understand something about poetic imagination, but also something about the human mind.

That the philosopher killed the poet in Coleridge is an often told tale. Wordsworth suggested it; Carlyle had his taunt about "transcendental life preservers, logical swim bladders"; it was repeated in substance by Professor Quiller-Couch: "He had landed in Germany a poet . . . he embarked from Germany not yet perhaps the 'archangel a little damaged' (as Charles Lamb described him some sixteen or seventeen years later) but already—and worse for us—a poet lost. . . . The man came back to England intensely and furiously preoccupied with metaphysics. *This,* I suggest and neither opium, nor Mrs. Coleridge's fretfulness, was the main reason why he could not recall his mind to poetry." [1] Coleridge indeed hinted as much himself in a letter to Southey, where he laments his loss of his poetic genius, "which I attribute to my long and exceedingly severe metaphysical investigations, and these partly to ill-

"Coleridge on the Growth of the Mind" by Dorothy M. Emmet. From *Bulletin of the John Rylands Library,* XXXIV, 2 (March 1952). Originally a lecture delivered in the John Rylands Library on December 12, 1951. Reprinted by permission of the author and the John Rylands Library.

[1] Introduction to *Biographia Literaria,* ed. by G. Sampson, pp. xxiv and xxviii.

health and partly to private afflictions which rendered any subjects, immediately connected with feeling, a source of pain and disquiet to me." [2] But is this meant as a stricture on the inner necessity Coleridge seems to have felt to try to understand the creative activity in his own mind? Or is he not rather referring to his attempt to escape from "private afflictions" by severe study? In this same letter, he continues by quoting from his *Dejection* ode:

> But now afflictions bow me down to earth,
> Nor car'd I that they robb'd me of my mirth.
>   But, oh! each visitation
> Suspends what nature gave me at my birth,
> My shaping spirit of Imagination.
> For not to *think* of what I needs must feel,
> But to be still and patient, all I can;
> And haply by abstruse research to steal
> From my own nature all the natural man,
> This was my sole resource, my wisest plan;
> And that which suits a part, infects the whole,
> And now is almost grown the habit of my soul.

But perhaps today critics are more prepared to accept the philosopher in Coleridge with all his sins on his head; or at least to realize that Coleridge could not have been Coleridge without him. And who is to say that his analytic interest killed the poet in him when out of it came the *Dejection* ode, surely both a very great poem and a very great piece of introspective analysis?

I shall try to argue that the heart of Coleridge's "metaphysical" interest was this need to try and understand something of the nature and conditions of the growth of the mind, and also of its frustration, and to struggle with the question of the relation between the world beyond us and the mind when it is working at its most creative in imagination: "the world without and the still more wonderful world within." [3]

One difficulty in estimating this side of Coleridge's reflections is to know how to take the terminology of German Kantian and post-Kantian philosophy in which he presents them. My own view is that this philosophy gave him a general intellectual apparatus with the help of which he tried to say what he had to say and to give a more systematic appearance to his empirical discoveries, but that he was not concerned to make himself into a post-Kantian idealist on the German model. True, in the collection of extracts from the notebooks called *Anima Poetae,* he says "In the preface of my metaphysical works, I should say: 'Once for all, read Kant, Fichte, etc., and then you will trace, or, if you are on the hunt, track me.' " [4] But here he is answering charges of plagiarism, and seeking to make a kind of *omnibus* acknowledgment while saying at the same time that the thoughts had been his own before he had heard of these writers. In any case the track of Coleridge is more complex than Kant and Fichte: among other paths it leads along the road to Xanadu. Moreover, we can add to this his saying that

> I can not only honestly assert, but I can satisfactorily prove by reference to writings . . . that all the elements, the *differentials,* as the algebraists say, of my present opinions existed for me before I had even seen a book of German Metaphysics, later than Wolf and Leibnitz, or could have read it, if I had.[5]

What then did Kant and the Kantians help him to say that he was already in essentials discovering for himself?

They helped him to see where he parted company with the empiricist philosophy of the mind with which he had grown up: the view of "ideas" (meaning here sensations), as joined by laws of association, by mechanisms controlled by resemblance and contiguity. Hartley was a symbol to him of this kind of empiricism. There was a stage in Coleridge's development when Hartley was his mentor, suggesting a way of trying to understand the working of the mind. He could even write of him (in 1794 in *Religious Musings*):

> he of mortal kind
> Wisest, he first who marked the ideal tribes
> Up the fine fibres through the sentient brain.

(Note "ideal tribes" for nervous currents conveying sensations; "ideas" were held to be somehow derivative from these.) Coleridge had an active interest all through his life in physiology and chemistry; he was fascinated as a schoolboy in his brother Luke's medical studies; he kept this interest at Cambridge, and followed it more thoroughly when he went to Göttingen; he kept up a friendship and correspondence with Sir Humphry Davy, and took interest in his experiments on respiration and gases. So it is quite untrue to think that he swam off into speculative

[4] *Anima Poetae,* p. 106.
[5] *Letters,* Vol. II, p. 735.

philosophy, and had no interest in the scientific and experimental study
of mind and body. I believe he was always more empirical than Professor Willey, for instance, allows; and his interest in precise observation
divides him decisively from the anti-scientific existentialist Kierkegaard
with whom Mr. Herbert Read links him. His quarrel with the Hartleian
sensationalist theory of the compounding of ideas was not that it was
empirical but that it was untrue to experience. "How opposite to nature,"
he writes,

> and to the fact to talk of the "one moment" of Hume, of our whole being
> an aggregate of successive single sensations! Who ever felt a single sensa-
> tion? Is not every one at the same moment conscious that there co-exist a
> thousand others, a darker shade or less light, even as when I fix my atten-
> tion on a white house or a grey bare hill or rather long ridge that runs
> out of sight each way. . . .[6]

And again, "A thing . . . must diffuse itself through the whole multitude of shapes and thoughts, not one of which it leaves untinged. . . .
Now this is a work of time, but the body feels it quicker with me." [7]
Probably few people now want to defend the notion that ideas are built
up by the association of atomic sensations through resemblance and contiguity. But as Professor Richards points out,[8] Coleridge was seeing the
limitations of this when it was the fashionable philosophy in this country.
And he was doing so not because he had imbibed speculative notions
from Germany, but because it was untrue to what he discovered in his
own experience. Or rather, as Richards says, "The contrast between
living power and lifeless mechanism was no abstract matter with him,
but a daily torment." The empirical associationist philosophy was "the
intellectual equivalent of his uncreative moods." [9] Hence he attacks the
mechanistic view of the chemistry of ideas, and the mechanistic view of
society as a contractual relation between isolated individuals which he
thought went along with this. There is a passage in the Philosophical
Lectures of 1818 where he guys this Social Contract view:

> Here are certain atoms miraculously invested with certain individual rights,
> from the collection of which all right and wrong is to depend. These atoms,
> by a chance and will of their own, were to rush together and thus rush-
> ing together they were to form a convention, and this convention was to
> make a constitution, and this constitution then was to make a contract, a

[6] *Anima Poetae*, p. 102.
[7] *Ibid.*, pp. 31-2.
[8] *Coleridge on Imagination*, p. 68.
[9] *Ibid.*, p. 60.

very sound contract, between the major atoms and the minor ones that the minor should govern them, but that the major should have a right to knock them on the head whenever they chose; and if there was any quarrel the major atoms were to assume the power of repulsion, suspending then the power of attraction, and dance the old Hay over again till they formed a new convention, which was to form a new constitution, which was to make a contract. . . .[10]

So Coleridge was seeking a view of the mind as an originative shaping activity, working upon images supplied through sensation, yet making something new and individual out of them. In his earliest interests in philosophy, he had found something like this in Plato and the Neo-Platonists. (The Neo-Platonists may also have interested him because of the strange and queer materials which came into their net. Coleridge was always fascinated by out of the way facts and beliefs, whether about the mind or nature.) And his concern to discover the role of an original shaping power of the mind may also account for the period when he was fascinated by Berkeley (Berkeley, it will be remembered, managed to be both an extreme idealist and an extreme empiricist: an instance of one of Coleridge's favorite maxims, "Extremes meet").

Hence Coleridge was looking for a philosophy to describe the active power of the mind before he came across the German idealists. And though Plato and what he calls his "dear, gorgeous nonsense" [11] never lost its appeal for him, it was Kant who helped him to find a way of expressing this which did greater justice to his genuine interest in exact observation of matters of fact and in scientific experiment. The main distinctions he took over from Kant were, first, the distinction between the Categories and the manifold of sensation; secondly, the distinction between the transcendent and the transcendental; and thirdly, the distinction between the Understanding and the Reason. Kant accepted the empiricist dictum that all our knowledge begins with experience, but not that it is entirely derived from experience. He diagnosed certain general forms of interpretation which we bring to bear on the material of given sensations, and with the help of which we can interpret our experience as a world of objects in space and time causally and reciprocally affecting each other. Coleridge seized on this conception of formative powers of the mind as necessary to the possibility even of simple perception (which he calls the "Primary Imagination"). But though the mind is active, Kant would not allow that there could be knowledge which transcended possible experience. The "transcendent" use of a concept

[10] *Philosophical Lectures,* ed. K. Coburn, p. 195.
[11] *Letters,* Vol. I, p. 211.

is purely speculative, i.e. the concept is being used to try to say something about what lies beyond all possible experience; and if we do this we shall run into antinomies, contradictory alternative views between which it is impossible to decide, because there is no evidence in experience to which we can appeal to decide one way rather than the other. By "transcendental" thinking, on the other hand, Kant meant the discovery of the conditions on which it is possible for us to have the experience we do have. So the argument that there must be some sense in which the human will is free is a transcendental argument from moral experience; the argument that the world had a First Cause and a beginning in time, or, alternatively, has existed infinitely with no beginning in time, is a transcendent argument. It is worth pointing out that Coleridge accepted Kant's distinction between transcendent and transcendental thinking, because he is sometimes accused of having been what Kant called a *Schwärmer*, that is, a person who allowed speculative metaphysical thinking free rein without observing the need for controls within experience. But he could write,

> Transcendental knowledge is that by which we endeavour to climb above our experience into its sources by an analysis of our intellectual faculties, still, however, standing as it were on the shoulders of our experience, in order to reach at truths which are above experience; while transcendent philosophy would consist in the attempt to master a knowledge that is beyond our faculties—an attempt to grasp at objects beyond the reach of hand or eye or all the artificial aids and as it were prolongations of eye and hand—of objects therefore the existence of which, if they did exist, the human mind has no means of ascertaining, and therefore has not even the power of imagining or conceiving; that which the pretended sages pass off for such objects being merely words from the senses variously disjoined and recomposed, or mere words expressing classes of these images and by addition of other words associated with obscure feelings—a process pardonable in poetry though even there quickly degenerating into poetic commonplace, as for instance, fountains of pleasure, rivers of joy, intelligential splendours, and the like, but as little to be tolerated in the schools of philosophy as on the plain high road of common sense.[12]

Also in *Aids to Reflection* he attacks the kind of speculative theology which produces ideas derived neither from the senses nor from examining our moral consciousness. Why we may ask, had the Inquirer not asked himself "by what appropriate Sense or Organ of Knowledge, he hoped to secure an insight into a Nature, which was neither an Object of his Senses, nor a part of his Self-consciousness! and so leave him to ward off shadowy Spears with the shadow of a Shield, and to retaliate the nonsense of Blasphemy with the Abracadabra of Presumption." [13] And he goes on to compare "the (so called) Demonstrations of a God" to "a species of logical legerdemain not unlike that of the Jugglers at a Fair who, putting into their mouths what seems to be a walnut draw out a score yards of Ribbon—as in the Postulate of a First Cause." [14]

Crabb Robinson once remarked that he was "altogether unable to reconcile his [C.'s] metaphysical and empirico-religious opinions." [15] Our belief is that the latter were the more important; the former mattered to Coleridge as a way of ordering and organizing what he had to say about his empirical, and in a sense religious, discoveries about the growth of the mind.

Here we come to the use he made of the further distinction he took over from Kant, the distinction between Understanding and Reason. To Kant, the Understanding orders the phenomenal world; that is, it enables us to explore a world appearing to the senses which we interpret by means of the Categories as a world of substances in Space and Time causally and reciprocally affecting each other. Coleridge accepts this in general. "By the Understanding," he says, "I mean the faculty of thinking and forming judgments on the notices furnished by the senses, according to certain rules existing in itself" (viz., in the Understanding). Reason, on the other hand, for Kant is the kind of thinking which seeks a completeness which can never be found in empirical knowledge. Empirical knowledge is essentially incomplete, both because it proceeds by adding bit to bit in our factual understanding of the phenomenal world, and because it can never tell us the nature of things in themselves, as distinct from their appearances. Reason makes us aware of this essential incompleteness by holding before us ideals, such as the ideal of the world as an intelligible whole, or of the Soul as an active unity behind the succession of states studied by empirical psychology. But these ideals of the Reason are to Kant *regulative* only; they hold before the mind ideals which would give satisfaction, but they are as it were intellectual carrots; they can never be reached by the empirical methods by which alone knowledge (as distinct from postulates of practical reason) is possible.

When Coleridge speaks of Reason and of the "Ideas of the Reason"

---

[13] P. 165 (1825 edition).

[14] *Ibid.*, pp. 176-77.

[15] Quoted from *Diary*, 11th Dec. 1811, by Shawcross, Introduction to *Biographia Literaria*, p. 1. References to *Biog. Lit.* throughout are to Shawcross's edition (Oxford), 1907.

he uses these expressions to mean neither "As If" concepts, nor formal principles of totality, but rather to express something like the dynamic power behind an actual way of thinking; that is to say, something which is not an objective concept at all. He was always making attempts at saying what he meant by "Ideas," and could never get it clearly and satisfactorily stated. For instance an Idea is "that which is deeper than all intelligence, inasmuch as it represents the element of the Will and its essential inderivability." [16] To ask for a conception of an Idea is like asking "for an image of a flavour or the odour of a strain of music." "Ideas and Conceptions are utterly disparate." So what Coleridge found in Kant, and before him in Plato, were ways of trying to show that there is an active, originative power at work in thinking. Both these philosophers used the term "Ideas," and though they meant very different things, to both "Ideas" indicated something not derived *a posteriori* through the senses but beyond and behind empirical knowledge. Coleridge uses the term to express what may be springs of the original active power of the mind, which is why he cannot present "Ideas" as objective concepts. To him they are more like energies of thinking and imagining, with the thinker's own individual style. Moreover, Coleridge was the first to use the term "Idea" to mean not just a definition, but an attempt to describe the inner ethos or quality of something, as when he writes of "The Idea of a National Church," and Newman after him was to write of "The Idea of a University."

All this seems obscure enough talk; but I think Coleridge is trying to find a way of indicating the productive energy which he believed lay behind the creation of something, whether an institution or a work of art, which had its own individual character. He was always trying to get nearer to understanding this productive energy, and testing what he said by a profound introspective analysis into his own mind; the states of mind in which productive energy worked, and equally insignificantly, the states in which it failed to work. And perhaps he can help us most when he is describing these states rather than when he is trying to put what he has discovered into a metaphysical language.

Perhaps not unnaturally he can tell us better what this creative power of the mind is *not* than he can tell us what it is; but we may thus indirectly get nearer to being able to say something about it. We have seen that it is not any mechanical association of ideas; nor is it even that conscious juxtaposition of ready-made images which he described as the work of the Fancy. (Coleridge's distinction between the Fancy and the Imagina-

---

[16] Quoted Snyder, *op. cit.,* p. 135, from autograph notebook MS. C.; cf. also Muirhead, *Coleridge as Philosopher,* pp. 97ff.

tion is generally familiar ground; and it has been recently discussed by critics far more competent than myself to judge its value.[17]) Whatever this power may be, it is likely to be effectively stopped by the varied means which people find for

> Reconciling the two contrary yet co-existent propensities of men, the Indulgence of Sloth with the Hatred of Vacancy; and which class, besides Novels, contains in it Gambling, Swinging or Swaying on a Chair, Spitting over a bridge, Smoking, Quarrels after dinner between husband and wife when *tête-à-tête,* the reading word by word all the advertisements of a Daily Advertiser in a Public House on a Rainy Day.[18]

Moreover, besides such "Preventive Substitutes of Occupation" which are the resources of what Coleridge calls the "Lazy Indolent," there is the unproductive business of the "Busy Indolent," who find ways of occupying their energies while never seriously rousing themselves to think. In contrast with both the Busy Indolent and the Lazy Indolent, the productive state of mind seems to alternate between extreme concentration and receptivity. He has a charming analogy to illustrate this.

> Most of my readers will have observed a small water-insect on the surface of rivulets, which throws a cinque-spotted shadow fringed with prismatic colours on the sunny bottom of the brook; and will have noticed, how the little animal *wins* its way up against the stream, by alternate pulses of active and passive motion, now resisting the current, and now yielding to it in order to gather strength and the momentary *fulcrum* for a further propulsion. This is no unapt emblem of the mind's self-experience in the act of thinking. There are evidently two powers at work, which relatively to each other are active and passive; and this is not possible without an intermediate faculty, which is at once both active and passive. (In philosophical language, we must denominate this intermediate faculty in all its degrees and determinations, the Imagination.)[19]

This may sound like the old Faculty Psychology; but I think that is due to a difficulty of language. Coleridge is describing a process of thinking where concentrated activity and receptivity alternate, but where the mind is throughout in control, and the Imagination as it were waits, hovering, to seize its chance—if its chance comes. Concerning the receptive stage, he wrote,

[17] Cf., for instance, Richards, *Coleridge on Imagination,* and B. Willey, *Coleridge on Imagination and Fancy* (Warton lecture to the British Academy, 1946).
[18] Rendered by Coburn, *Inquiring Spirit,* p. 206, from Egerton MS. 2800. A variant version of this occurs in *Biog. Lit.,* Vol. I, p. 34n.
[19] *Biog. Lit.,* I, p. 85.

A time will come when passiveness will attain the dignity of worthy activity, when men shall be as proud within themselves of having remained in a state of deep tranquil emotion, whether in reading or in hearing or in looking, as they are now in having figured away for an hour. Oh! how few can transmute activity of mind into emotion! Yet there are as active as the stirring tempest and playful as the may-blossom in a breeze in May, who can yet for hours together remain with *hearts* broad awake, and the *understanding* asleep in all but its retentiveness and *receptivity*. Yea, and (in) the latter (state of mind) evince as great genius as in the former.[20]

This productive receptivity is not just reverie, "the streamy nature of association." It is only possible in a disciplined mind, and one instrument of discipline is to care about the uses of words.[21] Another condition is that thoughts and images should be actively realized, not just carried along as what Professor Whitehead used to call "the burden of inert ideas."

In philosophy equally as in poetry it is the highest and most useful prerogative of genius to produce the strongest impressions of novelty, while it rescues admitted truths from the neglect caused by the very circumstances of their universal admission. Extremes meet. Truths, of all others the most awful and interesting, are too often considered as *so* true that they lose all the power of truth, and lie bed-ridden in the dormitory of the soul, side by side with the most despised and exploded errors.[22]

To realize thoughts is to appropriate them in feeling: and feeling of a physical and not only an intellectual kind. "Metaphysics," says Coleridge, "make all one's thoughts equally corrosive on the body, by inducing a habit of making momently and common thought the subject of uncommon interest and intellectual energy." [23] He used to speak (a veritably Coleridgean term) of his "Psycho-somatic Ology." [24]

There must be, too, a lively interest in the resemblances between things, especially resemblances of an unexpected kind; what Coleridge called "the sunshine comparative power." How great a part this flair for seeing unexpected resemblances played in the evocation of Coleridge's own images has been shown by Professor Livingston Lowes in *The Road to Xanadu*, where he tracks Coleridge down the queer by-ways of reading from which the elements of many of them were drawn.

[20] *Anima Poetae*, p. 66 (under 1804).
[21] Cf. *Biographia Literaria, passim:* and especially II, p. 116, where Coleridge speaks of the "beneficial after-effects of verbal precision in the preclusion of fanaticism" (an undisciplined mental emotion).
[22] *Aids to Reflection*, Aphorism I.
[23] *Anima Poetae*, p. 23.
[24] Coburn, *Inquiring Spirit*, p. 67. From MS. note for an essay on the Passions.

Yet a further condition of the creative growth of the mind is moral integrity. To Kant the Practical Reason, as man's sense of moral responsibility, may supply postulates to the Pure Reason; to Coleridge it permeates and conditions the whole work of the mind. Our thinking is bound up with our characters as morally responsible people.[25] Yet Coleridge can distinguish between the kind of conscientiousness which can stultify the growth of the mind and the kind which is its condition. A strong sense of duty may be "the effect of selfness in a mind incapable of gross self-interest. I mean the decrease of hope and joy, the soul in its round and round flight forming narrower circles, till at every gyre its wings beat against the *personal self.*" [26] *The decrease of hope and joy:* in writing of Pitt, Coleridge remarks that "his sincerity had no living root of affection"; and again, that "the searcher after truth must love and be beloved." [27]

For the creative power of the mind depends in the last resort on a deep underlying state which Coleridge calls Joy. Here the *locus classicus* is the *Dejection* ode. This ode is sometimes quoted (by philosophers, perhaps, rather than by literary critics) as an example of an Idealist philosophy in which nature is an expression of Mind, especially the lines

> O Lady, we receive but what we give
> And in our life alone does Nature live.

But the context makes clear that what Coleridge is describing is not an Idealist view of the production of what we call nature through the categories of the mind, nor is he denying that we live in an environment which is independent of our minds. He is trying to describe

> This light, this glory, this fair luminous mist,
> This beautiful and beauty making power

which makes possible creative vision, and it is Joy.

> Joy, virtuous Lady! Joy that ne'er was given,
> Save to the pure, and in their purest hour.
> Life, and Life's effluence, cloud at once and shower,
> Joy, Lady, is the spirit and the power,
> Which wedding Nature to us gives in dower
> A new Earth and new Heaven,
> Undreamt of by the sensual and the proud.

[25] Cf. *Aids to Reflection, passim.*
[26] *Anima Poetae*, p. 131.
[27] In *Essays on his Own Times.*

Coleridge could have agreed with Wittgenstein that "The world of the happy is quite another than that of the unhappy." [28] He may even go further: the actual empirical world we experience differs as we experience it through one underlying state of mind rather than another. (Richards in another connection quotes William Blake, "the fool sees not the same tree as a wise man sees." George Fox speaks in his *Journal* of how after one of his spiritual awakenings the whole creation seemed to have a different smell.)

The sources of such ways of experiencing must spring up in ourselves.

> I may not hope from outward forms to win
> The passion and the life, whose fountains are within.

Coleridge seems to have wondered whether Wordsworth realized how much of the "celestial light" in which he saw nature depended on his own inner power. In the Poem to William Wordsworth, said to have been "composed on the night after his recitation of a poem on the growth of an individual mind" (*sc. The Prelude*), he says,

> Of the foundations and the building up
> Of a human spirit thou has dared to tell
> What may be told, to the understanding mind
> Revealable; and what within the mind
> By vital breathings secret as the soul
> Of vernal growth, oft quickens in the heart
> Thoughts all too deep for words!
> > Theme hard as high.
> Of smiles spontaneous and mysterious fears
> (The first-born they of Reason and twin-birth)
> Of tides obedient to external force
> And currents self-determined, as might seem,
> Or by some inner Power; of moments awful,
> Now in thy inner life and now abroad,
> When power streamed from thee and thy soul received
> The light reflected, as a light bestowed.

Wordsworth of course also experienced the fading of his paradisical vision. But he believed that he could find a different kind of quiet, steady joy from which he could live.

> Though nothing can bring back the hour
> Of splendour in the grass, of glory in the flower.
> We will grieve not, rather find

---

[28] *Tractatus Logico-Philosophicus*, 6. 43.

> Strength in what remains behind;
> In the primal sympathy
> Which having been must ever be,
> In the soothing thoughts that spring
> Out of human suffering,
> In the faith that looks through death,
> In years that bring the philosophic mind.[29]

He, indeed, achieved a sympathy with fundamental human experience which stayed with him as a source of inspiration. Yet perhaps we can say that Wordsworth in his second wind did not know with Coleridge's devastating self-knowledge the times when he was being a failure. The only renewal of the power of feeling, of hope and joy, to which Coleridge can look has none of Wordsworth's calm assurance. Yet it is not just Dejection; there is at least the beginning of the rebirth of a power of feeling; of

> A tale of less affright
> And tempered with delight,
> As Otway's self had framed the tender lay.—
> 'Tis of a little child
> Upon a lonesome wild,
> Not far from home, but she has lost her way:
> And now moans low in bitter grief and fear,
> And now screams loud, and hopes to make her mother hear.

Coleridge, then, like Wordsworth, is trying to say something about the "deep power of joy" wherewith "we see into the life of things." And perhaps more clearly than Wordsworth he realizes that what he gives us in this mood is not a realist vision; but nor is it just "projectionist," a reading of our own feelings into nature. It is rather the possibility of entering into a deep *rapport* with something in the world beyond us,[30] seeing it with such loving sympathy that we make, as Coleridge says, the "external internal the internal external" [31] and out of this comes the possibility of the creation of imaginative symbolism. But the first condition of such creation is that we should be able not only to look, but to love as we look. The least touch of envy will be enough to stultify it. In his Philosophical Lectures of 1818, he says,

[29] *Ode on the Intimations of Immortality* (which provides a profoundly interesting comparison with the *Dejection* ode).

[30] This may be what lies behind the complicated pronouncements about the Subject-Object Relation in the "metaphysical disquisition" at the end of the First Part of *Biographia Literaria*.

[31] *Biog. Lit.*, II, p. 258.

The moment you perceive the slightest spirit of envy in a man, be assured
that he either has no genius or that his genius is dormant at that moment,
for all genius exists in a participation of a common spirit. In joy individuality is lost, and it therefore is liveliest in youth, not from any principle
in organisation but simply from this, that the hardships of life, that the
circumstances that have forced a man in upon his little unthinking con-
temptible self, have lessened his power of existing universally; it is that
only which brings about those passions. To have a genius is to live in the
universal, to know no self but that which is reflected not only from the
faces of all around us, our fellow creatures, but reflected from the flowers,
the trees, the beasts, yea from the very surface of the (waters and the) sands
of the desert. A man of genius finds a reflex of himself, were it only in the
mystery of being.[32]

I believe that Coleridge was concerned to explore not only a source
of the creative power of imagination shown in genius but also more generally the liberation of the mind from deadness and dereliction, a liberation on which its growth depends. Remember the passage on how the
renewal of hope comes to the Ancient Mariner (surely a poem of dereliction and grace—a very Coleridgean kind of grace):

> But where the ship's huge shadow lay,
> The charmed water burnt alway
> A still and awful red.[33]
>
> Beyond the shadow of the ship
> I watched the water-snakes:
> They moved in tracks of shining white,
> And when they reared the elfish light
> Fell off in hoary flakes.
>
> Within the shadow of the ship
> I watched their rich attire:
> Blue, glossy green, and velvet black,

---

[32] *Coleridge's Philosophical Lectures*, ed. K. Coburn, p. 179.

[33] J. L. Lowes, in *The Road to Xanadu* (p. 205), shows that the colors, the "still and
awful red" of the charmed water, and the "blue and glossy green" of the water snakes
possessed already another definite association in Coleridge's mind. "There is in the
Note Book a long passage from a 'Description of a Glory by John Haygarth,' transcribed
from the third volume of the *Manchester Memoirs*. . . ." "And the sun shining on a
surface of snow covered with a *hoar-frost* exhibit . . . beautiful brilliant points of
various colours, as, *red, green, blue*, etc., reflected and refracted at different angles."
This passage appears in Coleridge's notebooks along with jottings from Father Bourzes's
account of phosphorescent fishes, and of a rainbow in the spray. It is gratifying to
think that Coleridge's reading penetrated to the *Manchester Memoirs* (for 1790).

They coiled and swam; and every track
Was a flash of golden fire.

O happy living things! no tongue
Their beauty might declare:
A spring of love gushed from my heart
And I blessed them unaware:
Sure my kind saint took pity on me,
And I blessed them unaware.

The self-same moment I could pray;
And from my neck so free
The Albatross fell off, and sank
Like lead into the sea.

The Ancient Mariner has to be able to *look* at the snakes, contemplate them, and to be able to say *"happy* living things." And when he can say this, he finds he can bless and be blessed, and his liberation (though it must still be worked out purgatorially) has begun. Professor Irving Babbitt has some scathing remarks about "the Ancient Mariner, who, it will be remembered, is relieved of the burden of his transgression by admiring the color of water snakes." [34] Surely this just shows that Professor Babbitt is curiously blind to the fact that the grace which brings renewal of the power of hope can come in unexpected ways. And note also that the Ancient Mariner was able to be glad for the snakes, and to say from the bottom of his heart, *"happy living things"* (he "blessed them unaware") when he himself was undergoing profound misery. And to be able to do this may call for greater charity than to be able to feel compassion with suffering when you yourself are happy. As Coleridge himself says, "For compassion a human heart suffices; for full, adequate sympathy with joy, an angel's." [35] Kierkegaard asks, in *The Works of Love,* "Which of these two loves more: the happy who sympathizes with another's suffering, or the unhappy who truly sympathizes with others' joy and happiness?" [36] and he answers that it is the latter.

I believe that Coleridge's "empirico-religious" philosophy was concerned with exploring the conditions which make possible, and the conditions which frustrate this joy which underlies the creative growth of the mind. Hence his attempt to talk about "Ideas" as dynamic sources of mental energy. He tried to express this systematically in such theo-

[34] *Rousseau and Romanticism,* p. 287.
[35] *Anima Poetae,* p. 282 (1811-1812).
[36] *Works of Love,* translated by Swenson, p. 263.

logical and metaphysical language as was available to him and seemed
appropriate; but I doubt whether these attempts ever gave him full
satisfaction. He could even say "Our quaint metaphysical opinions in an
hour of anguish are like playthings by the bedside of a child deadly
sick" [37]; and of the somewhat formidable philosophical exposition of
the "Subject-Object" relation at the end of the first part of *Biographia
Literaria,* he remarked at the end of his life, "The metaphysical disquisition at the end of the first volume of *Biographia Literaria* is unformed
and immature; it contains fragments of the truth, but it is not fully
thought out." [38]

Coleridge was always talking of how one day his great systematic philosophy of mind in the universe, his *opus maximum,* would be fully
thought out, and written: it never was. But what he saw as "fragments
of the truth" remain, perhaps more in scattered notes and in the symbols
into which they were transmuted in his poems, than in his repeated attempts at "metaphysical disquisitions." Yet perhaps without his per-
sistent need to try to understand what he calls "facts of mind," "the
heaven descended KNOW THYSELF," even the symbols of his greater poems
could not have been created. The Ancient Mariner, Christabel, Kubla
Khan, give us above all symbols of dereliction and joy. Joy for Coleridge
was not just an "equipoise of the intellectual and emotional faculties," [39]
at any rate if this means the achievement of a balanced temperament,
which he sorely lacked. It was a state in which it was possible to bless
and be blessed; and to Coleridge there was no half-way house: its absence
was like the misery of a curse. And what he learnt about joy came as
much from his failure to achieve liberty of spirit as from the rare moments when he did achieve it. For most of the time he was a failure.
A remark of Wordsworth's, though patronizing, probably has its truth.
"It was poor dear Coleridge's constant infelicity that prevented him
from being the poet that Nature had given him the power to be. He
had always too much personal and domestic discontent to paint the sor-
rows of mankind. He could not afford to suffer with those he saw suffer." [40] Coleridge himself showed that he knew how often he was a failure
in his self-composed epitaph:

> Mercy for praise, to be forgiven for fame
> He asked, and hoped through Christ. Do thou the same.

[37] *Anima Poetae,* p. 3.
[38] *Table Talk,* 28th June 1834.
[39] E. H. Coleridge, edition of *Christabel,* p. 17.
[40] Quoted by De Selincourt, *Wordsworthian and Other Studies,* p. 65, from British
Museum MS. of Barron Field's *Memoirs of the Life and Poetry of W. W.*

There are hints from time to time in Coleridge's writings that he was seeking some means of showing that the growth of the mind he was trying to understand was continuous with a wider power of growth in nature. There is the saying in *Biographia Literaria*[41] that "the rules of the imagination are themselves the very powers of growth and production," and we may compare with this some passages in the Appendices to the *Statesman's Manual*. For instance, in contemplating nature, he says,

> I seem to myself to behold in the quiet objects, on which I am gazing, more than an arbitrary illustration, more than a mere *simile,* the work of my own fancy. I feel an awe, as if there were before my eyes the same power as that of the reason—the same power in a lower dignity, and therefore a symbol established in the truth of things. I feel it alike, whether I contemplate a single tree or flower, or meditate on vegetation throughout the world, as one of the great organs of the life of nature.

And he speaks of how a living thing ". . . with the same pulse effectuates its own secret growth" ". . . the plastic motion of the parts. . . ." [42]

And so, finally, "Whether Ideas are regulative only, according to Aristotle and Kant; or likewise constitutive, and one with the power and life of nature, according to Plato and Plotinus (ἐν λόγῳ ζωὴ ἦν, καὶ ἡ ζωὴ ἦν τὸ φῶς τῶν ἀνθρώπων) is the highest problem of philosophy, and not part of its nomenclature." [43]

There are echoes in all this of Schelling, who wrote of "the holy and ever-creating primal energy of the world," and could say that the creative power of genius in art is to be described as the intellectual correlative of the creative purpose in nature; Schelling looks on art as a way in which "the pure energy of things may flow together with that of our souls and both gush forth together as one stream." [44] But Schelling's expressions are *Schwärmerei* in a sense in which I believe Coleridge's are not. In spite of his metaphysical and theological language, Coleridge seems to be the more tentative, more empirical. He is impressed by the way in which, as he says, we find ourselves driven to talking teleologically about nature "with a feeling very different from that which accompanies a figurative or metaphorical use of words." "Without assigning to nature, as nature, a conscious purpose, (a thinker) may yet distinguish her

---

[41] II, p. 65.
[42] *Statesman's Manual,* Appendix C.
[43] *Ibid.,* Appendix E.
[44] Cf. especially Schelling's *Über das Verhältniss der bildenden Künste zu der Natur* (translated by A. Johnson, "On the Relation between the Plastic Arts and Nature").

agency from a blind and lifeless mechanism." [45] In the *Hints towards the Formation of a more Comprehensive Theory of Life* (an unfinished sketch in honor of John Hunter) he tries to describe life as "that sort of growth which takes place by means of a peculiar organisation," and illustrates this up and down the scale, from the stages of irritability and sensibility to nervous organization.

Hence when Coleridge seeks a relation between "the world without and the still more wonderful world within," he seems to suggest two ways (not mutually exclusive) in which this may be found. One way is the possibility of some kind of teleological continuity. "The rules of the imagination are the very powers of growth and production." The other way is by seeing how the imagination creates a new world of symbols out of a responsive *rapport* with the surrounding world of nature. The imagination does not mirror or copy or even combine elements in nature. It fuses its images into something new, a new world created out of the interplay between the mind and nature in alternate moods of receptivity and activity.

This suggests that what is called "poetic truth" is not a matter of correspondence with an external world, nor of coherence in the logical sense of the consistency of propositions. It is the creation of something new, and its truth consists in the authentic realizing and fusing of images in an individual vision. To the poet, this experience is, as Coleridge is always saying, a knowing which is at the same time a making. The poet, through discovering what he has to say, purifies and re-creates his own mind. Professor C. Day Lewis has recently described the truths of poetry as "operative" [46]; they involve "a search within the poet's self for the essential reality of that self, in the course of which the self is being constantly modified." Perhaps this self-knowledge, which is both purificatory and creative, is part of what may be meant by the "growth of the mind." Or indeed, it may even be more accurate to say that building up a power of this kind of knowing is what we mean when we speak of "the growth of the mind." Such power is found in that combination of activity and receptivity which Coleridge called joy: a state in which the imagination can wait, and watch for its chance. And if its chance comes, it may produce something which can exist independently and in its own right; but it may also achieve a leap forward in its own growth.

[45] *The Friend*, II, p. 10.
[46] *The Poet's Task*, p. 7.

Chronology of Important Dates

1772	Born 21 October, to the Rev. John and Ann (Bowdon) Coleridge.
1782	Attends Christ's Hospital.
1791-94	Sizar and scholar, Jesus College, Cambridge.
1795	Lectures publicly on religion and politics; meets Wordsworth; marries Sarah Fricker.
1796	*Poems on Various Subjects; The Watchman.*
1798	"Ancient Mariner" in *Lyrical Ballads; Christabel,* Part I, and possibly "Kubla Khan" written. To Germany.
1799	First Lakes tour with Wordsworth; meets Sara Hutchinson.
1800	*Wallenstein;* contributions to the *Morning Post;* Greta Hall, Keswick.
1802	*Dejection: an Ode.*
1803	Scottish tour with William and Dorothy Wordsworth.
1804-1806	In Malta; Acting Public Secretary.
1808	Lectures on literature at the Royal Institution.
1809	June to March 1810, *The Friend;* contributions to *Courier* to 1817.
1810	October: rupture with Wordsworth.
1811-12	Lectures on Shakespeare; last visit to the Lakes.
1813	*Remorse* at reopening of Drury Lane; lectures in Bristol (1813-14).
1816	*Christabel* published (3 editions); Highgate; *Statesman's Manual.*
1817	*Biographia Literaria, Sibylline Leaves, Zapolya;* Introduction to *Encyclopaedia Metropolitana.*
1818	*Friend* revised and enlarged. Three courses of lectures.
1825	*Aids to Reflection;* Royal Associate of the Royal Society of Literature.
1829	*On the Constitution of Church and State.*
1831	Attends first meetings of the *British Association.*
1834	Third edition of *Poetical Works;* death at Highgate, 25 July.

Notes on the Editor and Contributors

M. H. Abrams is Professor of English at Cornell University, editor of *English Romantic Poets: Modern Essays in Criticism* (1960), and author of *The Mirror and the Lamp: Romantic Theory and the Critical Tradition* (1953). He is editing the *Biographia Literaria* for the Collected Coleridge.

Edward E. Bostetter is Professor of English at the University of Washington, Seattle, editor of *George Gordon, Lord Byron: Selected Poetry and Letters* (1951) and author of *The Romantic Ventriloquists* (1963). He is editing Coleridge's Shorter Works for the Collected Coleridge.

Kathleen Coburn, Professor of English in Victoria College, University of Toronto, is editor of *The Notebooks of Samuel Taylor Coleridge,* Vol. I 1957, Vol. II 1961, Vols. III-V in progress, and General Editor of *The Collected Works of Samuel Taylor Coleridge,* more than twenty volumes, both works being published by Bollingen Foundation, New York, and Routledge & Kegan Paul, London. In 1949 she edited Coleridge's *Philosophical Lectures,* in 1951 *Inquiring Spirit,* and in 1954 *The Letters of Sara Hutchinson.*

Dorothy M. Emmet, until her recent retirement, was Professor of Philosophy in the University of Manchester, England, and is the author of *Whitehead's Philosophy of Organism* (1936), *The Nature of Metaphysical Thinking* (1945), *Function, Purpose, and Powers* (1958) and a contributor to philosophical journals.

Albert Gérard at the time of writing the article reprinted here was Professor in the Université Officielle du Congo, Elizabethville, Katanga. He is author of *L'idée romantique de la poésie en Angleterre: études sur la théorie de la poésie chez Coleridge, Wordsworth, Keats et Shelley* (Paris, Les Belles Lettres, 1955).

D. W. Harding is Professor of Psychology in Bedford College, University of London, and author of *The Impulse to Dominate* (1941), *Social Psychology and Individual Values,* and essays on poetry, *Experience into Words* (1963).

William F. Kennedy, Professor of Economics at the University of California, Santa Barbara, is author of *Humanist Versus Economist: the Economic Thought of Samuel Taylor Coleridge* (1958).

L. C. Knights is King Edward VII Professor of English Literature, Queen's College, Cambridge and author of various works on Shakespeare and other seventeenth century writers and dramatists, and of two collections of essays, *Explorations* (1946) and *Further Explorations* (1964).

Robert O. Preyer, Professor of English and American Literature at Brandeis

University, has written on Browning and other Victorians, and *Bentham, Coleridge, and the Science of History* (1958).

SIR HERBERT READ is a poet and critic of literature, painting, sculpture, and society, whose influence on contemporary taste and culture cannot be indicated by selected titles. Particularly pertinent to romantic studies are his *Wordsworth* (the Clark Lectures, 1930) and *The True Voice of Feeling* (1953). *The Contrary Experience* (1963), an autobiography, is full of Coleridge.

I. A. RICHARDS, C.H., Professor of English, Language Research Institute, Harvard University, advocate of Basic English and sometimes regarded as founder of the "New Criticism," is author of *inter alia, Basic English and Its Uses* (1943), *Principles of Criticism* (1925), *Practical Criticism* (1929), *Coleridge on Imagination* (1934), and two volumes of poems.

BENJAMIN T. SANKEY, JR. is Associate Professor of English, University of California, Santa Barbara. His essay "Coleridge and the Visible World" appeared in *Studies in Literature and Language* (Texas, 1964).

ELISABETH SCHNEIDER, Professor of English, University of California, Santa Barbara, is author of *The Aesthetics of William Hazlitt* (1933), *Aesthetic Motive* (1939), *Coleridge, Opium and Kubla Khan* (1953) and editor of a delightful anthology, *Poems and Poetry* (1964).

YASUNARI TAKAHASHI, is Associate Professor, College of General Education, University of Tokyo, Japan. A collection of his essays on literary subjects εκστασις, on the Metaphysicals, and on Wordsworth, Coleridge, Arnold, Eliot, and others, appeared in 1966.

GEORGE WHALLEY, Professor of English Literature, Queen's University, Kingston, Ontario, has published, as well as a volume of poems, *Poetic Process* (1953), *Coleridge and Sara Hutchinson and the Asra Poems* (1955). He is editing Coleridge's marginalia, in about four volumes, for the *Collected Works of S. T. Coleridge,* and the *Poetical Works.*

Selected Bibliography

Texts

The standard edition of the poems is the two-volume edition by E. H. Coleridge (1912). The Nonesuch *Coleridge. Poetry and Prose,* ed. Stephen Potter (1934), gives the first and final texts of *The Rime of the Ancient Mariner* on facing pages. The *Biographia Literaria* (1817), ed. Shawcross (1907), has many errors but includes some essays on aesthetics omitted in other editions. George Watson's edition (1957, revised 1961) omits the last two chapters on the ground that these were no part of Coleridge's original design. Of other prose works the only modern editions are: *The Statesman's Manual* (1816) and *A Lay Sermon* (1817), ed. R. J. White in *Political Tracts of Coleridge, Wordsworth and Shelley* (1953); *Confessions of an Inquiring Spirit* (1840), ed. H. St. J. Hart (1956). Coleridge's *Shakespearean Criticism* and his *Miscellaneous Criticism* were collected by T. M. Raysor from lecture reports, manuscript fragments, marginalia, and notebooks in 1930 and 1936 and revised, with some pejorative phrases removed, in 1960. Some of the marginalia appear in *Coleridge on the Seventeenth Century,* ed. R. F. Brinkley (1955). Coleridge's *Treatise on Method* (1934) and some passages from his manuscripts, in *Coleridge on Logic and Learning* (1929), were edited by A. D. Snyder. *The Philosophical Lectures* were first published in 1949, ed. Kathleen Coburn, and *Inquiring Spirit. A New Presentation of Coleridge from his Published and Unpublished Prose Writings* in 1951 by the same editor. *Aids to Reflection* (1825), *The Idea of Church and State* (1830), *The Friend, Essays on His Own Times* (newspaper contributions), *Table Talk, Theory of Life,* the essay *On the Prometheus of Aeschylus,* and most of the marginalia have never been given a modern scholarly editing and will appear, with all the other works, in the forthcoming *Collected Works of S. T. Coleridge* being sponsored by Bollingen Foundation. *The Collected Letters* (to be six volumes) being edited by E. L. Griggs is rich in biographical and critical material, as are the *Notebooks* (to be five double-volumes) being edited by the present editor.

Biographies

J. Dykes Campbell's *Samuel Taylor Coleridge. A Narrative of the Events of his Life* (1894) is still useful; E. K. Chambers' biography (1934) is good for details of times and places but limited by temperamental hostility; H. M. Margoliouth's *Wordsworth and Coleridge 1795-1834* (1953) gives compactly the dates and bare facts of the relationship; Lawrence Hanson's biography (1934) does not go beyond Volume I, i.e. 1800; Paul Deschamps carries his very interesting intellectual biography much farther in depth and a little farther in time, in *La Formation de la pensée de Coleridge* (1964). An article by J. R. MacGillivray, "The Pantisocracy Scheme and its Immediate Background" in *Studies in English by Members of University College, Toronto* (1931), is useful on that period, and on the Malta period there is a paper, "Poet into Public Servant" in the *Transactions of the Royal Society of Canada*, LIV (1960) by the present editor. T. M. Raysor's "Coleridge and 'Asra'" (see Introduction above, p. 10) and Virginia Woolf's two essays in the *New Statesman* (1940), "The Man at the Gate," and "Sara Coleridge" (both reprinted in her *The Death of the Moth*, 1942), deal with more intimate matters. For an attack on some assumptions, see also A. M. Buchan, "The Influence of Wordsworth on Coleridge (1795-1800)," *University of Toronto Quarterly*, XXXII (1963) and Sylva Norman "The Two Selves of Coleridge," *Texas Quarterly* (1964).

Books on Coleridge

There are numerous recent studies of Coleridge's intellectual life from various points of view. (Two are represented in the contents of this volume). Of preeminent interest are: J. A. Appleyard, *Coleridge's Philosophy of Literature 1791-1819* (1965); J. V. Baker, *The Sacred River: Coleridge's Theory of Imagination* (1957); John Beer, *Coleridge the Visionary* (1958); D. P. Calleo, *Coleridge and the Idea of the Modern State* (1966); John Colmer, *Coleridge, Critic of Society* (1958); R. H. Fogle, *The Idea of Coleridge's Criticism* (1962); Humphry House, *Coleridge: The Clark Lectures 1951-52* (1953); Gordon McKenzie, *Organic Unity in Coleridge* (1939); I. A. Richards, *Coleridge on Imagination* (1934); C. R. Sanders, *Coleridge and the Broad Church Movement* (1942); Elisabeth Schneider, *Coleridge, Opium and Kubla Khan* (1953); M. F. Schulz, *The Poetic Voices of Coleridge* (1963); Marshal Suther, *Visions of Xanadu* (1965); George Watson, *Coleridge the Poet* (1966); George Whalley, *Coleridge and Sara Hutchinson and the Asra Poems* (1955); Carl Woodring, *Politics in the Poetry of Coleridge* (1961).

Articles

Essays and articles are legion. On the poems: R. C. Bald, "Coleridge and *The Ancient Mariner*: Addenda to *The Road to Xanadu*," *Nineteenth Century Studies* (1940); David Beres, "*A Dream, a Vision and a Poem*: A Psychoanalytic Study of the Origins of the Rime of the Ancient Mariner," *International Journal of Psycho-Analysis*, XXXII (1951), 97-116; S. C. Wilcox, "The Water Imagery of the 'Ancient Mariner,'" *Personalist*, XXXV (1954); Bernard Smith, "Coleridge's *Ancient Mariner* and Cook's Second Voyage," *Journal of the Warburg and Courtauld Institute*, XIX (1956), 117-54; R. L. Brett, "Coleridge's *The Rime of the Ancient Mariner*," Chapter IV of *Reason & Imagination: A Study of Form and Meaning in Four Poems* (1960); Robert Penn Warren's introductory essay to his edition of *The Rime of the Ancient Mariner*, illustrated by Alexander Calder (1946) is a provocative interpretation that was replied to by, among others, Elder Olsen in "The Rime of the Ancient Mariner" *Modern Philology*, XLV (May 1948), reprinted in R. S. Crane *Critics and Criticism* (1952), E. E. Stoll, "Symbolism in Coleridge," *PMLA*, LXIII (March 1948); Kathleen Coburn, "Coleridge and Wordsworth and 'the Supernatural,'" *University of Toronto Quarterly*, XXV (1956), 121-30; E. E. Bostetter, "*Christabel*: The Vision of Fear," *Philological Quarterly*, XXXVI, 2 (1957), 183-94; D. F. Mercer, "The Symbolism of 'Kubla Khan,'" *Journal of Aesthetics*, XII (1953); C. R. Woodring, "Coleridge and the Khan," *Essays in Criticism* (1959); A. C. Purves, "Formal Structure in Kubla Khan," *Studies in Romanticism*, I (1962), 187-91; R. Gerber, "Keys to Kubla Khan," *English Studies*, XLIV (1963); Eli Marcovitz, "Bemoaning the Lost Dream: Coleridge's 'Kubla Khan' and Addiction," *International Journal of Psycho-Analysis*, XLV (1964), 411-25; E. de Selincourt, "*Dejection: an Ode*," *Wordsworthian and Other Studies* (1947); I. A. Richards, *Coleridge's Minor Poems*, "A lecture . . . in honor of the fortieth anniversary of Professor Edmund L. Freeman, Montana State University, 8 April 1960; Marshall McLuhan, "Coleridge as Artist," in *The Major Romantic Poets*, ed. C. D. Thorpe et al. (1956); G. M. Ridenour, "Source and Allusion in Some Poems of Coleridge," *Studies in Philology* (1963); Kathleen Coburn, "Reflexions in a Coleridge Mirror: Some Images in his Poems," in *From Sensibility to Romanticism, Essays presented to Frederick A. Pottle* (1965), 415-37. There was *A Coleridge Number* of *A Review of English Studies*, ed. A. N. Jeffares (Leeds 1966), with articles by E. Blunden, J. R. de J. Jackson, P. Kaufman, W. Schrickx, J. Shelton, G. Whalley, and C. Woodring.

ARTICLES ON THE PHILOSOPHY, LITERARY CRITICISM, AND OTHER PROSE

M. M. Badawi, "Coleridge's Formal Criticism of Shakespeare's Plays," *Essays in Criticism*, X (1959), 148-62; Nicholas Brooke, "Coleridge's 'True and Original Realism,'" *Durham University Journal*, LIII (1961), 58-69, disagrees with Basil Willey and Herbert Read on Coleridge's fancy-imagination distinctions; D. V. Erdman, "Coleridge in Lilliput: The Quality of Parliamentary Reporting in 1800," in *Speech Monographs* (1960); M. H. Fisch, "The Coleridges, Dr. Prati and Vico," *Modern Philology*, XLI (1943); Albert Gérard, "On the Logic of Romanticism," *Essays in Criticism*, VII (1957), 262-73; J. Isaacs, "Coleridge's Critical Terminology," *Essays and Studies by Members of the English Association* (1936); J. R. de J. Jackson, "Coleridge on Dramatic Illusion and Spectacle in the Performance of Shakespeare's Plays," *Modern Philology*, LXII, 1 (1964), 13-21; Ryotaro Kato, "Coleridge as Aesthetician," *Studies in English* (1962), 99-115; E. I. Klimenko, "The Language Reform in the Poetry of the English Romanticists Wordsworth and Coleridge," *First Leningrad Pedagogical Institute of Foreign Languages* (translation) (1940); A. O. Lovejoy, "Coleridge and Kant's Two Worlds," *A Journal of English Literary History*, VII (1940), 245-76, a most important article on Coleridge's voluntarism and its relation to Kant's,

answering, in this respect, J. H. Muirhead's *Coleridge as Philosopher* (1930),
R. Wellek's *Immanuel Kant in England* (1931), and E. Winkelmann's *Coleridge und die Kantische Philosophie* (1933); Masao Okamoto, "Coleridge and his
Theory of Imagination," *Doshisha Literature*, 24 (Kyoto, Japan, 1966), 1-22;
G. N. G. Orsini, "Coleridge and Schlegel Reconsidered," in *Comparative Literature* (1964), and also his "Coleridge, Fichte, and Original Apperception,"
Friendship's Garland, Essays Presented to Mario Praz (Rome 1966); Stephen
Potter, "On editing Coleridge," *The Bookman* (1934); Raymond Preston, "Aristotle and the Modern Literary Critic," *Journal of Aesthetics and Criticism* (1962);
C. R. Sanders, "Coleridge as Champion of Liberty," *Studies in Philology,* XXXII
(1835), 618-31; W. Schrickx. "Coleridge and Friedrich Heinrich Jacobi," *Revue
belge de Philologie et d'Histoire* (1958); Yasunari Takahashi, "Coleridge and
the Stream," *Studies in English Literature* (1965); Lucyle Werkmeister, "Coleridge and Godwin on the Communication of Truth," *Modern Philology,* LV
(1958), 170-77; Lucyle Werkmeister, "Coleridge on Science, Philosophy, and
Poetry: Their Relation to Religion," *Harvard Theological Review,* LXII (1958),
85-118; George Whalley, "Coleridge Unlabyrinthed," *University of Toronto
Quarterly,* XXXII, 4 (1963), 325-45, on the various kinds of manuscripts and
some of the problems and rewards of Coleridge work in general; George Whalley,
"The Integrity of *Biographia Literaria,*" *Essays and Studies* (1953); L. A.
Willoughby, "English Romantic Criticism: or Fancy and the Imagination," in
Weltliteratur: Festgabe für Fritz Strich (Berne, 1952); Basil Willey, "Coleridge
on Fancy and Imagination," *Proceedings of the British Academy* (1946); Kimiyoshi Yura, "The Involuntary Memory as Discovered by S. T. Coleridge," *Studies
in English Literature* XLII, 2 (1966), 133-43, arguing Coleridge's break from
Schelling and the *Naturphilosophie* and his anticipations of Freud, Bergson, and
Proust.

Books in Part on Coleridge

The numbers of books on "romanticism" in general almost precludes representation here, but a few have been selected for some special bearing. Coleridge
also comes into many books on subjects that concerned him but are not usually
thought of as being in the main line of march for him, such as those by W. F.
Kennedy and Robert Preyer in this selection. The dedication (32 pages) of the
second edition of F. D. Maurice, *The Kingdom of Christ* (1842) has been referred to in the Introduction here; it may be the best brief introduction to Coleridge. M. H. Abrams, *The Mirror and the Lamp* (1953); W. H. Auden *The
Enchafèd Flood* (1950); John Bayley, *The Romantic Survival* (1957); Kenneth
Burke, *The Philosophy of Literary Form* (1941); Justus Buchler, *The Concept of
Method* (1961) (on Bentham, Coleridge, Dewey and Whitehead); Alfred Cobban,
Edmund Burke and the Revolt against the Eighteenth Century (1929, 1960);
R. A. Foakes, *The Romantic Assertion* (1958); D. L. Munby, *The Idea of a
Secular Society* (1963), Chapter II: "Coleridge," *contra* T. S. Eliot, on Church

and State; Jean Pucelle, *L'Idéalisme en Angleterre de Coleridge à Bradley* (Paris, 1955); William Walsh, *The Use of Imagination: Educational Thought and the Literary Mind* (1959), Chapter 1: "Coleridge and the Age of Childhood," Chapter 3: "Coleridge and the Education of Teachers," Chapter 4: "The Literary Critic and the Education of an Elite: Coleridge, Arnold and F. R. Leavis."